THE **COMPLETE IDIOT'S GUIDE** TO

World Religions

Fourth Edition

by Brandon Toropov and Father Luke Buckles

ALPHA

A member of Penguin Group (USA) Inc.

ALPHA BOOKS

Published by the Penguin Group

Penguin Group (USA) Inc., 375 Hudson Street, New York, New York 10014, USA

Penguin Group (Canada), 90 Eglinton Avenue East, Suite 700, Toronto, Ontario M4P 2Y3, Canada (a division of Pearson Penguin Canada Inc.)

Penguin Books Ltd., 80 Strand, London WC2R 0RL, England

Penguin Ireland, 25 St. Stephen's Green, Dublin 2, Ireland (a division of Penguin Books Ltd.)

Penguin Group (Australia), 250 Camberwell Road, Camberwell, Victoria 3124, Australia (a division of Pearson Australia Group Pty. Ltd.)

Penguin Books India Pvt. Ltd., 11 Community Centre, Panchsheel Park, New Delhi—110 017, India

Penguin Group (NZ), 67 Apollo Drive, Rosedale, North Shore, Auckland 1311, New Zealand (a division of Pearson New Zealand Ltd.)

Penguin Books (South Africa) (Pty.) Ltd., 24 Sturdee Avenue, Rosebank, Johannesburg 2196, South Africa

Penguin Books Ltd., Registered Offices: 80 Strand, London WC2R 0RL, England

Copyright © 2011 by Brandon Toropov

International Standard Book Number: 978-1-61564-069-0
Library of Congress Catalog Card Number: 2010915379

13   12   11   8   7   6   5   4   3   2

Interpretation of the printing code: The rightmost number of the first series of numbers is the year of the book's printing; the rightmost number of the second series of numbers is the number of the book's printing. For example, a printing code of 11-1 shows that the first printing occurred in 2011.

Printed in the United States of America

Most Alpha books are available at special quantity discounts for bulk purchases for sales promotions, premiums, fundraising, or educational use. Special books, or book excerpts, can also be created to fit specific needs.

For details, write: Special Markets, Alpha Books, 375 Hudson Street, New York, NY 10014.

Publisher: *Marie Butler-Knight*

Associate Publisher: *Mike Sanders*

Executive Managing Editor: *Billy Fields*

Executive Editor: *Randy Ladenheim-Gil*

Senior Development Editor: *Phil Kitchel*

Senior Production Editor: *Janette Lynn*

Copy Editor: *Tricia Liebig*

Cover Designer: *William Thomas*

Book Designers: *William Thomas, Rebecca Batchelor*

Indexer: *Brad Herriman*

Layout: *Ayanna Lacey*

Proofreader: *John Etchison*

Contents

Introduction

We started working on this book with the hope that it would help build bridges.

Our aim was to increase mutual understanding, in an entertaining and informative way, among believers of a wide variety of backgrounds. Now that we've concluded the project, we find ourselves taken aback, not by the many differences the world's religions presented (although these certainly exist), but by the many similarities we've come across in the world's systems of faith.

Discussing unfamiliar religious matters has a way of making people feel tense and uncertain, perhaps because of the natural human tendency to withdraw from subjects they feel uninformed about. Sometimes this instinct can be a valuable one. When it comes to making contact with people of other religious backgrounds, though, it has its limitations. A lot of people, on encountering someone who holds to a different belief system, simply "shut down." It seems safer not to inquire, not to examine, not to explore—and not to learn. As a result, old, often degrading preconceptions recirculate, along with the assumption that "they" approach spiritual and religious matters fundamentally different than "we" do. Walls rise between communities of believers—and not always just figuratively!

We believe that when followers within religious system A stop listening and arbitrarily decide that people operating within system B don't revere life as a gift, or that their terminology for describing the Divine is flawed, or that they mislead others regarding true salvation, something tragic happens. The followers within system B are no longer representatives of a unique tradition with its own distinctive history, goals, and worldview; instead they are now proponents of a competing ideology. Too many needless conflicts have arisen from this familiar process of "drafting" religious adversaries. We offer this book as a tool for sidestepping this process and opening up to the world's faith systems. We hope to help you understand their idiosyncrasies and differing emphases, and penetrate to the common themes of grace, compassion, and transcendent purpose. We've tried to make the book interesting and of value to people who probably won't ever get an advanced degree in comparative religion, but we've also tried to make our assessments thorough, responsible, and consistent.

Remember, though, the book you're holding in your hands is only the beginning. There is a lot to learn—more than we could possibly set down in one book—so don't stop here. Use this book as a starting point for your own explorations of the world's great faiths. Use it to make your contacts with other traditions more fulfilling for both sides of the discussion. Use it to support and enhance your own spiritual journey. Use it to find new sources of insight. Use it to open up new doors. Use it to build new bridges.

For us, the discovery that the world's religions share much in common is a joyful one. To paraphrase an observation made during the Second Vatican Council:

> *The problems that weigh heavily on human hearts are the same today as in ages past. What is the human person? What is the meaning and purpose of life? What is upright behavior, and what is sinful? Where does suffering originate, and what end does it serve? How can genuine happiness be found? What happens at death? What is judgment? What reward follows death? And finally, what is the ultimate mystery, beyond human explanation, which embraces our entire existence, from which we take our origin and towards which we tend?*—Nostra Aetate, Declaration on the Relation of the Church to Non-Christian Religions

The authors of this book, both of whom have their own faith commitments, have, in writing it, come to understand not only the religions of the world but also each other. Both of us remember and celebrate another important message from the same publication of the Second Vatican Council: "The Church urges her children to enter with prudence and charity into discussion and collaboration with members of other religions. Let Christians, while witnessing to their own faith and way of life, acknowledge, preserve, and encourage the spiritual and moral truths found among non-Christians, (and) also their social life and culture."

Our prayer and our hope is that this book may serve all of us in the attainment of our true selves and that our extraordinary potential as communities of human beings will allow us to use the gift of life on this good earth and be blessed in journeying together with others while embraced by the Ultimate Mystery.

What You'll Learn in This Book

This book is divided into nine sections that will help you understand the world's religions.

Part 1, Opening Up to Other Traditions, shows you why you should bother to learn about other faiths in the first place, which basic ideas support virtually all the world's religious systems, and how to approach people from religious backgrounds that are unfamiliar to you.

Part 2, Judaism, offers an introduction to the world's first great monotheistic religion.

Part 3, Christianity, explores the rise and development of this diverse faith, whose influence in Europe and the Americas has been so profound, and which has become, in modern times, a truly global religion.

Part 4, Islam, helps you understand the history, principles, and practice of the religion founded by the Prophet Muhammad.

Part 5, Hinduism, examines the prehistoric origins of the dominant religion of India, and its development over thousands of years.

Part 6, Buddhism, traces the growth and development of a faith whose originator abandoned his life of luxury in favor of true self-realization.

Part 7, Other Influential Traditions, introduces you to the Confucian, Taoist, Shinto, and Sikh systems.

Part 8, Old Paths, New Paths, explores some traditional patterns of indigenous worship, as well as some exciting new religious forms that have emerged in recent years.

Part 9, A Matter of Life and Death, gives a summary of the responses of the major religious traditions to some of the thorniest questions of human existence. This part of the book also includes a revised and expanded essay on the important topic of religious extremism in our times.

Last, in the Appendixes, there's a glossary of keywords and definitions, as well as a timeline and some other helpful material.

Extras

You will probably want to take advantage of the little nuggets of information distributed throughout the text. They will help you gain an immediate understanding of some aspect of the topic under discussion. Here's how you can recognize them:

DEFINITION

Unless you've already studied the world's religions, you'll be running into a lot of unfamiliar terminology in this book. These boxes will help you make sense of it all.

SPIRITUAL SIGNPOST

Background facts or supporting information that can accelerate and streamline the exploration process. The key points here are about the tradition or approach under discussion.

ON THE PATH

Quotes from many different people who said it best.

BARRIER ALERT!

These boxes will alert you to common misconceptions and potential problem areas.

Acknowledgments

We thank the team at Alpha, and our technical reviewer Kenneth Garden, for all their help and support.

Two more individuals made outstanding contributions to this book. Judith Burros supplied invaluable research assistance and textual help, and her contributions are much appreciated. Leslie Hamilton-Tragert helped with research and illustrations. Without the efforts, insights, review, and encouragement of these two women, this book could not have been completed.

Special Thanks to the Technical Reviewer

The Complete Idiot's Guide to World Religions, Fourth Edition, was reviewed by an expert who double-checked the accuracy of what you'll learn here, to help us ensure that this book gives you everything you need to know about the world's religions. Special thanks are extended to Kenneth Garden, our technical editor on this project.

Trademarks

All terms mentioned in this book that are known to be or are suspected of being trademarks or service marks have been appropriately capitalized. Alpha Books and Penguin Group (USA) Inc. cannot attest to the accuracy of this information. Use of a term in this book should not be regarded as affecting the validity of any trademark or service mark.

Opening Up to Other Traditions

Each of the world's religions may seem foreign to "outsiders," but to an "insider" they represent a means by which both society and creation as a whole can be understood more completely. The fact that you're reading this book suggests that you are prepared for a mutual understanding of reality in today's diverse world. To make that search easier, this part gives you an overview of some of the commonalities—and some of the most important differences—you can expect to find among the world's major faith systems. It also offers a preview of the more detailed discussions to come.

Why Learn About Other Faiths?

In This Chapter

- The growth of religious diversity
- The approaches to "different" religions are changing
- The multi-faith society
- The ways this book can help you

If there was ever a time in human history when understanding the religions of other people was an advantage, this is that time.

In this chapter, you learn about the various ways this book can help you in approaching faith traditions with which you may be unfamiliar.

"I Read the News Today, Oh Boy"

News coverage of what were once seen as "alternative" traditions and patterns of devotion is seemingly at an all-time high in the United States. The reasons for this increase in coverage and interest are not hard to find. Current events are one factor. Following the terrorist attacks of September 11, 2001, for instance, a wave of discussions about Islam swept the globe, as did a number of painful questions for all people of goodwill about the nature of religious extremism in the new millennium.

Changes in demographics are another motivator for the increasing coverage of religious issues. An increase in Buddhist practice in the United States is just one example of the way non-Christian religions are gaining higher visibility in today's culture. According to the Pew Forum on Religion and Public Life, there are now roughly as many Buddhists in the United States as there are Jehovah's Witnesses.

SPIRITUAL SIGNPOST

"Religious tolerance" in America now means much more than simply acknowledging differences within the Judeo-Christian tradition. If you live in the United States today, you live in a nation in which there are about as many Hindu practitioners as Orthodox Jews, more Buddhists than Seventh-Day Adventists, and more followers of Islam than Episcopalians. (Source: World Almanac)

Changes in technology are yet another reason for the heightened visibility of religious issues in our society. The past decade or so has seen a marked increase in discussions about religious matters via the so-called social media channels. Most of these channels did not even exist when the first edition of this book came out, but they now serve as important points of contact for an increasingly connected, increasingly diverse society. Online engagement about the five major world faiths of Hinduism, Buddhism, Judaism, Christianity, and Islam is now quite vigorous, as are virtual discussions about more regionally oriented faiths such as Sikhism and Shinto.

Yet for all the news coverage, for all the new demographic information, for all the online traffic, there is often much more passion and emotion in our discussions about religious matters than there is sound understanding. In twenty-first-century America, we find ourselves citizens of a larger, more religiously pluralistic society than ever, yet we also find ourselves in greater need of good information about the various faith systems.

A spirit of what Christian believers might call *ecumenical* outreach sometimes seems missing in contemporary discussions about religion. That spirit—curious, not judgmental; patient, not rushed; open-minded, not out to score points—is what we are supporting with this book.

DEFINITION

The **ecumenical** movement promotes greater understanding and tolerance among the various branches of the Christian churches. In a broader sense, ecumenism sometimes refers to the process of attaining greater cooperation and understanding among widely differing faiths. Another, and perhaps more appropriate, term for this second sense is "interreligious dialogue."

Catching Up with the Constitution

Half a century ago, the various denominations of Christianity served as the guiding religious force in this nation, whose Constitution forbade a single official religion.

The diverse Christian tradition nevertheless exercised the single most important influence on religious life in the United States, as it had for all of American history.

Other faiths existed, of course, but with a clear "outsider" status. Notwithstanding their legal and *First Amendment right* to worship in any setting, few Americans envisioned a truly pluralistic religious tradition that actually placed Christianity on more or less equal social footing with other faiths in the everyday lives of U.S. citizens. Yet this is precisely what many of the Founding Fathers had in mind.

DEFINITION

First Amendment rights aren't just about freedom of speech and an unregulated press. The U. S. Constitution also guarantees the right to worship in any tradition, or none at all. In the words of the First Amendment: "Congress shall make no law respecting an establishment of religion, or prohibiting the free exercise thereof."

When Benjamin Franklin founded a strictly nondenominational religious meeting house, he drew attention to its nonsectarian nature with the following promise: "[E]ven if the Mufti of Constantinople were to send a missionary to preach Mohammedanism to us, he would find a pulpit at his service." These days, we would update the word "Mohammedanism" and use the name that religion's believers use—Islam—but Franklin's underlying message remains clear: America was to be a nation of equal access, individual choice, and utterly free practice when it came to the question of what, when, how, and whether to worship. In the twenty-first century, the Constitutional ideal of a truly pluralistic religious environment is still a target, rather than a reality, but the diversity of actual religious experience has become an undeniable (and occasionally chaotic) fact of American life.

If you lived in the United States of America 50 years ago, you could conceivably go a whole year without encountering someone whose religious tradition differed markedly from the one that was most familiar to you. Today, you are likely to supervise, be supervised by, meet on a social basis, or even suddenly find yourself related to someone whose religious tradition seems bewilderingly different from your own. What's more, you're likely to have little or no time to prepare for the new information that's coming your way.

Of course, America is not alone in this experience. Similar religious diversification is underway in the United Kingdom, Canada, France, and many other countries. As communication and economic barriers between members of various religious traditions fall away, the amazing diversity of the human religious experience becomes more and more exciting and more and more of a reality in our daily routine.

In an earlier era, unfamiliar religious systems could be dismissed as "foreign" and left for the scholars to explore. In this era, however, that is usually not a realistic option.

How This Book Can Help

This book is meant as a road map for a religiously pluralistic society—the society in which we all have found ourselves after the turn of the millennium. This book does not offer the final word on any of the rich traditions it discusses. Instead, it's meant to help you learn more about some of the most important aspects of each of the systems and disciplines we will be exploring. It's meant to pass along information that's likely to help everyone—not just people with advanced degrees—make sense of the various religions under discussion. And it's meant to continue the (welcome) recent trend of building bridges between faiths. There are fundamental differences between religious traditions, and discussion of those differences does not have to take place in a spirit of hostility. Instead, we believe these discussions can recognize differences and celebrate pluralism without encouraging division, and can emphasize commonality rather than discord.

This book will help you if ...

- You're a supervisor who must determine whether, when, and how to accommodate an employee who asks for time off to observe the Islamic holy period of Ramadan.

- You're a student who's supposed to develop a report on the history of the Church of Jesus Christ of Latter-Day Saints.

- You're an in-law who hopes to avoid awkward silences or unintended antagonism with a new member of the family whose faith is unfamiliar (or even a little intimidating) to you.

This book will also help you if ...

- You're comfortable with your own religious practice or tradition and want to learn more about where and how it connects with other faiths.

- You're experiencing doubts about your current religious practice and wish to learn about other faiths.

- You have deep doubts about religious structures as a whole, but are eager to discover the points of contact among the various traditions of the world and to learn how these commonalities may support your own personal search for meaning and coherence.

- You're curious.

"I Don't Need This! I'm an Atheist!"

Whether we like it or not, the religious traditions and structures of the people we meet can have a strong influence on our relationships with those people. This book is meant to help anyone—even someone who is undecided about the existence of God or convinced that there is no such entity—understand and respond intelligently to religious and cultural conventions and beliefs.

Not long ago, the world-famous astronomer Carl Sagan died. As part of its memorial service for Sagan, a radio talk show broadcast an old interview with the scientist in which he was asked whether or not he believed in God. Sagan responded that, while he rejected certain images of the Deity that had been presented to him as a child— the bearded man in the heavens dispensing lightning bolts—he did, as a scientist, have to acknowledge the possibility of a principle, or set of principles, that governed the universe. He also noted that a number of religious traditions—Buddhism, for instance—explicitly discounted the notion of God as a separate and distinct entity from the rest of creation.

DEFINITION

An **agnostic** is a person who believes that the existence of God, or a primal cause, can be neither proven nor disproven. The word comes from the Greek for "unknown" or "unknowable." An **atheist** is one who believes that there is no such reality as God or a primal cause.

Sagan politely declined the opportunity to set the world of rationality and the world of spirituality into opposition with one another. He also left open the possibility that the various religious traditions could offer important insights into the human condition.

Like the good scientist he was, Sagan was capable of keeping an open mind about big questions, and that definitely included questions of a religious nature. I like to think that this book would have stimulated and intrigued him. Certainly, the need to "build bridges" to initially unfamiliar traditions is shared by many nonbelievers who may be inspired to follow Sagan's example as well as by members of particular religious groups.

"Hey, This Sounds Familiar!"

Another reason to study the various faiths of the world is that the ways they influence, mirror, and support one another are, quite simply, fascinating. Sometimes, the true nature of a particular religious tradition can come into clearest focus when a seeker within that faith examines *another* tradition with a nonjudgmental approach.

Anyone who seeks in the writings of "unrelated" faiths for "contrary" opinions on such fundamental issues as, say, the attributes of a sage or a saint will often find surprising agreement. In the Islamic faith, the Qur'an (25.63–76) speaks of those patient "servants of the all-merciful" who "are neither prodigal nor parsimonious" and who dwell permanently in the high heaven, a heaven whose chief attribute is "Peace." A comparable Taoist scripture (Chuang Tzu 6) speaks of those sages who do not "rebel against want" or "grow proud in plenty."

Such parallels abound in the various scriptures. For all their doctrinal diversity, the major religions of the world appear to have much in common. Discovering and celebrating these life-affirming similarities is part of what has driven us to write this book, and we hope the same motivations encourage you to read it.

Learning about the ways in which the world's faiths reinforce one another can be very fulfilling indeed, even if you don't have an advanced degree in comparative religion.

The Academic Obstacle

Religious practices often seem unfamiliar because they've been introduced to us surrounded with a thick layer of "expert" academic explanation. There is a place for scholarship, of course, and we've certainly done our best to assemble the material in this book in a responsible and thorough manner. But we've also attempted to make certain that you don't need an advanced degree to understand the information we're passing along.

This book is meant as a beginning point, an initial introduction to the many and varied faiths of the world. It is not an academic treatise, but a guide to the lay reader. At various points, we'll point you toward more comprehensive works that will help you gain further insight into the practices and history of the tradition(s) under discussion.

Beyond Fear

Perhaps the most important reason to study faiths beyond one's own is that doing so is a marvelous way to replace fear with experience and insight. It's hard to be frightened by something you really understand.

A full study of religious intolerance over the centuries is beyond the scope of this book. However, it's fair to say that fear has all too often been a driving force behind acts that are not justified in any religious tradition.

Fear kills, in both the spiritual and physical senses of the word. And no one who has studied history will dispute that fear and mistrust of the unknown, and especially misunderstanding of the religious practices of others, has led to innumerable bloody conflicts. All too often, those conflicts accomplished nothing, except to demonstrate the futility of violently opposing what you don't understand.

ON THE PATH

"In the past thirty years the religious landscape of the United States has changed radically. There are Islamic centers and mosques, Hindu and Buddhist temples, and meditation centers in virtually every major American city…. The results of the 2000 census underscore the tremendous scope of ethnic change in our society, but tell us little about its religious dimensions or its religious significance.

"Pluralism has long been a generative strand of American ideology. Mere diversity or plurality alone, however, does not constitute pluralism. There is lively debate over the implications of our multicultural and multireligious society in civic, religious, and educational institutions. How we appropriate plurality to shape a positive pluralism is one of the most important questions American society faces in the years ahead. It will require all of us to know much more about the new religious landscape of America than we presently know."

—From the mission statement of The Pluralism Project (www.pluralism.org), a research project designed to engage students in studying the new religious diversity in the United States

The Other

When we know little or nothing about the religious beliefs of our neighbors, it can be easy to classify them as the *Other*, the misguided (or worse) victims or agents of alien and possibly immoral practices. When we define another tradition as Other, it's a short step to devaluing it, even dehumanizing it, unfairly. If we are to build viable bridges between one believer and another, we will have to try to understand and discuss more than one conception of the Divine.

DEFINITION

When a member of another religious tradition is relegated to the status of the **Other**, he or she is often seen as somehow less human or less worthy than we are. (Consider, for instance, the dehumanizing stereotypes associated with anti-Semitism over the centuries, or the current media bias against practitioners of Islam.) This denigrating process runs counter to the nearly universal injunction of most major religious traditions to honor and respect all human life.

The Other is usually the enemy, or at least a competitor. And when we make this designation, regardless of what words we use, we move from the world of spirituality to the world of human conflict, whether or not a blow is struck or a shot fired.

Words, Words, Words

Words like "pagan," "heretic," "heathen," and "savage" have typically marked this Other identification in the Western tradition. These words were frequently served up as justifications for acts of unspeakable violence and cruelty; they saw even more common service as markers of (supposedly) permanent division between "competing" traditions. Whatever their effect, these words and their many companions were used for one reason: fear of the unknown.

There is only one cure for this type of fear: knowledge. It's much harder to designate a particular religious tradition as the Other when you've taken the time to understand it. If this book hastens the process of knowledge and learning and helps to reduce the needless fear that arises when members of one tradition encounter members of another, it will have done its job.

The Least You Need to Know

- We live in a society in which true religious diversity is guaranteed by the Constitution of the United States, but is always a challenge to maintain.
- Building bridges to practitioners of other faiths is essential, because we often find ourselves in social or family relationships with those whose traditions are unfamiliar to us.
- Learning how the various religious traditions reinforce and support one another can be rewarding in and of itself.
- The more you know about other faiths, the less fear will be a factor in your dealings with people who practice those faiths. There are very real differences between religious traditions, and looking at religious difference is as legitimate as looking at similarities.

In This Chapter

- How most religions regard the fundamental truths (as inherited, rather than invented from scratch)
- What virtually all faiths have in common
- The limits of logic and reason
- Why an unfamiliar faith may be more accessible than it first appears

There are countless schools of religious thought, and yet a few common strands seem to run through them all. In this chapter, you learn about some of the key beliefs and spiritual principles shared by nearly all of the faiths discussed in this book.

Ancient Truths

A Shiite *Muslim* pursues a very different belief system than a member of the Greek Orthodox church, who in turn pursues a very different belief system than a Zen Buddhist practitioner. All the same, these believers all follow a spiritual path, and as such, embrace certain ideas that, when expressed openly and without preconception, can illuminate and clarify that path.

The vast majority of the traditions acknowledge that the fundamental message being passed along to believers is not new or unique, but ancient and impervious to change. This is not to say that all religions are identical. Far from it! It's important to remember, though, as you begin your tour of the world's religions, that the great faiths did not spring into existence without preparation. A people's culture and traditional wisdom provide a context for a prophet's message or a sage's advice.

DEFINITION

A **Muslim** is someone who practices the Islamic faith (see Part 4). The word *Muslim* is sometimes rendered *Moslem*; either way, the word means "one who submits (to God)."

Voices: The Timeless Ideas Behind the World's Great Religions

Notice the themes of continuity and timelessness in the quotes that follow:

Buddhism: "All Buddhas of the 10 parts of the universe enter the one road of Nirvana. Where does that road begin?" (Zen Buddhist *koan*)

Christianity: "God, who at sundry times and in divers manners spake in time past unto the fathers by the prophets, hath in these last days spoken unto us by his Son, whom he hath appointed heir of all things, by whom also he made the worlds." (Hebrews 1:1–2)

Confucianism: "The Master said, 'I have transmitted what was taught to me without making up anything of my own. I have been faithful to and loved the ancient ones.'" (*Analects of Confucius*, 7.1)

Hinduism: "I am born in every age to protect the good, to destroy evil, and to reestablish the law." (*Bhagavad Gita*, 4.7–8)

Islam: "Nothing is said to you (Muhammad) except what was said to the messengers who came before you." (The Qur'an, 41–43)

Judaism: "And Moses said unto God, 'Behold, when I come unto the children of Israel, and shall say unto them, The God of your fathers hath sent me unto you; and they shall say to me, What is his name? What shall I say unto them?' And God said unto Moses, 'I AM THAT I AM;' and he said, 'Thus shalt thou say unto the children of Israel, "I AM hath sent me unto you."'" (Exodus 3:13–14)

DEFINITION

A **koan** is a teaching riddle within Zen (or Ch'an) Buddhist tradition.

Each of the world's faiths must be understood and respected within its own context, of course. But it's important to note that the "we're-not-passing-along-anything-new-here-folks" message is a consistent theme among most of the faiths you'll be examining here.

That's not the only common note, either. On three additional points, the world's best-known religions (as well as the vast majority of the lesser-known ones) all agree. Let's look at them in detail now.

> **SPIRITUAL SIGNPOST**
>
> The longer you study the great religions of the world, the more you realize that each celebrates and refines concepts that reflect the same elemental truths. As the editors of *World Scripture: A Comparative Anthology of Ancient Texts* (Paragon House, 1991) put it, "Interfaith dialogue in our time is going beyond the first step of appreciating other religions to a growing recognition that the religions of the world have much in common. The common ground between religions becomes more apparent as the dialogue partners penetrate beneath superficial disagreements."

Humanity and the Eternal

In his play *Our Town*, Thornton Wilder has his Stage Manager point out what may be the single most important unifying concept shared by the great religions of the world. "I don't care what they say with their mouths," the Stage Manager says, "everybody knows in their bones that something is eternal, and that something has to do with human beings."

The Stage Manager's moving speech goes on to observe that this part of us that is *eternal* is "way down deep" in each and every one of us, and that the wisest souls have been repeating this simple message to their fellow humans for 5,000 years or so. ("You'd be surprised," he notes dryly, "how people are always losing hold of it.")

> **DEFINITION**
>
> A common understanding of the word **eternal** is "enduring forever," which is certainly one aspect of its meaning. But this definition is not complete. The primary sense of the word reflects a reality that is beyond time; that is, without beginning, end, or division. When the great religions of the world speak of a divine presence that exists eternally, they are speaking, as Einstein did, of the transcendence of time as human beings generally perceive it.

Voices: Humanity's Relationship with the Eternal

The idea that there is some aspect of the human identity involving contact with something changeless and beyond time extends across all doctrinal and dogmatic barriers. Notice the emphasis on eternity in the scriptural examples that follow:

Buddhism: "Coming empty-handed, going empty-handed: that is human. When you are born, where do you come from? When you die, where do you go? Life is like a floating cloud which appears. Death is like a floating cloud which disappears. The floating cloud itself originally does not exist. Life and death, coming and going, are also like that. But there is one thing which always remains clear. It is pure and clear, not depending on life and death. Then what is that one pure and clear thing?" (Cambridge Zen Center publication, "The Human Route")

Christianity: "I am the Alpha and the Omega, the beginning and the end, the first and the last." (Revelation 22:13)

Confucianism: "The exemplary person is not deceived by that which is transitory, but rather focuses on the ultimate." (*I Ching*, Hexagram 54)

Hinduism: "The great and unborn Self is undecaying, immortal, undying, without fear, and without end." (Brihardaranyaka Upanishad, 4.4.25)

Islam: "(God) is the First and the Last and the Ascendant (over all) and the Knower of hidden things, and He is Cognizant of all things." (Qur'an, 57.3)

Judaism: "Hark! One saith: 'Proclaim!' And he saith: 'What shall I proclaim?' 'All flesh is grass, and the goodliness thereof is as the flower of the field; the grass withereth, the flower fadeth; because the breath of the Lord bloweth upon it; surely the people is grass. The grass withereth, the flower fadeth, but the word of God shall stand forever.'" (Isaiah 40:6–8)

Taoism: "Without sound and without form, (the Tao) depends on nothing and does not change." (Tao te Ching, 25)

Our contact with and connection to the eternal, despite the seemingly transitory nature of human existence, is a consistent notion within the faiths of the world. Even those who reject organized religion or the "existence of God" may find themselves agreeing instinctively with the proposition that there is something deep within us that endures despite the fact that our physical bodies and the world around us obviously do not.

Interconnectedness with All Creation

Are you the same as, or different from, the book you're reading right now? The question may be trickier than it sounds. Another "big idea" embraced by many of the world's faiths is that of an intimate connection with all created entities in the universe.

Most faiths also acknowledge the difficulty of reconciling this "connected" divine reality with our own perceived, and seemingly legitimate, day-to-day experience, in which we see ourselves as separate and autonomous entities. Even "acknowledging" some form of common identity with the book you're holding in your hands may reinforce separate notions of "book" and "reader." All the same, the primal cause is held to permeate every conceivable aspect of creation.

The joint message of the world's great religions is clear and unmistakable: All of creation is linked together in a fundamental and unalterable way, and the journey of the sincere seeker can be said to trace and illuminate the reality of that linkage.

SPIRITUAL SIGNPOST

Despite massive cultural differences, despite innumerable doctrinal disputes, despite the occasional heated conflict with representatives of other factions and traditions, virtually every organized faith honors the notion of the individual believer's contact with something eternal.

Voices: Interconnectedness in All Creation

Here are just a few of the (numerous) passages, scriptural and otherwise, that embody this idea of interconnectedness.

Buddhism: "Banzan once walked through the marketplace and heard a butcher talking to one of his customers.

> "'I want the very best piece of meat you have in the shop,' the customer demanded.

> "'Every piece of meat in this shop is the best,' the butcher responded. 'You will never find a piece of meat here that is not the best.'

> "Upon hearing this, Banzan attained enlightenment." (Zen story)

Christianity: "In the beginning was the Word, and the Word was with God, and the Word was God. The same was in the beginning with God. All things were made by him; and without him was not any thing made that was made." (John 1:1–3)

Hinduism: "Our existence as embodied beings is purely momentary; what are a hundred years in eternity? But if we shatter the chains of egotism, and melt into the ocean of humanity, we share its dignity. To feel that we are something is to set up a barrier between God and ourselves; to cease feeling that we are something is to become one with God." (Mahatma Gandhi, quoted in *Be Here Now*, by Ram Dass [Lama Foundation])

Islam: "His (God's) throne comprises the heavens and the earth." (Qur'an, 2.255)

Judaism: "Holy, holy, holy is the Lord of hosts: the whole earth is full of His glory." (Isaiah 6:3)

Taoism: "All things in the world came from being; and being comes from nonbeing." (Tao Te Ching, 40)

Interestingly, just about *every* religion makes a point of emphasizing an all-encompassing plan of the Divine that connects anything and everything, including you, this book, and that cup of coffee you're planning to have once when you're finished reading. Admittedly, the logical basis of this contention is sometimes hard to grasp, but the notion of total interconnectedness is nevertheless an important common theme.

Beyond Words, Beyond Mind

Yet another oft-repeated message of the great religions of the world—one often echoed by people whose work points them toward "ultimate" conclusions about the physical universe—concerns the limitations of human intellect. Ultimately, the great faiths counsel, childlike simplicity, rather than overbearing intellect or rigorous logic, is required for true union with the Divine.

Variations on this observation appear countless times, and in countless ways, in the religious practices, writings, and commentaries that have come down to us through history. A representative sampling follows.

Voices: The Limits of the Logical Mind

Notice the skepticism of human logic and reason in the quotes that follow:

Buddhism: "The true path is only difficult for those who make distinctions. Do not like, do not dislike. Then everything will become clear." (*"On Trust in the Heart,"* Master Seng Ts'an)

Christianity: "Eye hath not seen, nor ear heard, neither have entered into the heart of man, the things which God hath prepared for them that love him." (1 Corinthians 2:9)

Confucianism: "The presence of the Spirit: It cannot be surmised. How may it be ignored!" (*Doctrine of the Mean,* 16)

Christianity: "All that the imagination can imagine and the reason conceive and understand in this life is not, and cannot be, a proximate means of union with God." (St. John of the Cross)

ON THE PATH

I didn't arrive at my understanding of the fundamental laws of the universe through my rational mind.—Albert Einstein

Hinduism: "Eye cannot see him, nor words reveal him; by senses, austerity, or works he is not known." (Mundaka Upanishad, 3.1.8)

ON THE PATH

An African traditional faith: "There is no need to point out God to a child."— Ghanian proverb

Islam: "He is far above the conceptions of those who refuse His existence, and also of those who imagine His attributes in various expressions of nature." (Nahjul Balagha, Sermon 54)

Judaism: "Behold, I go forward, but He is not there; and backward, but I cannot perceive Him; on the left hand, when he doth work, but I cannot behold Him; he turneth himself to the right hand, but I cannot see him." (Job 23:8, 9)

Taoism: "The True Man of ancient times knew nothing of loving life, knew nothing of hating death. He emerged without delight; he went back in without a fuss. He came briskly, he went briskly, and that was all. He did not forget where he began; he did not try to find out where he would end. He received something and took pleasure in it; he forgot about it and handed it back again." (Chuang Tzu, 6)

SPIRITUAL SIGNPOST

At some point in its scripture or philosophy, each of the major faiths we will discuss refers to the limited power of human reason as a final vehicle for contact with the infinite. Something simpler and more innocent is required for true realization, something beyond logic.

One More Thing

Let's touch on one more important commonality before moving on. Most traditions may be more flexible than you imagine, regardless of what it looks like at first from the outside.

There are a number of reasons for this. For one thing, developing a personal spirituality—a meaningful relationship, if you will, with one's true self—is an ongoing process. Lessons have a way of appearing when one is ready to receive them. (A pertinent saying in one tradition points out that "You can't rip the skin off the snake.") The odds are good that a given religious tradition has some mechanism for dealing with people of a wide variety of interests and levels of experience, including yours.

Religions that are rigid and completely inaccessible tend not to spread very far or adapt well to cultural changes over the years. It's certainly true that religious institutions may emphasize fixed rituals and sets of references that can confuse an outsider, but it's also true that the tradition usually has some point of entry that will make sense to anyone unfamiliar with the faith.

BARRIER ALERT!

Assuming that members of an unfamiliar religious tradition are inherently hostile to well-intentioned, open-minded outsiders is usually a big mistake. If you keep an open mind, you'll almost always find ordinary people who are willing to talk to you about what they believe and why.

In other words, there is one Roman Catholic church, operating under a distinctive set of rituals and principles; there are thousands upon thousands of local emphases and accommodations to local Catholic practitioners. The same principle operates, to a greater or lesser degree, for many other faiths that have become widely dispersed over the earth.

Of course, it's always possible to find a particular sect that is hostile to newcomers, one that makes no attempt to adjust responsibly to the evolving spiritual needs of its practitioners, one that briskly rejects those who have honest questions about how and why its followers do what they do. But it's not exactly common, either.

In the next chapter, you'll find specific advice for approaching and communicating with someone whose religious traditions are unfamiliar to you.

The Least You Need to Know

- The vast majority of religions acknowledge that their core precepts are timeless, rather than new and unrelated to any existing tradition.
- The notion of humanity's connection to something eternal is a common one among the great religions of the world.
- The notion that all of Creation is somehow interconnected is common among the great religions of the world.
- The notion that rigorous, adult logic alone is not a sufficient tool for comprehending divine truths is also common among the great religions of the world.
- An unfamiliar faith may be more accessible than it first seems.

Speaking Softly and Dropping the Stick

Chapter

3

In This Chapter

- Why external differences are less imposing than they may seem
- The most common barriers to interfaith communication
- What's most likely to alienate someone of another faith
- How to ask the questions that build bridges between people of different belief systems

So you're interested in approaching someone to learn more about his or her faith, but you're a little perplexed about exactly how you should go about this. After all, most of us are counseled from an early age to avoid two topics with those who aren't family members or close friends: religion and politics. Why? People get so touchy!

Truth be told, they sometimes do. This chapter won't be of much help to you if your aim is to reach out to a member of an opposing political faction, but it will offer you some pragmatic strategies for reaching out to learn more about someone's religious practices.

Non-Sectarian Knees

Not long ago, a Catholic priest teamed up with a Zen Buddhist teacher to conduct a Christian/Buddhist meditation retreat. After the retreat ended, the priest found himself in a discussion with a Buddhist practitioner who wanted to know why mainstream Christians didn't take greater notice of certain elements of Buddhist theology and practice.

For a while the priest tried to deflect the questions tactfully, but when his questioner persisted, it was clear the priest had to respond directly somehow. Finally, the priest told his companion, "I'm not very big on 'why,' and I'm not very big on labels, either. You and I just spent a whole day sitting in meditation together. As long as it was just knees and legs and pillows we were sitting on, we had no problem. The minute we start sitting on Christian knees and legs and pillows or Buddhist knees and legs and pillows, though, things start to get complicated."

The same wisdom can easily be extended to Islamic knees, Quaker knees, Jewish knees, or any number of knees of other denominations. All of them bow in reverence or sit in meditation with the same level of efficiency. To the extent that people fixate on labels, on explanations, on differences that really ought to be reconciled, interfaith contact is difficult. To the extent that people focus on a sincere spiritual commitment that can take many expressions, interfaith contact can be fairly easy.

SPIRITUAL SIGNPOST

Showing a willingness to look beyond externals and penetrate to the core concerns of a person's faith is a great way to build bridges.

When talking with someone whose faith is unfamiliar to you, remember that most of the objectives behind the religion are almost certainly similar (or identical) to the tradition you are comfortable with.

There's an old joke about a rabbi who upbraided a young man named Isaac, a member of his congregation. Isaac loved to ridicule the Christians he encountered regularly at his print shop. Isaac's jokes with his friends about the "goys" invariably painted all of Christianity as an ill-informed, logically absurd religion that routinely went out of its way to persecute Jews.

One day, after hearing the latest of these jokes, the rabbi decided to share a joke of his own with Isaac. He took the young man aside, winked at him conspiratorially, and said, "Isaac, do you know why Christians make a habit of hitting the salt-shaker on the side, while Jews always tap it on the bottom?"

Isaac smiled, expecting a good joke at the expense of the "goys" he dealt with every day. "No, rabbi," he replied. "Why is that?"

"To get the salt out," the young man's spiritual guide answered quietly.

Six Paths to Alienation

Here are six common traps even well-meaning outsiders fall into when dealing with practitioners of an unfamiliar faith. Following each, you'll find some advice on taking a more constructive approach.

1. Fixate on "Why."

"Why do you people dress like that?"

As the priest at the Christian/Buddhist retreat knew, "why" questions are often loaded questions. It's quite possible that the person you're talking to really has no clear fix on the ultimate reasons behind a particular practice. It's also quite possible that he or she will presume your question has some unfriendly intent.

Instead of focusing on "why," ask questions that will encourage your acquaintance to open up and start discussing nonthreatening aspects of his or her practice. ("It's wonderful to see you here. Are you a member of Temple Beth-Israel?")

2. Follow the (Unflattering) Lead of the Media.

This means holding an individual responsible for any recent bad press generated by some representative of his or her faith.

Media coverage of religious figures is often sensational and irresponsible. (For that matter, media coverage of the very idea of personal or group spirituality is often sensational and irresponsible.)

Biased reports about a particular religious group often leave its adherents feeling as though they are under siege. "Current events" may seem like a harmless enough way to begin the conversation, but it won't be if your conversational partner perceives you as one of the attackers. A fundamentalist Christian probably won't take kindly to your assumption that he or she is willing to defend, or even discuss, a publicly disgraced member of the clergy within his denomination. A Muslim who worships at a mosque in your neighborhood may not appreciate being interrogated about yesterday's arrest of a religious extremist operating in Pakistan or Yemen. These are complicated topics that you may eventually find the opportunity to address, but they are not great opening subjects if your goal is to build a new relationship.

Play it safe. Assume the best, and use neutral conversation-starters.

3. Stare.

There's not much that makes someone feel more like an outsider than being gawked at. Maintain appropriate, friendly, intermittent eye contact, but don't use your gaze to burrow through the person.

4. Talk About What's "Normal."

"Would you say you're a typical Catholic?"

How can a question like this be answered without polarizing a conversation? Words like "normal" and "typical" can sabotage otherwise promising exchanges. How would you feel if someone asked you whether or not close friends or relatives who worshipped within a particular tradition dressed "normally," or acted as "typical" members of that faith would?

The implication behind such language, of course, is that the practices of the person you're talking to aren't "normal," whatever that means. Acknowledge the validity of the other person's experience and traditions and stay away from language that implies there is one and only one way to categorize religious or cultural issues.

5. Use Attack Language to Describe Someone's Faith.

There are numerous loaded words you can use to describe someone else's religious practices, words that will serve only to convince your conversational partner that you're not interested in learning anything more about the tradition under discussion.

Stay away from words like *sect, cult, recruit, programming, alien,* or *terrorist* in reference to the person's beliefs—even if you're just quoting someone else. The person with whom you're speaking may assume that you're eager to polarize the conversation, just like those you're quoting.

6. Stomp on Toes That Are Already Bruised.

That is to say, ask the most obvious, and most sensitive, question right out of the gate. The point here is to avoid asking questions or raising issues that will cause the other person to sigh (audibly or internally) and think, "Oh, great. Another one who has to talk about such-and-such."

A Christian Science practitioner may eventually be interested in discussing his or her beliefs concerning faith as a counterpart to contemporary medical treatment.

A member of the Church of Jesus Christ of Latter-Day Saints (the Mormons) may eventually take part in a stimulating discussion with you about that tradition's history and initial acceptance of polygamy. But why try to initiate a dialogue by raising such issues?

At the beginning of your relationship with someone whose religious background differs from your own, your best approach is probably to avoid sensitive or overplayed issues. Establish contact with the person first, and make it clear that you're interested in human-to-human contact, not sparring and preconceptions.

Ask Questions!

Appropriate questions that focus on "how" and "what" rather than "why" may be your most powerful tools when it comes to building bridges with people of other faiths. Intelligent questions, unlike statements or aggressive pronouncements, let others know your mind is open and ready to listen. The right questions work to develop relationships. Questions that don't threaten, intimidate, or cross-examine let everyone know you're interested in gathering information, rather than dispensing judgment.

Questions that show you have a genuine curiosity about the other person's faith and practices will make it easier for you to develop a person-to-person, rather than *proselytizer-to-proselytizer*, relationship.

DEFINITION

To **proselytize** is to make an effort to convince another to convert, typically to another faith or sect. Initial encounters between those of different faiths are sometimes needlessly polarized when one or the other parties believes that proselytizing is taking place or about to take place. You'll be most likely to keep communication open if you make it clear you're engaged not in proselytizing, but in its opposite: open-minded, nonjudgmental discussion and curiosity.

Questions allow you to explore and celebrate commonalities, rather than highlight divisions. Here are some examples of nonintrusive, nonthreatening questions and their more abrasive counterparts. One group will help you encourage the person with whom you're talking to open up. One group will ensure plenty of furtive looks and granite silences.

Whenever you can, choose open questions rather than closed questions. The following is a list of open and closed questions about an unfamiliar faith:

Open: "Where are you planning to celebrate such-and-such a holiday this year?"

Closed: "So you really believe such-and-such, huh?"

Open: "I'm curious: When do children in your tradition begin wearing such-and-such a garment?"

Closed: "I'll bet you have a heck of a time trying to talk your kids into wearing that kind of clothing to school, don't you?"

Open: "Is there anything I should know about dietary restrictions in setting the menu for our get-together?"

Closed: "Why don't you eat meat?"

Open-minded questions—posed intelligently and early—can also help you develop appropriate behavior patterns during the various rituals or ceremonies in which you may be taking part. Don't assume that a particular level of participation or response will be accepted simply because that standard represents what works in your own tradition!

And Now, a Word from the Federal Government

Just a reminder: It is completely inappropriate (and usually illegal) to question someone who reports to you about the whys and wherefores of his or her religion as it relates to workplace performance. Stay on the right side of the law. Do not give even the barest impression that you are judging someone's performance, or potential as a candidate for a job opening, on his or her religious beliefs.

> In the United States, the relevant statute is Title VII of the Civil Rights Act of 1964, as amended, which forbids employers to ...1. [f]ail or refuse to hire or to discharge any individual, or otherwise to discriminate against any individual with respect to his compensation, terms or conditions, or privileges of employment, because of that individual's race, color, religion, sex, or national origin; or
>
> 2. limit, segregate, or classify his employees or applicants for employment in any way which would deprive or tend to deprive any individual of employment opportunities or otherwise adversely affect his status as an employee, because of such individual's race, color, religion, sex, or national origin.

BARRIER ALERT!

If you're unfamiliar with the protocol around a particular religious event such as a wedding or funeral, by all means ask someone (either an officiant or a member of the group) what should happen and how you should respond in a certain situation. That beats improvising your way through the ceremony and drawing unhappy stares from others. The earlier you ask, the better off you'll be. Can you take photographs during a particular service? Is the type of clothing you have in mind suitable for the ceremony? Are there some parts of a ritual you'll be expected to participate in? If so, which? Don't put off questions like these. Ask for help!

We're All in the Same Boat

The simplest and most reliable principle to bear in mind during your initial encounters with representatives of other traditions is easy to remember: *When you listen, you can't make a mistake.*

Adopting a humble, open-minded attitude toward the practices of others does not represent a betrayal of your own faith. On the contrary, this approach allows you to deepen your understanding about other outlooks and will very likely result in a more profound appreciation of your own tradition's distinctive features.

Remember that, at the end of the day, religious traditions of all varieties represent a profoundly human attempt to address fundamental questions about life, growth, maturity, and death. In the final analysis, regardless of the undeniable differences among the believers who pursue different faiths, every religious practitioner faces the same basic human obstacles and dilemmas.

If you come in contact with a tradition that seems utterly foreign to you, remember that each and every person within that tradition shares the following challenges with you:

- The common heritage of physical birth.

- The common destiny of physical death.

- The common desire to find meaning and purpose within the daily activities of life.

No matter your background, no matter your religious upbringing, no matter your past experience with members of this group, you already have much more in common with these people than you probably imagine. You, like each of the members of the faith you have encountered, are a participant in the dance of life—someone who delights in the birth and growth of children; someone who gazes through the vast and forbidding distances of a cold starry night and wonders at the immensity of creation; someone whose relationships with friends, family, and daily acquaintances are sometimes easy and sometimes hard.

You, like each of the members of the tradition you now wish to understand more fully, have your good days and your bad days. You can recall choices from your past that make you proud and choices that have separated you from others and filled your heart with remorse. You have been born, and you will someday die.

All of this is true for you. And it is also true for each and every member of the group you are studying now. If you can bear these points in mind as you interact with the representatives of that group, you will learn more about them—and perhaps learn a little more about yourself as well.

The Least You Need to Know

- Showing a willingness to look beyond externals and penetrate to the core concerns of a person's faith is a great way to build bridges.
- "Why" questions may be more provocative than you realize.
- The unintentional use of loaded questions and "attack" terminology can undermine even a sincere effort to reach out to someone of another faith.
- Open-ended questions that don't threaten your conversational partner probably represent your best opportunity for contact.
- When in doubt, remember: we're all in the same boat.

Judaism

Within Judaism, we find stories about God's active and ongoing presence in human affairs: the patriarch Abraham, the great prophet Moses, the story of the Torah—the laws that have exerted authority from biblical times onward—and much more about the people whose social and religious codes developed in response to the requirements of the single God. Practicing Jews believe that, in return for their love and obedience, God promised to establish and sustain them as His people. In this part of the book, you learn the basics of this rich, and varied, covenant faith.

The Roots of Judaism

In This Chapter

- The history of the world's oldest monotheistic faith
- How Judaism has influenced other traditions
- Understanding the Ten Commandments
- The distinctive elements of this enduring faith

Like Christianity and Islam—two later traditions that also explicitly trace their lineage to the patriarch Abraham—Judaism is a faith that has encompassed many historical events, factions, movements, and countermovements. In this chapter, you learn about the history and development of this diverse Covenant faith.

The Hebrews

The Torah (the Five Books of Moses that begin both the Hebrew and Christian Bibles) teaches that the Hebrew people are descended from Abraham, the patriarch with whom God formed the *Covenant*.

The Torah also tells how, long after Abraham's time, the descendants of Abraham and his son Isaac moved to Egypt, where they were eventually enslaved. After centuries of persecution, the Hebrews were released from the Pharaoh's power and led back to Canaan (or Palestine) by Moses—with the help of the same single true God who had spoken to Abraham. On Mt. Sinai, the book of Exodus reports, God gave Moses ten commandments meant to guide the conduct of God's people, and initiated a solemn Covenant with this people.

DEFINITION

As recounted in the Bible, God made **covenants**, or agreements, not only with Abraham, but with Noah and Moses as well. The covenant with Abraham, as described in the book of Genesis, was an agreement under which God would establish a chosen people, a "great nation," from Abraham's descendants. In return, Abraham and those who followed would offer the one true God complete obedience. According to scripture, the covenant has been restated and renewed at various times in Jewish history.

Abraham is regarded as the founding patriarch of the Israelites and other ancient peoples, including the Ishmaelites, Edomites, and Midianites. His story is related in the book of Genesis.

Today, it is common for Judaism, Christianity, and Islam to be designated as "Abrahamic religions" because of the critical role Abraham plays in texts central to these traditions. Believers from all three faiths consider Abraham a major prophet and the father of the people of Israel through his son Isaac. In addition, Muslims consider Abraham to be an ancestor of Muhammad through his son Ishmael, born to him by Sarah's handmaiden, Hagar. The narrative of Abraham's receiving an angelic vision demanding the sacrifice of his son is also of great importance in all three faiths, though the Qur'an tells the story differently than the Hebrew scriptures do.

> 1 And it came to pass after these things, that God did prove Abraham, and said unto him: 'Abraham'; and he said: 'Here am I.' And He said: 'Take now thy son, thine only son, whom thou lovest, even Isaac, and get thee into the land of Moriah; and offer him there for a burnt-offering upon one of the mountains which I will tell thee of.' And Abraham rose early in the morning, and saddled his ass, and took two of his young men with him, and Isaac his son; and he cleaved the wood for the burnt-offering, and rose up, and went unto the place of which God had told him. On the third day Abraham lifted up his eyes, and saw the place afar off. 5 And Abraham said unto his young men: 'Abide ye here with the ass, and I and the lad will go yonder; and we will worship, and come back to you.' And Abraham took the wood of the burnt-offering, and laid it upon Isaac his son; and he took in his hand the fire and the knife; and they went both of them together. And Isaac spoke unto Abraham his father, and said: 'My father.' And he said: 'Here am I, my son.' And he said: 'Behold the fire and the wood; but where is the lamb for a burnt-offering?' And Abraham said: 'God will provide Himself the lamb for a burnt-offering, my son.' So they went both of them together. And they came to the place which God had told him of; and Abraham built the altar there, and laid the wood in order, and bound Isaac his son, and laid him on the

altar, upon the wood. And Abraham stretched forth his hand, and took the knife to slay his son.

And the angel of the LORD called unto him out of heaven, and said: 'Abraham, Abraham.' And he said: 'Here am I.' And he said: 'Lay not thy hand upon the lad, neither do thou any thing unto him; for now I know that thou art a God-fearing man, seeing thou hast not withheld thy son, thine only son, from Me.' And Abraham lifted up his eyes, and looked, and behold behind him a ram caught in the thicket by his horns. And Abraham went and took the ram, and offered him up for a burnt-offering in the stead of his son. And Abraham called the name of that place Adonai-jireh; as it is said to this day: 'In the mount where the LORD is seen.' And the angel of the LORD called unto Abraham a second time out of heaven, and said: 'By Myself have I sworn, saith the LORD, because thou hast done this thing, and hast not withheld thy son, thine only son, that in blessing I will bless thee, and in multiplying I will multiply thy seed as the stars of the heaven, and as the sand which is upon the seashore; and thy seed shall possess the gate of his enemies; and in thy seed shall all the nations of the earth be blessed; because thou hast hearkened to My voice.' So Abraham returned unto his young men, and they rose up and went together to Beersheba; and Abraham dwelt at Beersheba.

—Genesis 22:1–19 (The Tanakh, Jewish Publication Society, translated 1917)

The Star of David.

Ten Enduring Rules

The Ten Commandments (or *Decalogue*), which also appear in the Hebrew Bible's book of Deuteronomy, now serve as the moral compass for the entire Judeo-Christian tradition. They are regarded by both Christians and Jews as having been delivered to Moses by God Almighty. It is worth noting here, as well, that Islam regards Moses' prophetic mission as an instance of divine revelation to humankind. (Moses is, as it turns out, the prophet most frequently mentioned in the Qur'an, the holy text of the Muslims.) Although there is no specific mention of the Ten Commandments in the Qur'an, there is ample support for all ten of them in the text of this religious scripture.

It's fair to say, then, that the Ten Commandments set forth in the books of Exodus and Deuteronomy and ascribed directly to God speaking to Moses occupy a position of unparalleled importance, embraced by all three of humankind's major *monotheistic* traditions!

> **DEFINITION**
>
> The **Decalogue** is another word for the Ten Commandments. **Monotheism** is the belief in a single personal God, usually a figure seen as unifying the entire universe. It is not to be confused with the practice of identifying or worshipping a chief god within a group. The worship of many gods simultaneously is known as *polytheism*. Although many polytheistic traditions elevate a single god to a position of dominance, the Hebrew Bible's early emphasis on a single true God is distinctive.

The Ten Commandments

Even though, for most Westerners, the Ten Commandments are pretty familiar material, not many of us today can recite them all by heart. Given the immense influence of these principles on religious practices around the world, they're worth reviewing in their entirety.

Let's look now at all 10 of these rules, which represent the very heart of the Law in the Jewish tradition and have profoundly influenced religious practice and social interaction in so many other religions, as well.

Note: The division points between the commandments vary between Jewish and non-Jewish observance. The Jewish divisions of the text are used here.

1. I am the LORD thy God, who brought thee out of the land of Egypt, out of the house of bondage.

2. Thou shalt have no other gods before Me. Thou shalt not make unto thee a graven image, nor any manner of likeness, of any thing that is in heaven above, or that is in the earth beneath, or that is in the water under the earth; thou shalt not bow down unto them, nor serve them; for I the LORD thy God am a jealous God, visiting the iniquity of the fathers upon the children unto the third and fourth generation of them that hate Me; and showing mercy unto the thousandth generation of them that love Me and keep My commandments.

3. Thou shalt not take the name of the Lord thy God in vain, for the Lord will not hold him guiltless that taketh His name in vain.

4. Remember the sabbath day, to keep it holy. Six days shalt thou labor, and do all thy work; but the seventh day is a sabbath unto the Lord thy God, in it thou shalt not do any manner of work, thou, nor thy son, nor thy daughter, nor thy man-servant, nor thy maid-servant, nor thy cattle, nor thy stranger that is within thy gates; for in six days the Lord made heaven and earth, the sea, and all that in them is, and rested the seventh day, wherefore the Lord blessed the sabbath day, and hallowed it.

5. Honor thy father and mother, that thy days may be long upon the land which the Lord thy God giveth thee.

6. Thou shalt not kill.

7. Thou shalt not commit adultery.

8. Thou shalt not steal.

9. Thou shalt not bear false witness against thy neighbor.

10. Thou shalt not covet thy neighbor's house; thou shalt not covet thy neighbor's wife, nor his man-servant, nor his maid-servant, nor his ox, nor his ass, nor any thing that is thy neighbor's.

—Exodus 20:2–17 (The Tanakh, Jewish Publication Society, translated 1917)

The Kingdom and the Dispersion

The Israelites established a stable kingdom. A period of political continuity and self-determination, under the kings Saul, David, and Solomon, followed. Division of the kingdom and domination by Assyrian and Babylonian forces in the eighth and sixth centuries B.C.E., respectively, led eventually to a dispersion of the Hebrews beyond the borders of their former nation. When the Hebrews finally returned to their homeland, Israel was a political power no more. A period of Roman domination led to a dispersal (known as the Exile) of large numbers of Hebrews beyond the borders of their former nation and the destruction of their sacred Temple in Jerusalem. A new Temple was built in Jerusalem, but under Roman rule, believers suffered the destruction of this sacred edifice (in 70 C.E.) and the eventual neutralization of all organized Jewish opposition.

The ideas that guide Judaism are animated by a belief that God directs all aspects of human activity, public and private, individual and collective. A "religion," understood as a limited set of beliefs, or as a separate entity from a kingdom or a tribe, was not the point. At issue instead was unswerving devotion to the will of God in any and every aspect of one's life. This single-minded devotion to a single all-powerful Deity may well have been one of the features that enabled the Hebrews to perpetuate and extend their faith even after the disappearance of what a modern observer would consider to be a "political" structure.

Despite the dissolution of their country as a political entity, however, the faith of the Israelites in their destiny as a "chosen people," and their commitment to the idea of a single true God, endured. That faith supported, and probably reinvigorated, a set of core traditions and observances that have remained in place from the Diaspora (the "scattering" that followed the Babylonian captivity) to the current time. For more than two and a half millennia, the traditions and observances ascribed to Abraham and his people have continued to thrive in societies around the globe, many of them distinctly hostile to Jewish practice and belief.

The Prophets

Within the Jewish tradition, the revelation of the *Law*—the first five books of the Hebrew Bible—was reinforced and supported by the revelation of the Prophets. According to scripture, certain people were chosen by God to remind the people of the Creator's love for them, and of the necessity of their obedience to the Law.

DEFINITION

In the Jewish tradition, the **Law** is the Torah, the Five Books of Moses. These represent the written account of the revelation of God, who is regarded as having been active in every aspect of human development and history, and as being active in the same way today.

Fundamental Precepts

Regardless of denomination or sect, practicing Jews believe that ...

- There is one and only one God, with Whom each individual has direct personal experience, and to Whom prayers may be addressed.

- God is the ultimate authority and possesses final dominion over the universe.

- Life is holy.

- The Torah (a term that usually means the scroll containing the Five Books of Moses, but may also refer to accumulated sacred writings through the centuries) is a guide to correct and upright living and a source of continued revelation of the word of God. The act of studying the Torah is the practical equivalent of prayer.

- Group worship and prayer are indispensable elements of a righteous life.

- Jews around the world, regardless of nationality, share a broad common destiny and a sense of collective purpose and responsibility to one another.

SPIRITUAL SIGNPOST

Over time, writings reflecting the message of the prophets—a phrase that usually refers both to a specific prophet and his accompanying school—were received and celebrated within the community of believers. Their messages were diverse and sometimes, as in the book of Isaiah, included the promise of a national reawakening under the righteous leadership of a Messiah who would redeem Israel and all human beings. Throughout this diverse scriptural heritage, the final emphasis has been on the single nature of the divine entity.

Despite these common bonds, the truth is that Judaism has been and still is a remarkably diverse faith that accommodates a wide variety of beliefs expressed by practitioners the world 'round. Beyond the major points previously laid out, there really is no single unifying dogma or brief summary of principles embraced by all practicing Jews.

Some broad and universally accepted ideas, however, arise from the principles just outlined, and these are worth reviewing in detail now.

Some Key Aspects of Judaism

The first timeless dimension of Jewish spirituality is the appreciation of the proclamation known as the Sh'ma: "Hear, O Israel, the Lord is God, the Lord is One." (Deuteronomy 6:4–9) Amidst many neighbors with different beliefs, the ancient Hebrews proclaimed that their God was one. The absolute primacy of this one God was a distinctive component of this tradition, the world's oldest monotheistic faith.

The prohibitions against idolatry in the Hebrew Bible reflect a deep and abiding concern that no limited entity or belief be mistaken for the one true God by His chosen people. In their fullest sense, these warnings serve as injunctions against pursuing anything other than the Lord, who had been divinely revealed to Abraham in the desert, to Moses at Mt. Sinai, and again and again through the prophets. This single, transcendent God's demands were (and are) simple and nonnegotiable: Obey the laws and commandments I have set down for the good of all my chosen ones.

The Mishna is the recorded assemblage of (originally) oral legal interpretation within Judaism. When taken together with some important commentaries, the Mishna constitutes the Talmud, a vitally important collection of studies, commentary, anecdote, allegory, and elaboration that forms a fundamental guide influencing day-to-day Jewish observance and thought.

ON THE PATH

"The Jewish community of Palestine suffered horrendous losses during the Great Revolt and the Bar-Kokhba rebellion. Well over a million Jews were killed in the two ill-fated uprisings…. This decline in the number of knowledgeable Jews seems to have been a decisive factor in Rabbi Judah the Prince's decision around the year 200 C.E. to record in writing the Oral Law. For centuries, Judaism's leading rabbis had resisted writing down the Oral Law….(W)ith the deaths of so many teachers in the failed revolts, Rabbi Judah apparently feared that the Oral Law would be forgotten unless it were written down.

"In the Mishna, the name for the sixty-three tractates in which Rabbi Judah set down the Oral Law, Jewish law is systematically codified, unlike in the Torah. For example, if a person wanted to find every law in the Torah about the Sabbath, he would have to locate scattered references in Exodus, Leviticus, and Numbers. Indeed, in order to know everything the Torah said on a given subject, one either had to read through all of it or know its contents by heart. Rabbi Judah avoided this problem by arranging the Mishna topically."—Joseph Telushkin. *Jewish Literacy: The Most Important Things to Know About the Jewish Religion, Its People and Its History.* NY: William Morrow and Co., 1991.

The Covenant

Another key idea in Judaism is to be found in the notion of the Covenant. God called forth a people, a community, who received God's revelation both through the sign of the Covenant and through the Law.

In the Jewish tradition, the notion that God acted to bestow the Covenant and the Law upon a particular nation and that these gifts represent examples of divine intervention for and blessings to that people, are vitally important. A believer's ability to keep the Law demonstrates his or her conformity with the will of God and serves as a sign of belonging as a member of the community.

A Community Gathered

Yet another distinctive aspect of Judaism has to do with the emphasis on the group identity assumed by believers regarded as the descendants of Abraham and Isaac. This tradition emphasizes community-based experience and worship in a truly remarkable way.

The constantly reinforced sense of belonging, not just to a happenstance social arrangement but to a people of the Lord, takes on great significance within the Jewish faith. This tradition does not, of course, reject the idea of a single individual's relationship with the Deity, but it does place a profound emphasis on the social phenomena that encompasses (and often regulates) both daily worship and daily social interaction among believers.

In other words, Judaism nourishes a community-based form of religious practice. Distinctive social customs (such as circumcision among male members of the community) reinforce this sense of belonging. The individual operates not merely within a set of precepts, admonitions, or philosophical principles, but as part of a coherent, constantly reinforced community of fellow believers. In that community, the written account of the divine revelation is proclaimed and seen.

ON THE PATH

Education and study are important elements of the Jewish experience. The Book of Proverbs counsels believers, "Train up a child in the way he should go." (Proverbs 22.6)

Of vital importance in Judaism is the sense of being called into the community to make appropriate contributions on a number of levels: in the *synagogue* or temple, as part of a family, and as a member of a Jewish citizenry. Prayer life in the Jewish tradition takes place both in formal settings, such as at synagogue, and also at home. The idea of attentive worship through predetermined, and usually written, prayer is also a distinctive and important one in this faith. This practice supports Judaism's emphasis upon a specific written liturgy to celebrate the community's ongoing relationship with the one true God.

DEFINITION

A rabbi is a respected teacher and leader of worship, usually connected to a particular **synagogue** (house of learning and prayer).

The Least You Need to Know

- The history of Judaism is intimately related to, but not synonymous with, the history of the ancient kingdom of Israel. The lineage of Judaism can be traced back to the patriarch Abraham.
- The Torah teaches about Abraham and the Covenant he formed with God.
- The importance of the Covenant (God's agreement with the chosen people of Israel) and the Law (the written account of God's revelation) cannot be overstated within this faith.
- The Ten Commandments—the core of Jewish Law—have profoundly influenced not only Judaism, but Christianity and Islam as well. These ten injunctions can be seen as central elements not only of the Jewish tradition, but of the entire monotheistic tradition.
- According to the Hebrew Bible, prophets were chosen by God to remind the people of the love of God and of the necessity of their obedience to the Law.
- Judaism is a distinctively community-based tradition.

Modern Jewish Experience

In This Chapter

- How Judaism has developed in modern times
- The Orthodox, Conservative, Reform, and Reconstructionist branches
- The guiding ideas behind each of these movements in the Jewish faith
- The different approaches practicing Jews take to adjust their practices in the modern world

Throughout its long history, Judaism has proven to be one of the world's most remarkably resilient and enduring traditions. It has united believers through good times and bad, in hostile surroundings, and in times of peace, plenty, and harmony. Yet, through the centuries, a fateful question has always arisen: how much should non-Jewish surroundings be allowed to influence Judaism's distinctive practices? This question has resulted in a many-layered set of answers.

In contemporary times, the faith has evolved into a number of branches, each of which has taken a different approach to the difficult matter of whether, and how, to accommodate the various influences of the outside world. These influences, of course, were and are incredibly varied, because Jewish observance takes place in a bewildering array of social and cultural settings. In this chapter, you can read about the major contemporary movements within the faith, and how modern Judaism has defined itself.

Reactions to the Modern World

European Jews of the nineteenth century encountered cultural, scientific, and technological influences that profoundly influenced their daily lifestyles. The European Enlightenment, among many other factors, led a number of believers to press leaders within the faith to take up a sensitive issue: whether a practicing Jew must always strive to live within the dictates of the vast and complex religious code laid out in the Hebrew Bible.

Not surprisingly, a strong set of voices within the Jewish tradition answered that question with a resounding "yes."

> **BARRIER ALERT!**
>
> Judaism is a diverse faith, and the labels we apply to it are only useful up to a point. The major movements we'll be discussing in this chapter carry out certain basic ideas and principles as part of modern Jewish practice, but making broad generalizations about these schools is dangerous. Other schools of thought also exist within the Jewish faith, and none of the major branches can claim complete accord among those who pursue the faith.

The Orthodox Tradition

Members of the *Orthodox* movement, which remains strong to this day, maintain that they are bound to preserve ritual, tradition, and doctrine as received from rabbis of the past, all the way back to the very beginnings of the faith. Practitioners within this community see themselves as willing and eager to preserve the faith exactly as revealed to the people of God in antiquity.

> **DEFINITION**
>
> **Orthodox** Jews take what might be called a "literalist" or "fundamental" approach to issues of faith. The notions of unswerving faith to the written word of God, and to established religious tradition, with no alteration, are important ones within the Orthodox branch of Judaism.

The core of the Orthodox experience can be found in its emphasis on complete, uncompromising conformity to the dictates of God. This branch of the faith tends not to recognize any possibility of accommodation to social changes or influences in what others might refer to as "the outside world." For Orthodox Jews, Judaism *is* the world, inside and out. The emphasis on complete observance of God's will within all aspects of the community, and not merely a supposed "religious sphere," is an ancient idea in this faith. (It's important to understand, however, that this idea was widespread among all religions, and indeed in most cultures, until the modern period.)

Within the Orthodox community, obedience to the will of God—and complete conformity to God's revealed commands—is the world. The primary and overriding influence is to the Law and the traditions that have grown up around it.

The Orthodox tradition reflects a reverence for custom, a deep concern with the word of God, a profound obligation to carry out God's dictates to the letter, and a further obligation to pass on, without alteration, the rituals that have been in place for centuries within the tradition. Distinctive clothing and firmly established social and family structures are expressions of this reverence for custom.

Within the Orthodox Jewish tradition, strong and unalterable gender roles prevail. Certain roles and activities are reserved exclusively for males; others are open only to women. During public religious ceremonies, segregation of the sexes into two groups is the rule. And in both home and synagogue worship, there are liturgical roles based strictly on gender.

Hebrew characters representing the Ten Commandments.

The Orthodox approach can be summed up as a desire to live according to the faith, tradition, and liturgy associated with the Law and to pass those conventions on to the next generations. Both Reform and Conservative Judaism have made observance of at least certain elements of the Law optional; Orthodox Judaism has not. The point is not to keep the entire modern world at bay, but rather to maintain adherence to the Law in its original form.

Conservative Judaism

In *Conservative* Judaism, the notion of absolute adherence to past traditions is not the guiding principle, as it is in the Orthodox branch of the faith. But a strong sense of tradition and continuity still prevails.

Here, the emphasis is on preserving and honoring appropriate traditions from the past, with favor always given to retaining as much as possible of the "old ways"—but not all the "old ways."

Like Orthodox Jews, Conservative adherents affirm the primacy of tradition within their religious experience. They are, however, willing to acknowledge the importance of judiciously chosen adjustments to the world in which they live, and they are not as interested as those within the Orthodox tradition in building a "closed" socioreligious system.

DEFINITION

Conservative Jews do not observe Orthodox standards completely, but nevertheless strive to retain a significant number of the traditions of historic Judaism. The Conservative movement can be seen as representing the "middle ground" in the reform debate within Judaism that took place in the nineteenth century.

Jews in the Conservative tradition truly are "conservative" in the sense that they aim to hold on to (conserve) as much as possible, while still making some accommodation with social realities that appear to have nothing contrary to Judaism.

Conservative Jews have also been known as adherents of the "historical school" of Judaism. They acknowledge the role of history and contemporary social development and are willing to make adjustments to important trends and practices that appear in contemporary life. At the same time, they are keenly aware of Judaism's own history and its demands upon its followers. They argue that tradition and change have been intimately connected throughout the development of the faith.

Reform Judaism

Reform Judaism is the most pragmatic of the three major strands of the Jewish faith today and is the most open to dialogue and interaction with contemporary society. If the Orthodox tradition is focused upon absolute, unwavering adherence to the many dictates of the Law, and the Conservative tradition is concerned with retaining as much as possible of the ancient traditions, the Reform approach can be described as an attempt to retain those essential elements of Judaism that make the most sense in a contemporary setting.

Of course, Reform Jews do not reject the Law as embodied in the Hebrew scriptures and commentaries. They do, however, take a distinctive approach to the interpretation of these injunctions, choosing to accept them in a larger ethical sense that permits each individual believer a greater degree of autonomy than in the Orthodox and Conservative traditions. Followers of Reform Judaism are also the most likely to adapt traditions to current social circumstances and values.

DEFINITION

Within **Reform** Judaism, the entire Torah is accepted as inspired by God, but it is also seen as open to the study and interpretation of the individual. Reform Jews see God's relationship with the Jews as an ongoing process, and emphasize the broad moral messages of the Jewish tradition.

Reform Judaism arose in mid-nineteenth-century Europe, but it experienced its most explosive growth in the United States, where immigrants from Europe helped to propagate it. The Reform branch's willingness to embrace the idea that Jews were citizens of the nations where they lived, and its rejection of the idea that practitioners must be bound by the narrowly interpreted laws of historic Israel, were probably important factors in the movement's growing popularity.

ON THE PATH

"My job as a Reform Rabbi is to share the historic heritage of our people: its laws, its stories, its traditions, its ethics, and its hope for the future."

—Rabbi Cory Weiss

The Pressures of the Outside World

Reform, Conservative, and Orthodox Jews take strikingly different approaches to the specific social questions that arise in contemporary life. The issue of gender-based roles within religious worship itself, for instance, shows the various approaches these three wings of contemporary Jewry take to matters of "social accommodation."

Suppose a woman has great faith and sincere purpose, is as knowledgeable as her male counterparts on spiritual and scriptural issues, and is eager to become a teacher. The question arises: Why can't such a woman become a rabbi?

The debate would be an easy one to resolve in the Orthodox tradition. An Orthodox Jew would probably address this issue by pointing out that "outside" notions of sexual equality in contemporary society simply don't matter in God's community. What has worked in the past can be counted on to work in the future, and believers have an obligation not only to reinforce but to pass along existing patterns of worship, regardless of what outsiders have to say about who should be permitted to become a rabbi.

An Orthodox believer of either sex might argue, "Centuries of tradition have established certain distinct roles for men and women, roles that are not open to debate or alteration. Within the community of Jews that has been established and supported by God's intervention, women have never become rabbis, and so long as that tradition is maintained and faithfully passed along, women probably never will become rabbis. After all, if the word of God is represented within our tradition—and we certainly believe that it is—then tinkering with any aspect of the tradition to accommodate modern notions is foolish and unthinkable." As a matter of recent history, the Orthodox ordination of women as rabbis has (so far) remained off-limits.

SPIRITUAL SIGNPOST

Some elements of the culture in which Reform Jews live are seen as part and parcel of their identities as people of God. Reform Jews, then, attempt to take a pragmatic approach by balancing modern viewpoints and social conclusions more or less equally against established tradition, all the while hoping to honor, illuminate, and reinforce the fundamental truths of the faith. Their focus is on engaging in contemporary realities as they present themselves, rather than on pre-written prayers and rituals for every conceivable situation.

A Conservative Jew would be more willing to make "judgment calls" arising from outside influences when it comes to the larger issue of the relative social roles of men and women, but would nevertheless insist upon a firm base of tradition as the best means of making these decisions. Thus, strict gender stereotyping is less pronounced within the Conservative tradition than within Orthodox Jewry, because scriptural arguments can be made that accommodations on such issues may be, at some level, in keeping with the teachings of the Prophets.

A member of the Conservative tradition, then, would be likely to approach this issue as follows: "Yes, I live in Boston in the twenty-first century, and yes, I am aware of the fact that I live in a society that places great importance on the fundamental equality of men and women. In evaluating issues such as this one, I also take into account the Lord's injunction to love my neighbors as myself." Although the issue of ordaining female rabbis has remained highly controversial within the Conservative branch of the faith, a number of Conservative women have in fact assumed that role. A member of the Reform wing, by contrast, would be far more likely to ask about the *purpose* a given tradition is serving.

A Reform Jew, in addressing the question of whether female rabbis are appropriate, would not ignore the centuries of tradition that point toward male rabbis and only male rabbis. By the same token, the Reform movement does not allow the fact that "things have always been done that way" to assume fundamental importance when it comes to meeting the spiritual needs of contemporary Jews.

Reform Jews reject the claim that they are "tampering" with the scriptures or with doctrine and argue instead that they are allowing the scriptures to be lived more fully and more deeply by not erecting barriers likely to prove intimidating to modern-day practitioners. Reform Judaism makes far fewer social demands on its practitioners than the Orthodox and Conservative branches do. Very few Reform practitioners attempt to encompass every aspect of daily life in their customs and traditions, as so many members of the Orthodox school do.

SPIRITUAL SIGNPOST

The role of the rabbi has evolved over the many centuries of Judaism's development. In ancient times, rabbis were fundamentally instructors in, and explainers of, the Law. In later years, important responsibilities connected to the spiritual life of the community as a whole became important. Although preaching and administrative work have assumed greater prominence for rabbis in modern times within many communities (including Orthodox ones), Orthodox rabbis have always historically emphasized their roles as interpreters and instructors of the Torah.

A Reform practitioner might consider the issue this way: "Is the possibility of a radical revision in gender roles, such as female rabbis, really in opposition to the fundamental ideas and values of my faith? Or does such a change instead have a chance to make that faith more accessible to me and to others in my community? If I can answer affirmatively to the second question, then there is probably no good reason not to alter tradition and practice in this area."

In the end, Reform Jews are likely to ask themselves something similar to this: "How can those of us who live life in contemporary society best be brought into contact with the ancient truths?" It's not surprising, then, that Reform Judaism has formally accepted women as religious teachers since 1922, having first debated the idea in the late nineteenth century.

The Diversity of "Jewishness"

There are many, many forms of observance within Judaism. We've only touched on a few of the main strands. To try to define and isolate the "essence" of Jewish practice in its many diverse disciplines and innumerable social settings is to miss something fundamental about the faith. Certainly it cannot be done without oversimplifying and perhaps seriously misreading the ancient traditions—and misreading "Jewishness" itself. Indeed, the very words "Jew" and "Judaism" appear nowhere in the Torah! The effort to refine, expand, and perpetuate this Covenant faith, however, despite obstacles and persecutions, extends in an unbroken chain from the mists of antiquity to the present century.

In addition to the well-known Orthodox, Conservative, and Reform traditions, a number of other currents within the Jewish faith claim significant numbers of followers. The Reconstructionist school, a movement of the twentieth century, holds that Judaism is a fundamentally social (rather than God-centered) religious civilization. They see Judaism as a cultural phenomenon and boldly reject some core ideas about God embraced by other Jews. Reconstructionists do not, for instance, accept the contention that the Hebrew Bible is the word of God. They share with Reform Jews a belief in the fundamental equality of male and female rights.

Other important traditions include those of the *Sephardic* Jews, whose distinctive traditions and practices evolved centuries ago in Spain and Portugal, and the *Hasidic* Jews, members of a sect that originated in Poland in the eighteenth century, who continue to emphasize religious mysticism and joy in prayer.

Two Extraordinary Modern Events

Two twentieth-century occurrences have profoundly affected contemporary Jewish life. The first was the rise of *Zionism,* a philosophy that made its first appearance in the nineteenth century and gained dramatically in influence after the turn of the century. Zionism embraced without apology the goal of reestablishing the state of Israel. This goal was realized a few years after the conclusion of the Second World War. (For a closer look at the Zionist movement, see Chapter 7.)

The second influence, of course, and one that, like Zionism, can probably never be fully separated from the origins of the modern state of Israel, was the Holocaust. Hitler's virulently anti-Semitic Nazi German state pursued and perpetuated across Europe a brutal policy of systematic murder. The Nazis' assembly line brand of genocide resulted in the deaths of millions of Jews, along with a significant number of non-Jews. After the defeat of the Germans, Jews around the world vowed never to forget, or permit a repetition of, the unspeakable horrors of the concentration camps.

The Least You Need to Know

- Judaism is a vibrant and diverse faith with many strands, a tradition that is continually rediscovering itself in both new and old expressions.
- Orthodox Jews take a fundamental approach to the dictates of the Law, seek to pass along existing traditions without changing them, and strive to incorporate the dictates of their faith into a wide range of daily activities and social interactions.
- Conservative Jews acknowledge the need to make some accommodations to external society, but nevertheless grant an important and usually dominant role to the traditions of the past.
- Reform Jews do not see the dictates of the Hebrew Bible as specific, binding regulations on daily contact with others, but rather seek to honor tradition and faith by making religious observance accessible to contemporary practitioners.
- Other important movements within Judaism include the Reconstructionist school and the Sephardic and Hasidic traditions.

Jewish Ritual and Celebration

In This Chapter

- Jewish tradition and life itself as a ceremony
- Jewish rituals
- Jewish observances
- Jewish holidays

In this chapter, you learn about the specifics of religious observance within the Jewish tradition; about holidays such as Passover, Rosh Hashanah, and Yom Kippur; and about the rituals that mark important landmarks in the life of practicing Jews.

Life: The Ultimate Religious Ceremony

As you've seen, one distinctive aspect of Judaism is its emphasis on a detailed code of conduct rooted in the survival of the ancient people of the original kingdom of Israel. Judaism celebrates specific guideposts by which the community is to perpetuate itself, and it embraces its traditions as both worthy in themselves and reflections of an all-pervasive daily spirituality within the members of the community as they interact with one another.

Today, of course, the role played by Jewish ritual and by predetermined forms of worship varies depending on the nature of the emphasis on the Law accorded by contemporary traditions. At the foundation of all Jewish practice, however, is an all-encompassing approach that seeks to translate the incredible detail and diversity of God's creation to a holy form of human celebration, often quite detailed itself. The basic aim of Jewish worship, then, is to see all of life as *liturgy*.

DEFINITION

Liturgy is public worship or ritual.

The overarching religious belief of Judaism is that all life should be seen as a ritual in honor of the Creator. Orthodox, Conservative, and Reform are in agreement on this point, but their emphases and their definitions of the word "ritual" differ.

Worship in the Orthodox tradition places a heavy emphasis on word-for-word recitation of specific prayers in specific situations. There are specific prayers to be recited upon awakening and before eating. There is even a prayer of thanksgiving following a trip to the bathroom, in which the believer praises God for the wonder of the body and its functions.

The Conservative approach to worship is less formalized but still keyed to tradition. The Conservative practitioner's approach to questions of formal religious worship embraces ritual as one expression of values like loving God and helping others, rather than a commitment to specific prayers for every conceivable situation. Conservative Jews could be said to follow the popular saying, "There's a time and a place for everything."

Reform Jews, while embracing some specific forms of religious worship, are just as likely to find legitimacy in an unscripted response to day-to-day activities—a response rooted in the idea that action itself is a form of prayer. Members of the Reform movement arfe more prone to see prewritten, predetermined prayer designed for particular day-to-day situations as something that distances one from the actual experience of God's creation.

The Reform school is not anti-prayer—far from it. It's just that the multiplicity of instruction and repetition found in the other two traditions, and particularly in Orthodox Judaism, tends to be seen by Reform Jews as an obstacle to spiritual growth rather than an aid.

Every branch of the faith is sincere in its approaches. The question is how to realize the principles laid down in scripture and tradition.

Dietary Laws

Just as prayer and common worship had a distinct social advantage to subjects of the ancient kingdom of Israel (social cohesion and a sense of purpose within the community), specific dietary rules served a purpose as well. The dietary rules set down in the Hebrew Bible may have seemed unusual to the Israelites' neighbors, but they ensured the health and well-being of the people, and served as yet another example of the fulfillment of God's promises to his people.

SPIRITUAL SIGNPOST

The word *kosher* refers to that which is in accordance with the established standards of Jewish ritual, typically food and its preparation. Meat that is kosher comes from animals that both chew a cud and have cloven hoofs (such as sheep and cows), and that are killed in accordance with special slaughtering procedures. Kosher meat must be prepared in such a way as to remove all traces of blood. Seafood is considered kosher if the animals caught have scales or fins. Poultry is kosher if it is slaughtered and prepared in the same manner as meat. Kosher dietary guidelines prohibit the consumption of dairy products at the same time, or immediately before or after, a meal including meat products. Separate cooking and serving utensils are required for dairy and non-dairy meals.

Ritual cleanliness and the avoidance of unclean animals remain all-important parts of the Jewish tradition, just as they were an important part of survival in Biblical times. Like the circumcision of males, specific dietary demands help to define and distinguish both the individual and the community he or she is a part of. To the practitioner, however, such considerations are secondary. These injunctions are, first and foremost, God's Law.

What Happens in the Service?

Group prayer is extremely important in the Jewish tradition. The number, complexity, and purpose of the prayers recited during a service at a synagogue varies according to the hour of the day, the day of the month, and the branch of Judaism in question. Those wishing to pray alone may do so, but must eliminate certain prayers meant for group recitation.

Hebrew is the sacred language of Judaism. Orthodox services incorporate the most Hebrew in the ceremony; Reform tends to use the least. Similarly, Reform and Reconstruction services tend to be shorter than their Orthodox and Conservative counterparts. According to long-observed custom, a communal service requires a quorum, or *minyan*, of at least 10 adults (persons over the age of 13) to proceed. Orthodox Jews, as well as many Conservative practitioners, require 10 *men* for a minyan.

The basic service consists of …

- The *Amidah*, a group of grateful salutations and prayers of praise to God.

- The *Sh'ma*, a pledge of faith, the centerpiece of which is the all-important declaration from Deuteronomy: "Hear O Israel, the Lord is our God, the Lord is One."

- A public reading of a passage from the Torah. The *aliyah*, or "going up," refers to the act of being summoned to participate in this reading, a distinct honor.

A rabbi leads the service. A cantor sings and leads the congregation in song.

SPIRITUAL SIGNPOST

The fundamental elements of the service in a synagogue/temple may be presented in brief or lengthy variations, depending on the demands of the situation and the particular branch of the Jewish faith. Morning, midday, and sunset prayer services typically run from 15 to 30 minutes; Friday evening or Saturday morning services are considerably longer.

Shabbat

The Shabbat, or "repose" that follows six days of workday activity, parallels the account in the book of Genesis of God's rest after the Creation. The day begins on Friday at sunset and continues until nightfall on Saturday. Work is prohibited at this time, but the definition of "work" can very quickly become a matter of (intricate) discussion among practitioners. Buying, selling, and negotiating, however, are all acknowledged as prohibited activities for Jews during this period, which is also known as the Sabbath.

Regardless of the branch of Judaism under discussion, prayer services undertaken on the Sabbath are the longest and most intricate of them all. Friday evening services may last anywhere from half an hour to three times that long. The Saturday morning service may go as long as three full hours.

Major Observances

Following are thumbnail sketches of some of the most important observances within the Jewish faith. For more detailed information on Jewish rituals and celebrations, see the fine books *How to Be a Perfect Stranger* (Arthur J. Magida, Editor, Jewish Lights Publishing, 1996) and *This Is My God: The Jewish Way of Life* (Herman Wouk, Pocket Books, 1974).

Rosh Hashanah

This is the Jewish New Year, a holiday that takes place on the first and second days of the Hebrew month Tishrei, roughly the middle of September to the middle of October. (The Hebrew religious calendar is based on the phases of the moon, not on the Gregorian calendar we go by in daily life.)

Rosh Hashanah celebrates both the religious New Year and the creation of the earth as described in the early chapters of the book of Genesis. Some branches celebrate both days of this holiday; others (the majority of Reform congregations) only the first day. Work is not performed.

SPIRITUAL SIGNPOST

Jewish congregations require males (even males of another faith) to wear a small headpiece called a *yarmulke* (YAM-uh-kuh) during services. Orthodox congregations require that men and women sit in separate areas.

Yom Kippur

On this day, which takes place shortly after Rosh Hashanah on the tenth day of Tishrei, practicing Jews the world over observe the Day of Atonement. From the sundown that marks the beginning of Yom Kippur until the sundown of the following day, believers forgo food and drink, do no work, and repent for misdeeds of the year just past.

BARRIER ALERT!

The habit many Gentiles have of referring to Chanukah as the "Jewish Christmas" can be a source of frustration among practicing Jews. The celebration of this (minor) holiday involves the commemoration of events that precede the birth of Jesus by more than 150 years.

Sukkot

The harvest celebration known as the Feast of Booths lasts for eight days and generally takes place late in the month of October (using the secular Gregorian calendar). It is common to perform no work at the beginning and end of the celebration, but the number of days observed in this manner varies. By the way, the "booth" is a small hut (sukkah) erected for the occasion; meals are eaten in it.

Chanukah (Hanukkah)

The beneficiary, perhaps, of undue media attention because of its (coincidental) placement near the Christian observance of the birth of Christ, Chanukah is often presented as a "Jewish alternative" to Christmas. This is unfortunate, as the Festival of Lights deserves honor, attention, and recognition on its own terms and within its own tradition. The holiday known as the Festival of Lights celebrates the victory of the Maccabees over the Syrians in the second century B.C.E. It begins on the twenty-fifth day of the Hebrew month of Kislev (usually early- to mid-December). Work is permitted during Chanukah.

The menorah is used during the festival of Chanukah.

Purim

A festival celebration commencing on the fourteenth day of the Hebrew month Adar (usually late February or early March), Purim commemorates the deliverance of Persian Jews from destruction, as recounted in the book of Esther. This joyous festival is preceded by a day of fasting, and soon gives way to general merrymaking. Members of the community, especially children, dress up in costume and go to temple for a reading from the book of Esther. Work is permitted on Purim.

SPIRITUAL SIGNPOST

Purim is marked by gift-giving and generosity toward those in need.

Pesach (Passover)

This major holiday, which begins on the fifteenth day of the month of Nisan, honors the delivery of the Jewish people from slavery in Egypt. According to the book of Exodus, God issued a set of instructions for the Israelites: They were to prepare a special feast in great haste before the departure from Egypt. With no time for bread to rise, the bread at the meal would have to be unleavened.

Exodus also reports that God arranged for the Angel of Death to destroy the first-born males of the Egyptians, and to "pass over" the marked houses of the Israelites, killing no one within. The Passover celebration, during which practicing Jews abstain from foods prepared with yeast or any other leavening agent, is observed (usually beginning in late March or early April) for seven days by Reform Jews and for eight by members of the other major branches. Many Jews (especially those who follow the Orthodox tradition) perform no work on the first and last two days of the period, but observances vary.

Shavuot

This holiday celebrates both the spring harvest season and God's gift of the Torah. It takes place on the sixth and seventh days of the month of Sivan, which corresponds to May or June in the secular Gregorian calendar. As a general rule, Orthodox Jews do no work on these days; a number of Conservative and Reconstructionist practitioners follow the same practice, but Reform Jews celebrate Shavuot for a single day.

Life Rituals

The baby boy is at the center of the *brit milah* (covenant of circumcision), the ritual removal of the foreskin enacted in accordance with Genesis 17:10. This ceremony takes place on the eighth day of the baby boy's life. A parallel naming ceremony for infant girls is known as the *brit hayyim* (covenant of life) or *brit bat* (covenant of the daughter). This, too, occurs on the eighth day of life.

At the age of 13, a Jewish male marks his entry into the community as an adult during his *bar mitzvah* (son of the commandment). The female counterpart is known as a *bat mitzvah* (daughter of the commandment), and can be held for females as young as 12. The bat mitzvah was first celebrated in the twentieth century.

The Jewish marriage ceremony is known as the *kiddushin* (sanctification). It takes place under a wedding canopy known as a *huppah*, and incorporates the ritual breaking of a glass underfoot, an act that commemorates a sad event in Jewish history, the destruction of the Temple in Jerusalem in 70 C.E.

Funeral observances in the Jewish tradition follow distinct guidelines that may vary depending on the branch of Judaism in question. (Reform Jews, for instance, permit cremation, while Jews of most other traditions observe injunctions against the practice.)

The Least You Need to Know

- Jewish customs, rituals, and dietary guidelines provided both social cohesion and rules for law-abiding life among ancient Israelites, just as they do for practicing Jews today.
- The moment-to-moment celebration of life itself, in all its diversity, underlies Jewish worship, observance, and ritual.
- Different branches of Jewish faith take different approaches to the ideal forms of celebrating life.
- Major Jewish holidays include Rosh Hashanah, Yom Kippur, and Passover.

Breaking Down Barriers to Judaism

In This Chapter

- Zionism
- Judaism and the position of women
- "Judeo-Christian" used as a term
- Anti-Semitism

There are many misconceptions, myths, and stereotypes associated with Judaism. In this chapter, five of the most common are covered.

Misconception #1: Zionism equals Judaism.

People who are unfamiliar with the historical and political differences between Judaism and *Zionism* sometimes make the newcomer's mistake of assuming that the two are one and the same. They are not. In addition, many who disapprove of the policies of the Israeli government speak of Jewishness and the desire to maintain a Jewish state as though these two things are identical. Very often, this is not an innocent mistake, but rather a deliberate slur against Judaism and those who practice it.

Although the overwhelming majority of Jewish people support (and believe in defending) the State of Israel, one can be a practicing Jew without arguing in favor of an internationally recognized Jewish homeland. A number of prominent Jews oppose the principles of Zionism, though they are certainly in the minority. (The author Noam Chomsky is perhaps the best-known American example.)

The movement known as Zionism was launched in 1896 by a man named Theodor Herzl, and has since become a central part of modern Jewish history. The high point of the movement was, clearly, the founding of the Jewish state in 1948. It's important to understand that Zionism is a specific political movement that advocated the segregation of the Jewish people in a specific national setting. To support the modern expression of Zionism is to believe that it is important to maintain "a publicly and legally assured home" in present-day Israel.

The idea of a Jewish nation in Palestine has many scriptural references in the Hebrew Bible, which is one reason for the historically strong support of Jews around the world for the state of Israel. Scriptural arguments alone, however, do not mean all Jews are Zionists. For more information on this complex subject, see the excellent article "The Difference Between Judaism and Zionism," by G. Neuberger, available at www.jewsnotzionists.org/differencejudzion.html.

In the meantime, bear in mind that many observant Jews embrace and applaud the Zionist movement and its aims; other Jews have no opinion on it, and still others have reservations about its goals or methods. One's status as a Jew is not determined by one's position on contemporary political issues.

Misconception #2: The Jewish people are guilty of deicide.

A gross slander has been directed at the Jewish people over the last 2,000 years of their history. It is the common claim that they are responsible, as a people, for the execution of Jesus Christ, and are therefore guilty of *deicide*.

It is worth noting that the claim has been condemned by all but the most rabidly anti-Semitic Christians, and was explicitly denounced by the Roman Catholic Church in the Second Vatican Council in the 1960s.

Today, the claim that the Jewish people are guilty, as a group, of the execution of Jesus of Nazareth simply identifies those who make the claim as religious bigots who promote hatred and intolerance.

Misconception #3: Judaism views women in a negative way.

Many people consider Orthodox and Conservative Jewish religious practices to carry the shadow of negative attitudes toward women. Yet female practitioners of these schools of the Jewish faith overwhelmingly reject the characterizations, and frequently point out that they have chosen to pursue their own spiritual path in a setting that emphasizes integrity, autonomy, and personal growth before God.

Women in Judaism enjoy a rich and rewarding spiritual legacy. The idea that they are the participants in their own oppression carries little weight among Jewish women themselves, who reject the notion. (See similar discussions on Islamic gender issues in Chapter 18.)

It is worth noting as well that Jewish women who follow Biblical injunctions on separation from the rest of the community during the menstrual cycle view this practice not as a matter of being "unclean"—a translation that is not borne out by the original scripture text—but as an opportunity to pray and become closer to God during an important time. When the remains of an ovum that could have become a human being is being expelled from the body, believers maintain, this is a time for mindful observance of the passing of a human soul.

SPIRITUAL SIGNPOST

The Rabbis of the Talmud believed that women maintain a variety of spiritual insight known as *Dinah* that, if developed properly, surpasses the parallel perceptive ability of men. The skill is basically that of being able to tell the difference between elements or occurrences that seem to be identical or very close in nature.

Misconception #4: "Judeo-Christian" means, basically, "Christian."

Many assume that the common term "Judeo-Christian" has been used for centuries to describe the development of the religious component of Western civilization. In fact, the phrase only dates back to 1899. It came into vogue during World War II as the media of the Allied nations tried to come to grips with the enormity of the Nazi Holocaust against the Jews. The term should be used carefully.

It tends to be used much more frequently by Christians than by Jews, in contexts that seek to emphasize the continuity of the Christian and Jewish faith traditions. Jewish people, however, sometimes resent the phrase, because it often seems to suggest that Jews and Christians follow in essence the same religious practices. This is, of course, untrue.

The best advice here is simply to think before using the term. At all costs, one should strive to avoid the mistake of one prominent fundamentalist Christian group, which circulated press materials emphasizing its devotion to "Judeo-Christian values." As proof of this, it provided a list of a series of beliefs, none of which, Jewish readers were quick to point out, had anything whatsoever to do with Judaism!

BARRIER ALERT!

If you decide to use the term "Judeo-Christian," be sure that you are actually making reference to, and comparing, the traditions of both Judaism and Christianity.

Misconception #5: Judaism is monolithic.

A vast array of ominous fantasies have proceeded from the (ridiculous) argument that Jewish people think, work, invest, write, and organize as a single, conspiratorial group. This belief is, perhaps, the founding principle of *anti-Semitism*.

DEFINITION

Anti-Semitism is hatred of or discrimination against Jewish people. It is often rooted in the belief that the global body of Jewish believers is operating with a single, usually nefarious worldview, and that it pursues coordinated objectives.

Jewish people, as with Buddhists, Hindus, Muslims, Christians, and members of other faiths, pursue widely divergent political, social, and educational goals. They do not act as a single group, nor do they control entire industries or social institutions to manipulate them to the ends of some global Jewish bureaucracy. Anyone who denies the staggering plurality of the modern Jewish experience has simply not been exposed to that experience in any meaningful way.

The Least You Need to Know

- Zionism is not the same as Judaism.
- Judaism does not view women negatively.
- Use the term "Judeo-Christian" with care.
- Judaism is not a monolithic or dangerous global movement.

Christianity

Virtually no nation on earth is without some community of Christian believers. Although its adherents can be found around the world, and acceptance of Jesus as the Messiah, the Son of God, is central to the faith, Christianity's "basic doctrines" defy simple explanation. In part, this is because of the many divergent traditions and structures that have emerged over the centuries as the result of disagreements over doctrine and practice; and in part, it is because the role and teachings of Jesus himself remain, after two millennia, part of a fundamental mystery.

Christian Beginnings

In This Chapter

- The man at the center
- The origins of organized Christianity
- The historical development of the various branches of the Christian church
- The diversity of Christian observance

Christianity grew from a tiny sect in first-century Palestine to become one of the world's great faiths. In this chapter, you learn about how that faith system has developed, what forces have influenced it, and some of the diverse pathways it has traveled during the first 2,000 years of its existence.

The Man at the Center of the Faith

The simple and familiar name "Jesus Christ" offers a great deal of information about the influences that shaped Christianity.

"Jesus" is a Latinized form of the Greek "Iesous," a transliteration of a Hebrew name most contemporary Christians probably would not recognize: Y'shua. And "Christ" is not a name at all, but a description—a variation on the Greek word "Christos," which means "the anointed one." This word is, in turn, a translation of the Hebrew "Messiah"—in Jewish tradition, a figure chosen and anointed by God who would bring salvation to Israel.

The Holy Spirit, pictured as a dove. The New Testament describes a dove (the "Spirit of God") descending upon Jesus at his baptism.

A few historians have suggested that all we can know for certain about Jesus of Galilee is that he was crucified in Jerusalem—probably on charges open-ended enough to sound like blasphemy to the Jewish religious leaders of his day and like sedition to the Roman authorities. However, most scholars now accept the basic Gospel picture of Jesus—that he conducted a ministry that embraced sinners and social outcasts; that he was popularly regarded as a healer and teacher; that he occasionally challenged the religious authorities of the day; and that he promoted love, tolerance, and faith. Jesus' claim to be the Messiah won him bitter enemies as well as followers, and was probably one reason for his execution.

Christians believe that Jesus was both God and Man, born on Earth to redeem the human race. Christians celebrate the mystery of the Incarnation—the notion that, by the power of the Holy Spirit, the Virgin Mary conceived and gave birth to a son who is a divine person with both a divine and a human nature. They accept and celebrate Jesus' ethical teachings, which emphasize unfailing mercy and forgiveness. They also believe that after Judas Iscariot betrayed him and Pontius Pilate condemned him to death, Jesus rose again from the dead, enabling humans to achieve true salvation. Christians anticipate the return, or Second Coming, of the risen Jesus.

The name "Jesus Christ" represents a fateful (and, at the time, controversial) moment in the history of the church. These two words served to introduce Jesus, and the

Jewish concept of a redeemer for the subjugated nation of Israel, to a distinctly non-Jewish audience. The various messages sent to that audience laid the foundations of modern Christianity. In other words: the figure at the center of this faith is described at a distance, in translation, as the result of Greek cultural influences in the Mediterranean societies where the faith first gained wide acceptance among non-Jews. After this phase of its development, Christianity began the ascent that would lead to its status as one of the world's major religions.

Who was the "real" Jesus? A feeling of removal from Jesus the person sometimes arises among some of today's Christians, and understandably. Today, we may expect written history to be an attempt at a neutral accounting of events, but this is a modern value we can't expect to find in the sacred writings of antiquity. The compilers of the *Gospels* didn't set out to answer the modern questions, "What was Jesus really like?" and "What was the precise sequence of the events in his life, historically speaking?" Assembled from various sources a generation or two after Jesus' ministry, and written in Greek, rather than the Aramaic he spoke, the Gospels are part history, part faith testimony—not contemporary journalism or biography.

DEFINITION

The four New Testament **Gospels** of Matthew, Mark, Luke, and John are the received accounts of the life and ministry of Jesus. None were assembled, at least in their current form, during Jesus' ministry. The sources, dates of composition, and degrees of interrelationship of the various Gospels have given rise to centuries of scholarly work. The first three accounts share such strong similarities of material and viewpoint that they are regarded as "synoptic" (i.e., "same eye") Gospels. John presents a notably different, and probably later, tradition.

A brief aside: A series of publications by a group of New Testament academics has led to some passionate contemporary debates about the Gospels. On one side of the discussion are groups of scholars who believe that certain parallel passages appearing in both Matthew and Luke point to the existence of an earlier source Gospel (or "sayings Gospel"), which they believe is now lost. These scholars call this hypothetical ancient text Q, from the German word *Quelle*, or source, and they have attempted to reconstruct it based on the texts of Matthew and Luke. On the other side of the debate are a group of more traditional believers and scholars who see promotion of any "hypothetical Gospel"—and that of Q in particular—as an attempt to rewrite Christian theology under the guise of academic research.

For a fuller examination of the debate, and some contemporary Christian responses to it, consider visiting these websites:

- "The End of the Theology of Q?"
  http://ext.sagepub.com/content/113/1/5.full.pdf+html

- "The Canonical Status of Q"
  http://virtualreligion.net/forum/q_canon.html

SPIRITUAL SIGNPOST

By and large, Christians accept the Bible as the inspired word of God. The Christian Bible includes 39 sacred Hebrew and Aramaic books, as well as 27 books from the years following the ministry of Jesus. Christians refer to the first group of books as the *Old Testament,* and the second group of books as the *New Testament.* A number of books and fragments frequently grouped with the Old Testament, known as the Apocrypha, are also considered to be holy scriptures by some Christians.

The Christian Mystery

We've seen how the name "Jesus Christ" reflects a "translation" challenge faced by the early Christians. The challenge goes well beyond the question of how to refer to Jesus. Think of the many difficulties associated with integrating the religion of one culture into a separate (and very different) culture. In the case of the Gospels, faith in Jesus had to be translated from the Judaism of first-century Palestine to the Greek- and Latin-speaking (or "Hellenistic") culture of the late Roman Empire.

An aura of mystery appears to have surrounded Jesus from the moment he emerged in Palestine as a teacher. For many believers, the same aura attaches itself to his teachings to this day. In first-century Palestine, many people apparently could not encounter Jesus without asking, "What kind of man is this?"

SPIRITUAL SIGNPOST

Christians believe that Jesus, in dying and rising from the dead, overcame human sin and made world redemption a reality, allowing whoever believes in him and follows his way to enter the kingdom of heaven.

For 2,000 years, Christians have worked to lessen the distance between their own hearts and the demanding, puzzling figure at the center of their faith. Whether they lived in cultures that oppressed and persecuted followers of Christianity, cultures that claimed to follow Jesus' teachings as their social blueprint, or cultures that took no position one way or the other, Jesus' followers have had to make their own journeys to resolve fundamental questions about the man whose ancient ministry continues to exert a profoundly modern influence.

Christianity in the World

Christianity is a rich, diverse faith that, like the other major religions, encompasses many schools and points of view. It is, today, a global religion. Some of the major events within the history of that faith are identified in this chapter.

Cultural and Historical Adaptability

Jesus has sometimes been called the most influential person in Western civilization. This is probably because of the extraordinary reach and influence of the religion that sees him as its founder.

The word "Christianity" certainly applies to a staggeringly wide range of worship, and the religion has been a powerful social force for centuries in widely varying settings. (In his book *The 100: A Ranking of the Most Influential Persons in History*, Michael H. Hart observed that "[t]here is no question that Christianity, over the course of time, has had far more adherents than any other religion.") Because Christianity is an adaptable faith, however, it's extremely difficult to make across-the-board statements about it or, perhaps, logical assessments of its fundamental ideas.

An Unfinished Faith

One reason to be wary of the use of logical tools to describe Christianity is that it is not (for most believers) a closed, finalized system. Christians, in living out their faith, do not look backward to a specific historical period but forward to redemption and resurrection through Jesus.

This orientation not only affirms the conviction that good will ultimately prevail over evil but also calls believers to be vigilant in living out the Gospel message in daily life. Christians are reminded that their faith is a direction, not a static set of principles. Some would even say Christianity is a "work in progress."

With these cautionary points in mind, you're ready to take a closer look at the history and development of this influential monotheistic faith.

Peter and Paul—and Beyond

It is very important to recall that Christianity began as a form of Judaism and that not only Jesus but his earliest followers were observant Jews. Christians today often overlook this fact and may not always realize the impact of early arguments concerning Jesus within Judaism.

The Apostle Peter, a disciple of Jesus (*Apostle* means "messenger" or "envoy"), is today regarded as the first bishop of Rome. The Christian congregation in Rome was to play a leading role in the survival and development of the faith. Another apostle, Paul, was a contemporary of Peter, although he never met Jesus. A devout Jew, Paul gave up persecuting Christians after receiving a call from Christ to preach salvation to the Gentiles. Paul went on to become the foremost Christian theologian of the faith's early years and the main architect of the faith's expansion into the Gentile community.

Intermittent persecution by Roman authorities followed Christianity's emergence as a religion separate from Judaism, and both Peter and Paul are assumed to have died martyr's deaths in Rome. Although the extent of persecution has sometimes been exaggerated, Christians were seen by many Romans as disloyal and even immoral. Sporadic local persecutions and occasional imperial crackdowns brought suffering to Christian communities, including torture, loss of property, and very often violent death. Such measures proved ineffective, however, in halting Christianity's progress.

SPIRITUAL SIGNPOST

The Pauline Epistles are ancient letters attributed to Paul, offering guidance to particular congregations of the day and to the Christian church as a whole. The epistles are part of the New Testament and have had an immense impact on Christian doctrine and practice.

Development, Conflict, and Acceptance

The majority of members of the early church appear to have belonged to the lower classes and were looked down on as such. Their communities were small, poor, and scattered among the cities of the empire. Inner spirituality formed a large part of

Christian experience. Understanding and interpreting the mystery of Christ and of salvation often led to sharp conflicts and divisions.

Upper-class skeptics marveled at how members of a religion that emphasized love could put so much energy into attacking other Christians, especially while their faith was still under attack. Then in 312 C.E., something dramatic happened. A future emperor named Constantine converted to the Christian faith following a vision that told him that he would gain a military victory. After defeating his military rivals, Constantine assumed political power and issued decrees forbidding the persecution of Christians. His actions made Christianity respectable in the Empire and encouraged conversions to the faith among all classes of people.

With the weakening and failure of imperial power in Western Europe after 400 C.E., the popes, retaining religious leadership, also began to emerge as a powerful social and political force in their own right. Over the next several centuries, Christianity expanded and developed under papal leadership. At the same time, however, disputes between the Latin-speaking church of the West and the Greek-speaking church of the Byzantine Empire in the East were leading to separation. Pope Gregory VII, who was successful in undertaking ecclesiastical reforms in the West, was unable to prevent this division. Formal *schism* came in 1054. By that time, missionary efforts had brought Latin Christianity to most of Western Europe.

DEFINITION

A **schism** is a division or state of disunion within a church. In Christianity, the schism between the Eastern and Western wings of the church (1054) led to separate groupings today known popularly as the Orthodox and Catholic churches.

The **Crusades** were a series of military conflicts initiated by European powers during the eleventh to the thirteenth centuries. Their stated aim was to gain control of the holy places in the land where Jesus had lived—regions then under the control of Muslims. Although the Crusaders managed to take Jerusalem briefly in 1099 and establish a Latin Kingdom in Palestine that lasted 200 years, they were eventually repelled, leaving Muslim rulers in charge.

As city life revived in the thirteenth century after centuries of stagnation and decay, new religious orders of layfolk and clerics were formed to teach and preach the faith. This period also saw the building of great cathedrals and the founding of the major universities of Europe.

The life of St. Francis of Assisi, born in Italy in the late twelfth century, has inspired many Christians. As a young man, Francis relinquished a life of wealth, choosing instead a life of joyous poverty. Francis saw the suffering of Jesus in the poor and the sick, and the beauty of Jesus in nature. He eventually founded the Franciscan Order. Francis is one of the most beloved figures in Christianity.

The century of St. Francis and St. Dominic saw the papacy assume a position of extraordinary prominence in both the culture and political life of Western Europe. This time was marked by stability, intellectual openness on certain topics, and unchallenged religious and social authority. But these same years also gave birth to the *Crusades* and the first of the Inquisitions, under which the church conducted secret trials to identify and eliminate heretics. This period of church history was also marred by various forms of institutional corruption.

DEFINITION

The **Crusades** were a series of military conflicts initiated by European powers during the eleventh to the thirteenth centuries. Their stated aim was to gain control of the holy places in the land where Jesus had lived—regions then under the control of Muslims. Although the Crusaders managed to take Jerusalem briefly in 1099 and establish a Latin Kingdom in Palestine that lasted 200 years, they were eventually repelled, leaving Muslim rulers in charge.

The later Middle Ages witnessed a papal schism and a series of bitter power struggles in Rome, resulting in competing claims for what had become the most powerful office in Europe. The papal office itself was claimed by two, and, for a while, three, claimants. Finally, an extraordinary council was called (at Constance, 1414–1418) both to end the papal schism and to reform the church in head and members. The council was able to secure unity in the papacy, but not to reform church abuses.

By the beginning of the sixteenth century, calls within the church for reform were becoming ever more insistent. Complaints about abuses, both in Rome and elsewhere, were loud. These complaints centered on a bloated, money-hungry bureaucracy; unblushing office seeking; the practice of concubinage by too many members of a clergy sworn to celibacy; and a series of entangled religious and military alliances. Doctrinal misunderstandings concerning practices like indulgences (too often seen as a kind of payment to excuse sin) and about the grace won by Christ for all believers were viewed with dismay by many. European Christianity was ripe for the Protestant Reformations.

The Protestant Reformations

The Reformations began, as their name implies, as an attempt to reform the excesses of the Roman Church *internally*. The result, instead, was the formation of a number of churches separate from papal authority. The roots of the movement actually extended far into the past. John Wyclif, for example, had headed a dissident movement in the fourteenth century. The catalyst of the Protestant Reformations, however, was Martin Luther's famous 95 theses, which may or may not have been posted on the door of the castle church at Wittenberg in 1517, but which certainly sparked a firestorm of controversy.

Luther, a professor of theology, did not intend to separate from the Roman Church when he wrote his 95 theses. His purpose was to address matters of salvation that concerned him deeply. Luther was a firebrand, however, and he refused to back down when his call for debate on doctrinal issues led him into direct conflict with church authorities. In 1519, he openly denied the authority of the church on religious matters; in 1520, he was excommunicated by the pope and condemned by the Holy Roman Emperor. By then, however, Luther had many supporters. In 1521, an attempt to heal the rift only led to greater support for the revolt against Rome.

Luther's doctrines (examined in Chapter 9) gained wide support in Germany and elsewhere, and a number of political leaders embraced his cause, not least because they stood to gain economically by confiscating church property. A new class of capitalists, too, looked to benefit from a more open, less centralized social structure.

But to read too much into these economic motives would be a mistake. The criticisms Luther and his colleagues launched against corruption were shared by many laity and clergy. His revolutionary insistence on direct communication with God, unmediated by a priest, struck a chord with believers throughout Europe. Tragically, matters of conscience led to decades of bloody warfare between rival Christians.

Eventually, the rift did lead to significant reforms within the Roman Church. Doctrinal orthodoxy became an imperative, and clerical celibacy became more of a reality. But the religious divisions in Europe remained deep.

Profound war-weariness, commercial interest, and skepticism about competing religious claims eventually ended the religious wars. In Europe, territory was divided among the various factions. England became guardedly pluralistic, although the rise of Puritanism showed there was plenty of energy left in that country for religious debate. In the aftermath of the European Reformations, and in North America especially, varieties of Protestantism proved a rich source of new Christian thought and worship.

Beyond the Divisions

In the long period following the Protestant Reformations, the leaders of the various Christian factions have attempted to transcend old conflicts, with varying degrees of success. To one degree or another, most of the divisions of Christianity have had to come to terms with the demands and opportunities of life lived in a time of rapid social and technological change.

Today, an increasingly vigorous *ecumenical movement* has helped to unite disparate factions of the church in ways that would once have been considered unthinkable. Representatives of prominent Protestant and Orthodox Eastern churches, for instance, were in attendance as observers during the Second Vatican Council in Rome, which convened in 1962 and opened the way to significant new reforms within the Roman Catholic Church.

In the modern era, scientific inquiry and heavy secular and commercial influence have discouraged the faith of some Christians while reinforcing and strengthening the faith of others. As the global church enters the new millennium, it finds itself gaining adherents in lands that once seemed far beyond its influence. "Christianity" may never again be the religious wing of a mighty political empire, but its essential principles endure. Empires crumble, but great religions go on. The Christian emphasis on mercy, forgiveness, reconciliation, and love has transcended even the (serious) limitations of the institutions that have propagated the faith over the centuries.

 DEFINITION

The **ecumenical movement**, an ongoing effort to promote unity among the various Christian denominations, has been a potent force in twentieth-century Christianity.

The Least You Need to Know

- The figure at the heart of Christianity, Jesus, has been the subject of mystery and veneration for centuries, and categorical pronouncements about him should be treated with skepticism.
- The Western, or Latin, Christian church emerged as the dominant religious force in Western Europe and held that position for centuries.
- Disagreements with the Eastern church in 1054 led to one major rift in Christianity; the Protestant Reformations of the fifteenth century created another.
- The excesses and limitations of the various Christian churches have not prevented the faith promulgated by those churches from becoming one of the world's most important religions.

The Many Christian Denominations

In This Chapter

- The ancient roots of the Roman Catholic faith, and its distinctive doctrines
- The world of Orthodox Eastern Christianity
- The amazingly diverse world of Protestantism
- The commonalities and differences among Christian believers

Christianity can be divided into three main branches: the Roman Catholic Church, the Orthodox Eastern churches, and the Protestant churches. In this chapter, you find out about all three.

Roman Catholicism

The word "catholic" originally referred to the global community of Christian believers and is still used this way in some contexts.

When Roman Catholics use the word Catholic, they are usually referring to the huge worldwide group of Christians who identify themselves as being in communion with the bishop of Rome, the pope. This group accounts for roughly half of all Christians on the planet. In this chapter, the terms "Catholic" and "Roman Catholic" will refer to this group of believers.

What Catholics Believe

Roman Catholics, like all Christians, accept Jesus Christ as the Son of God. Many aspects, however, of Catholic faith and observance stand in contrast to the practices of other Christians. Here are some of the most important distinguishing characteristics of the Roman Catholic faith:

- Acknowledgment of and participation in particular sacraments: baptism, confirmation, the Eucharist (that is, sharing in the 'transubstantiated' body and blood of Christ offered in Holy Communion during Mass), penance (also referred to as confession), the anointing of the sick, marriage, and holy orders (for those entering the clergy).

  What remains of the Eucharist after a Roman Catholic mass is reserved in the tabernacle for later distribution for the sick, and as a focus for personal prayers of adoration of the presence of Jesus Christ in the sacrament.

- Acceptance of the church as the repository of complete, divine revelation.

- Acknowledgment of the spiritual authority of the pope and the bishops of the church as coming directly from Christ, who assigned earthly dominion over spiritual matters to the Apostles (also known as *apostolic succession*). One of these Apostles was Peter, regarded as the first bishop of Rome.

- Acceptance of the human soul's immortal status, with each person accountable for his or her actions and choices.

- Belief that God exists in an objective sense, and is understood as triune in nature.

- Celebration of the grace of God as poured forth in the hearts of believers, who are so changed as to become the children of God.

- Celebration of the message of Christ as both a belief and a way of life.

DEFINITION

The doctrine of **apostolic succession** holds that, in transmitting authority to the Apostles, Jesus initiated a chain of authority that has extended in an unbroken line to current Catholic bishops. The group of bishops, united with the pope, form a body called the Episcopal College. Roman Catholics believe that the members of this body have been given the commission to pass down the teachings of Christ and, at special times, to articulate matters of doctrine with the assistance of the Holy Spirit.

This list sets out the most obvious "external" or "institutional" features distinctive of the Roman Catholic Church. It is worth noting, too, that Catholics accept that ...

- The church is committed to a divine mission.

- God is concerned with human affairs and can be reached through prayer.

Roman Catholics, along with Orthodox believers and some worshippers in the Anglican and Lutheran traditions, venerate Jesus' mother Mary in a special way, regarding her as the Mother of God. This veneration arises from the faith understanding of the divine and human natures united in the person of Jesus. Roman Catholics believe that, because of the redemption brought by Jesus, Mary, like her son, was preserved from the stain of original sin, which is seen as touching all other members of the human family. This view of Mary is known as the doctrine of the Immaculate Conception. The Roman Catholic Church also teaches that, having finished the course of her earthly life, Mary was assumed, body and soul, into heaven. This teaching is known as the doctrine of the Assumption.

ON THE PATH

"Christianity, with its doctrine of humility, of forgiveness, of love, is incompatible with the State, with its haughtiness, its violence, its punishment, its wars."

—Leo Tolstoy

The Trinity

The distinctively Christian notion of the "triune" God is both important and fundamentally mysterious. Catholics have always regarded it as one of the profound truths of their faith and are joined in this by many other Christian believers.

The Profession of Faith that says that the Son, Jesus Christ, is truly God and truly human was debated in the third, fourth, and fifth centuries. Many councils were called during this period to defend the full mystery of the Incarnation of the Son, the Second Person of the Trinity, maintaining a full divine and human nature of Jesus Christ united in one divine person.

SPIRITUAL SIGNPOST

The Trinity of Father, Son, and Holy Spirit should not be interpreted as meaning that Catholics (or believers within other Christian systems) view God as an essentially male deity. The divine essence is not considered as having a gender.

Similarly, the three dimensions should not be seen as somehow separate and incompatible with one another. The triune God is both one *and* three. If such a doctrine seems to defy rational explanation, this may be just as well. The dogma (teaching) of the Trinity is held by Catholics to transcend logical analysis or philosophical demonstration.

In discussions of the Trinity, contemporary Catholics (along with many other Christians) hold that the light of reason or logical analysis is not dismissed by this doctrine. Rather, they maintain that the light of reason is not contradicted, but is simply not powerful enough to begin to accept the mystery of the Trinity. This mystery, believers maintain, can only be accepted by the light of faith.

Expansion—and a Rift

For the first centuries of its existence, the church's history was essentially identical with that of organized Christianity, which evolved in an atmosphere of passionate debate (see Chapter 8).

From its earliest beginnings, Christianity can be seen as a religion on the move, spreading rapidly, if not always gently, into many nations. In part, this was because of the universality of the faith, but it was also, in part, because church authorities were willing to incorporate local traditions and imagery within the broader context of established Christian worship.

In 1054, the Western church formally split with the Eastern wing of the faith. Serious divisions between the two had, however, been in evidence long before.

Challenge and Change

From the ninth century C.E. to the early sixteenth century, the Western church was the religious component of Western European society. Because clear divisions did not yet exist between religious bodies and other social institutions, the church was often a dominant social influence within the kingdoms of that era.

SPIRITUAL SIGNPOST

Religious orders within the Roman Catholic Church have served to energize and reinvigorate the institution for hundreds of years. Members of these orders, which include (among many others) the Dominican, Benedictine, Franciscan, and Carmelite movements, seek to imitate the life of Jesus: they own no property, pursue a celibate lifestyle, and follow a discipline of obedience, according to the constitutions of each particular religious order.

The Protestant Reformations, which led to a long and bloody military struggle, as well as a new pluralism within European Christianity, began as an internal attempt to reform the "Mother Church." The Reformations were neither the first nor the last campaigns mounted by believers to reform church practices.

A pattern of vigorous reform, growth, complacency, and renewed reform is not difficult to make out over the centuries of the Catholic Church's development. Catholics view the seemingly countless cycles of change and reform within their faith as part of an ongoing historical process of development, one fully in keeping with the church's divinely appointed role.

The most recent, and perhaps the most dramatic, of the reforms took place in the early to middle 1960s, with the Second Vatican Council (Vatican II). As a prelude to any review of Vatican II, it is worth remembering the work of the First Vatican Council, which began in 1869.

The First Vatican Council is remembered chiefly for its expression of the doctrine of papal infallibility, a much-discussed (and routinely oversimplified) statement that when the pope speaks officially ("ex cathedra") on matters related to faith or morals, he acts as pastor of the universal church and is given a special gift of the Holy Spirit to preserve the teaching from error.

SPIRITUAL SIGNPOST

Among the most prominent of the Catholic orders has been the Society of Jesus, whose members are commonly known as *Jesuits*. The intellectual accomplishment and energetic missionary work of the Jesuits have been two of the high points of modern Catholic history. The order was founded in response to the Protestant Reformations by Ignatius of Loyola.

The idea that Catholics consider the pope to be correct in his every utterance is a common misconception. Only formal pronouncements concerning faith or morals fall under the doctrine of papal infallibility, which speaks about a special gift of the Holy Spirit. A pope could not use this doctrine to enforce compliance with a decree that God is not three persons but two, or to declare that Jesus was born in Dayton, Ohio. Such fundamental issues are beyond the reach of the pope's authority. (See Chapter 11 for a fuller discussion of the doctrine of papal infallibility.)

BARRIER ALERT!

Although most people understand on an intuitive level what is meant by the words "Catholic" and "Orthodox," careless use of the terms without their initial capital letters can lead to confusion. Followers of the Eastern tradition emphasize the Catholicism (universality) of their faith, just as believers within the Roman Church realize the value of embracing and understanding orthodoxy (established and accepted belief) in addressing important faith challenges.

For critics, the doctrine of papal infallibility epitomizes what they see as a kind of rigid orthodoxy within the church. The Second Vatican Council, however, openly embraced some long-ignored initiatives for change—taking many observers, both within the church and outside it, by surprise.

Among the most important reforms were the acceptance of contemporary local language (rather than Latin) in the Mass, and a forthright embrace of broad ecumenical principles. The council also issued a direct condemnation of anti-Semitism.

The Orthodox Church

The Orthodox Church (or, as it is also known, Orthodox Eastern Church) represents the dominant form of Christian worship in Greece and in a large region of Eastern Europe. As a church, it claims an unbroken history dating from Apostolic times when the Christian message was carried to such Greek-speaking communities as Ephesus, Antioch, and Corinth. The Orthodox system is also present in parts of the Middle East.

Shared Origins, Different Rites

Because the Eastern and Western churches were united during their first thousand years of existence, they agree on many significant matters of doctrine. Their most important differences have to do with emphasis and practice.

Long before the formal split with the Western church in the eleventh century, for example, Eastern churches differed with Rome on the use of unleavened bread during religious ceremonies (Orthodox services today employ leavened bread), on the West's alteration of the Nicene Creed to include explicit reference to the Holy Spirit's "proceed(ing) from the Father and the Son," and on the role of the pope.

Another obvious difference is the Eastern tradition's embrace of the liturgies of St. John Chrysostom and St. Basil. The Orthodox liturgy is sung, rather than spoken, and it is not generally a matter of daily observance.

Parish priests in the Orthodox tradition may marry before they are ordained. Infants may receive communion.

Orthodox places of worship are renowned for their beauty and elaborate ornamentation. Icons, gilding, carved ornamentation, incense, and screens veiling the high altar are some common elements of Orthodox liturgy and sacred space and serve to emphasize the transcendent nature of the Divine.

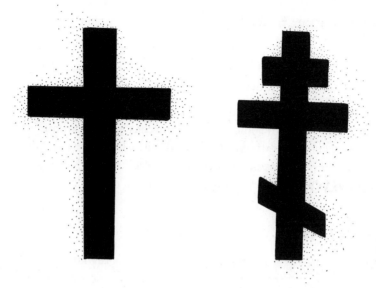

Western cross (left), Eastern cross (right).

Organization

On an organizational level, the Orthodox tradition is less centralized than its Catholic counterpart. This is because it developed over the centuries through a number of *patriarchates,* a form of regional religious administration under the leadership of patriarchs.

In fact, within the Orthodox Eastern tradition, individual national churches operate with great independence from their counterparts, and national identity plays an important role in daily worship. The Russian Orthodox Church, which represents the largest community of Orthodox believers, was ruthlessly suppressed during much of the Soviet era. It reemerged, significantly, during World War II, and flourishes in the period following Communist rule.

The Orthodox Church Today

A number of national Orthodox churches exist today, each representing the traditional patriotic traditions of its believers. Among these, the Greek and Russian branches are the most prominent.

Several autonomous Orthodox groups have established separate hierarchies in the United States, and although some of these churches are in communion with one another, no single confederation of Orthodox faiths has emerged. Given the nationalistic and cultural emphasis of most Orthodox traditions, it's likely that a variety of Orthodox voices will continue to add to the richness of America's religious life.

Protestantism

From a single point of origin—the European religious revolutions of the 1500s—the religions designated as "Protestant" form the most diverse strand of the three great divisions within Christianity. The variety can be more than a little intimidating, because the collection of Protestant views presents a rich profusion of Bible-based traditions. Does it really make sense to group Episcopalians with the Amish, Seventh-Day Adventists with Congregationalists, and Lutherans with Quakers?

Only up to a point. All these groups, of course, reject the authority of the pope, but generalizations about any faith system are dangerous, and broad statements about the Protestant traditions can be particularly tricky. In this family, denominations incorporate stark differences in doctrine and approach. The authors respect and honor the validity and devotion of the many Protestant traditions, but we can't identify all of them here.

"Protestantism" is an umbrella term for a set of traditions that came into existence after the Reformations. If there is a single common thread among the traditions in this group, it is probably rooted in ideas of group autonomy and respect for individual experience. It has been said, for example, that Catholics come to Christ through the church, while Protestants come to the church through Christ.

This is not to say that most early Protestants believed in religious toleration and pluralism. (In the sixteenth and seventeenth centuries, such ideas were reserved for the radical fringe.) The guiding accents in the Protestant experience have been the formation of communities and the power of direct experience. Protestants claim "the priesthood of all believers," by which they assert that lay believers have the same access to God as clergy—that all have a religious vocation, whether farmers, factory workers, parents, or ministers.

SPIRITUAL SIGNPOST

Lutherans appealed to the New Testament writings of the Apostle Paul in support of the notion of "justification by grace, through faith." The dispute over whether a human's good works could augment God's grace, or be accumulated in surplus by the church (like a bank account), was a matter of intense dispute between Luther's followers and the Catholic Church.

Two other fundamental doctrinal points set Protestant Christians apart from believers in the Roman Catholic tradition. The Bible itself is regarded as the source of infallible, received truth, and the believer is justified by God's grace, obtained through his or her faith in Christ—not by good deeds or the mediation of any religious institution.

In practice, the vast majority of Protestant denominations have also rejected the notion of clerical celibacy. A few, including the Shakers, advocated celibacy among all believers, relying on the recruitment of outsiders to perpetuate the faith.

A word of warning: What follows is a beginner's summary. The outlines of major Protestant movements and doctrinal issues that follow are meant as an introduction to the group in question, and not as the last word on any tradition or practice.

Faith, Not Works

Martin Luther, the first and one of the foremost Protestant reformers, interpreted certain passages of the New Testament to mean that God's grace alone, and not the good works of individuals, served as source of salvation through faith. Luther's doctrine won an immediate following among academics, clergy, and laity.

John Calvin was another reformer of significant influence. An exiled French theologian of the generation after Luther, Calvin devoted his life to the ideal of building a truly Christian society based on charity, humility, and faith.

For Calvin, theology was important, but it was the starting place, not the goal. His vision of a church governed by elders (in Greek, *presbyteros*) led to the founding of the Presbyterian Church. "Reformed" churches in Holland, Germany, and France look back to Calvinist roots.

SPIRITUAL SIGNPOST

In 1536, John Calvin wrote the highly influential theological work *Institutes of the Christian Religion,* which explicitly rejected the authority of the pope and set out the doctrine of predestination for which Calvinism is well known.

Other Major Denominations

The Anglican Church, whose American branch is known as the Episcopal Church, rejects the authority of Rome but agrees with Roman Catholicism on many issues of doctrine. Followers of both the Anglican Communion (in England) and the Episcopal Church (in the United States) have embraced a commitment to positive social change.

For millions of Christians, worship and practice have been profoundly affected by the *Book of Common Prayer,* the service book of the Anglican Communion.

The Methodist Church was founded by the English cleric John Wesley. This denomination emphasizes repentance, individual faith, and responsibility for the betterment of society at large. The tradition takes its name from the commitment of Wesley and his colleagues to lead lives governed by "rule and method" in religious study. Methodism is among the largest Protestant denominations in the United States.

Baptists, of which there are many varieties, represent the largest American Protestant denomination. Unlike most other branches of the Christian faith, Baptists insist that baptism, to be valid, must be a conscious adult choice that accompanies full acceptance of Jesus as one's personal savior.

SPIRITUAL SIGNPOST

The Great Awakening, a period of religious revival and highly emotional preaching styles during the eighteenth century, led to rapid growth for a number of Protestant denominations. One of the greatest preachers of this period included the Congregationalist Jonathan Edwards and the Presbyterian William Tennent.

Many Baptist traditions (as well as other denominations within the Protestant tradition) place heavy emphasis on New Testament passages that highlight the importance of being "born again." Baptists often see a direct, conscious acknowledgment of Jesus as Savior as the best means to this end.

Congregationalism, which traces its lineage from the Nonconformist movement in England, honors the Christian community as a covenant of faithful individuals. Each local church operates autonomously, acknowledging only Christ as its head, and respecting the relationships of the various congregations as interactions between members of the Christian family. Fellowship and cooperation are at the heart of Congregationalism.

In the twentieth century, two important movements within Protestantism have had profound influences on Christian worship in the United States. One is Fundamentalism, which holds that all statements in the Bible are literally true. Fundamentalist approaches to Christianity are broadly popular in the United States.

Pentecostalism is a global movement emphasizing an ecstatic experience of God, often resulting in *glossolalia* (speaking in tongues). Major Pentecostalist denominations include the Church of God in Christ and the Assemblies of God.

"Distinctive" Protestant Movements

The Quakers (or Friends) reject the necessity of ordained ministers and external sacraments, viewing all aspects of life itself as sacred. This pacifist tradition holds that every believer is gifted with "inner light." Friends gather in weekly meetings to pray silently together and to share revelation as the Spirit dictates.

Extraordinary piety and a commitment to live as simply as possible mark the practices of active Mennonites, who refuse, on religious grounds, to hold public office or serve in any military capacity. The Mennonite tradition traces its roots to the radical fringe of the early Reformation, the Anabaptists. Another such group is the Amish, who reject many modern technological advances and severely limit contact with the outside world.

SPIRITUAL SIGNPOST

One person's comfortable orthodoxy may be the force that galvanizes another to launch a new religious movement. Protestantism contains countless examples of such movements; some have endured, some have not. The varieties of these movements, each with its distinctive approach to doctrine and practice, are seen by some as instances of Christian fragmentation, and by others as a source of tremendous richness and strength.

The Unitarian Universalist Association, which includes both Christian and non-Christian members, is among the most open and tolerant of Protestant religious traditions. Unitarian Universalists reject the doctrine of the Trinity, seeing Christ as a great teacher, not a divine incarnation. They tend to avoid dogma as restrictive and even presumptuous, choosing to emphasize inclusiveness and understanding rather than a specific religious creed.

The Christian Science movement, founded by Mary Baker Eddy, holds that the spiritual world is the true reality, compared to which the material world is an illusion. Christian Scientists believe that sin and illness can be overcome by spiritual powers. For this reason they tend to avoid medicines and medical procedures in favor of divine healing.

SPIRITUAL SIGNPOST

An influential movement (particularly during the 1960s and 1970s) was the ecumenical mission, which sought to promote union and acknowledgement of common spiritual principles among Christians.

Seventh-Day Adventists celebrate the Sabbath on Saturday (rather than Sunday) and anticipate the imminent Second Coming of Christ.

Jehovah's Witnesses accept the Bible as factually true in every detail and anticipate the coming of God's kingdom after the battle of Armageddon, which is considered imminent and which is expected to be followed by a thousand-year reign of Christ on Earth.

Followers of the Church of Jesus Christ of Latter-Day Saints (the Mormons) pursue a system of beliefs that accepts the divine revelation of the Bible but differs markedly from the doctrines accepted by most other Christians. Church tradition holds that an angel dictated a new and contemporary revelation, the *Book of Mormon*, to the American founder of the faith, Joseph Smith. Mormon practices and beliefs, which originally sanctioned polygamy, were extremely controversial during the nineteenth century. The sect endured hardship and persecution, and eventually relocated in a dramatic westward migration under the leadership of Brigham Young.

ON THE PATH

"I believe in Christianity as I believe that the Sun has risen: not only because I see it, but because by it I see everything else."—C. S. Lewis

The Quilt of Many Squares

Hundreds of movements, countermovements, splits, and alliances have occurred within the Protestant tradition over the centuries. Only the best known can be touched on here. We close by reminding you that Protestantism can be thought of as a quilt of many squares, each square distinctive and important. To appreciate the quilt fully, any observer must first acknowledge its extraordinary complexity, and then the rich history of diversity to be read along the many seams.

The Least You Need to Know

- Roman Catholicism draws its energy not only from its ancient practices and teachings, but also from a tradition of internal reform, which periodically re-invigorates the faith.
- For the first period of its organized existence, the history of Christianity was identical with the history of the Roman Church.
- The Orthodox Eastern Church of today is a grouping of autonomous churches, many with strong national identities.
- Protestantism's emphasis on revelation and the formation of community has led, over the centuries, to an astonishing variety of religious expression.

Christian Celebration

In This Chapter

- The major Christian holidays
- When the most important holidays occur
- The most important observances
- The religious significance of various Christian celebrations

No single chapter in a book such as this can say all there is to say about Christian ritual and celebration, or about every tradition's religious calendar. This chapter offers a brief look at the major Christian holidays, what they mean, and how observances can vary. So without further ado …

Advent

In Western churches, this season of preparation for Christmas begins on the Wednesday nearest November 30 (St. Andrew's Day) and lasts until Christmas Day. Catholics observe Advent with fasting and repentance but also with joy, in anticipation of the feast of the Nativity, or birth of Jesus. This event is described in the Gospels of Matthew and Luke. Most Christians view Jesus' birth as the fulfillment of certain prophecies enshrined in Hebrew scripture. The New Testament relates Jesus' birth as miraculous, in that his mother, Mary, was a virgin when she conceived.

Orthodox believers observe Advent with a 40-day fast from meat and dairy products.

Since medieval times, Advent has also been acknowledged as a time for preparation for the Second Coming of Jesus and an opportunity to acknowledge his presence in the daily lives of believers.

Christmas

Perhaps the most familiar of all Christian holidays to secular Western society, Christmas, the feast of the Nativity, is less important than Easter in the Christian religious calendar. The manner of its observance—austere or jubilant, serene or Bacchanalian—was a matter of intense dispute in England after the Protestant Reformations.

Catholics and Protestants celebrate Christmas on December 25, shortly before Epiphany. (In the Eastern Christian tradition, Epiphany originally incorporated the celebration of Christ's Nativity.) The familiar date is celebrated in the West as the date of the birth of Christ, and as an opportunity to exchange gifts, but it is worth remembering that the observance did not gain wide acceptance until the fourth century C.E.

SPIRITUAL SIGNPOST

Secular influences on the Christmas holiday began to emerge noticeably in the nineteenth century, and in the United States, the approach of the "big day" has assumed heavy commercial and economic overtones. Many Christian churches have felt it necessary to undertake campaigns to remind believers of the spiritual nature of Christmas. Even in our advertising-driven era, however, the day is observed by means of certain distinctively Christian elements. One of these is the créche, the scene of the infant Christ Child in a manger in Bethlehem. This presentation was originally made popular by Franciscan monks.

Christmas emerged in the Middle Ages as the preeminent popular festival of the year, and it has featured strong secular as well as religious influences from that time to the present day. Despite its contemporary commercial overtones, Christmas has a profound meaning that transcends materialism. It is the time when Christians, reflecting on the mysteries and paradoxes of Christ's Incarnation, respond with generosity, renewal, gratitude, and celebration.

For a fascinating essay on the Christian history of the Christmas holiday and its origins, see "Is Christmas Christian?" by Hank Hanegraaff, *Christian Research Newsletter*, Volume 6: Number 5, 1993. The article is also posted on the following website: www.iclnet.org/pub/resources/text/cri/cri-nwsl/crn0056a.txt.

ON THE PATH

"Are you willing to believe that love is the strongest thing in the world—stronger than hate, stronger than evil, stronger than death—and that the blessed life which began in Bethlehem nineteen hundred years ago is the image and brightness of the Eternal Love? Then you can keep Christmas."

—Henry Van Dyke

Epiphany

Epiphany, celebrated each year on January 6, commemorates the visit of the Wise Men to the newborn Jesus as recounted in the Gospel of Matthew. "Epiphany" means "manifestation" or "showing forth," usually of divine nature. The word has been used for centuries to describe gentiles' encounter with Jesus, symbolized by visitors from the East coming to humble themselves before the infant Messiah.

The first historical reference to the Feast of the Epiphany dates to 361 C.E., but it was certainly celebrated long before that.

DEFINITION

An **epiphany** may also describe a manifestation of the Divine in one's own experience, through a vision, for example.

The time of Epiphany, in addition to celebrating Jesus' appearance as king to the gentiles, also commemorates Jesus' own baptism and his first miracle, the transformation of water to wine at Cana as described in the Gospel of John. All three events are aspects of Jesus' manifestation to the world.

The eve of Epiphany is often referred to as Twelfth Night, a name most know now only as the title of a play by Shakespeare. As a celebration, Epiphany is considerably older than Christmas. Although often relegated to footnote status in the aftermath of the (highly secularized) Western Christmas, Epiphany remains an important, if little publicized, Christian feast day.

Lent

Lent is a season of repentance and fasting that serves as a spiritual preparation for the joy of the Easter festival. The observance of the first day of Lent on Ash Wednesday, the seventh Wednesday before Easter, is of ancient origin. In a number of Christian settings, it is marked by the imposition of ashes, a ritual in which worshippers come forward to receive a smudge of ashes on their foreheads. By this act the church echoes the words in Genesis regarding human mortality: "Dust thou art, and to dust shalt thou return."

SPIRITUAL SIGNPOST

If you haven't actually received ashes yourself on Ash Wednesday, you have probably encountered Catholics who have. Sometimes the bearer of the ashes finds herself fending off the well-meaning handkerchief: "Yes, I know I have something on my forehead …"

But did you know where the ashes of Ash Wednesday come from? They are the ashes of the palms that were carried in the previous year's Palm Sunday celebration. In this way, believers acknowledge, with a touch of irony, Jesus' abandonment by even his closest followers during the final days and hours of his life—just one week after his royal welcome to Jerusalem.

Palm Sunday

Palm Sunday is the final Sunday of Lent and the last Sunday before Easter. It is a day of acclamation and rejoicing, but also of somber anticipation. Palm Sunday marks the first day of Holy Week, the week in which the betrayal and suffering of Jesus are remembered.

The palm, traditional Western symbol of Christ's triumphal entry to Jerusalem. (Worshippers in Eastern churches, for whom palms are scarce, use other plants.)

The New Testament relates that, as Jesus entered Jerusalem for Passover, crowds hailed him as a savior, scattering palm leaves in his path. In commemoration of the event, and as a prelude to the events of Holy Week, many Christians carry palm fronds on that day.

Good Friday

The Friday before Easter recalls the death of Jesus on the cross. It has been marked since ancient times by fasting and other penitential rituals, as well as by meditation on the Stations of the Cross, a series of 14 images depicting the passion, or suffering, of Christ.

Orthodox, Anglican, and Catholic churches do not celebrate the Eucharist on Good Friday. The gift of Holy Communion they receive on that day is consecrated the day before, to reserve Good Friday as a day of mourning.

SPIRITUAL SIGNPOST

As of this writing, the calendar observance of the Orthodox Eastern celebration of Easter differs from that of Catholic and Protestant practice. (As a general rule, Orthodox Easter occurs some weeks after the Western holiday.) There is, however, a movement to unite the dates of celebration.

Easter

Easter is the single most important holiday of the Christian year. It celebrates the resurrection of Jesus after his crucifixion and proclaims the spiritual rebirth of believers through their union with the risen Christ.

Easter is a springtime holiday. The Sunday on which it is celebrated is a time for joy and praise from the faithful at the perpetuation and renewal of life through God's grace. It is a commemoration of the power of Christ to conquer death itself.

SPIRITUAL SIGNPOST

The holiday Westerners know as Easter is celebrated as Pascha by Orthodox Eastern Christians.

Pentecost

Derived from the Jewish festival of Shavout celebrating the spring harvest, the Christian feast of Pentecost commemorates the gift of the Holy Spirit on the disciples following Jesus' resurrection and ascension. By this gift, the church believes itself to be in union with the risen Christ, who, through the Holy Spirit, guides, upholds, comforts, and enlightens the faithful on earth. The holiday, which marks the birth of the Christian church, is held to be second in importance only to the Easter festival.

The New Testament, in the Acts of the Apostles, relates that on the day of Pentecost the Holy Spirit descended on Jesus' disciples in the form of tongues of flame, accompanied by a sound like rushing wind. Filled with the Holy Spirit, the disciples began proclaiming Jesus' resurrection in all the languages of the world, so that the crowds who listened to them marveled. The feast of Pentecost celebrates the church's call to bring the good news of Christ to all people.

> **SPIRITUAL SIGNPOST**
>
> For Jehovah's Witnesses, the memorial of Christ's death is the one day of the year set aside for religious observance. It takes place on the first evening of the Jewish Passover.

Pentecost is observed on the Seventh Sunday after Easter. In some traditions it is accompanied by vigils of penitence. An English name for Pentecost is Whitsunday.

The Feast of the Assumption

This feast, held on August 15, is the oldest feast in honor of Mary. It is celebrated both in the West and in the East; Roman Catholics in particular commemorate Mary's assumption, body and soul, into heaven. Roman Catholics and Orthodox believers alike see Mary as the first human to receive the full fruits of life in Jesus' resurrection.

> **ON THE PATH**
>
> "St. Juvenal, Bishop of Jerusalem, at the Council of Chalcedon [451 C.E.], made known to the Emperor Marcian and Pulcheria, who wished to possess the body of the Mother of God, that Mary died in the presence of all the Apostles, but that her tomb, when opened, upon the request of St. Thomas, was found empty; wherefrom the Apostles concluded that the body was taken up to heaven."—St. John of Damascus

For Roman Catholics, the Feast of the Assumption (August 15) and the Feast of the Immaculate Conception (December 8) establish Mary as the image of the worldwide church. Believers within the Catholic faith see in her the realization of what the church (the "bride of Christ") will be.

New Year

The official beginning of the Orthodox church year is September 1. Believers within this branch of the faith celebrate this new beginning in a religious context. There is no equivalent New Year celebration in the Western church.

Is that it? Well, no. There are scores of other holidays within the various Christian traditions. The Catholic faith, in particular, is known for its profusion of holidays in honor of particular saints. The celebrations described here represent the major dates of observance familiar to Christians, however, and are a good beginning point for those just encountering or rediscovering the faith.

The Least You Need to Know

- Easter is the most important Christian holiday.
- As of this writing, Easter (or Pascha) is celebrated according to one calendar tradition among believers in the West, and another among Orthodox believers.
- Along with Easter, other important Christian observances include Christmas, Epiphany, Ash Wednesday, Good Friday, Pentecost, and the Feast of the Assumption.
- Despite strong influences from consumer society, Christmas retains its special spiritual character.
- In addition to the major holidays discussed in this chapter, Christianity is enriched by many variant traditions within the manifold expressions of the faith.

Breaking Down Barriers to Christianity

In This Chapter

- The question of unanimity
- Confession
- Attitudes toward homosexuality
- Distinctive beliefs of certain Christian faith communities

In this chapter, you will find factual responses to a number of common oversimplifications, stereotypes, and misconceptions related to Christianity.

Myth #1: The Christian faith is unanimous.

There are so many varieties of Christian practice that the single most common barrier to understanding Christianity is to underestimate its extraordinary diversity. Many non-Christians (and yes, some Christians) overlook or minimize the ability of this faith's practitioners to hold contrary views.

Christians can and do differ with one another on important matters of emphasis and sectarian doctrine. In fact, as a general rule, if you hear the phrase "Christians believe …", and then hear that sentence conclude with virtually any statement other than one emphasizing a) the saving role of Jesus Christ or b) the authority of the Bible, then you are probably well advised to confirm the accuracy of the statement by researching the matter yourself.

Christians agree on essential matters of faith. Virtually all of them, for instance, accept John 3:16, which states, "For God so loved the world that he gave his one and only Son, that whoever believes in him shall not perish but have eternal life." (The word "virtually" is used here because the Unitarian Universalists—some of whom consider themselves Christians—hold that Christ is divine only in the sense that all human beings possess goodness indicative of a "divine spark.")

Christians frequently do, however, have profound differences about such basic issues as the definition of sin and the requirements of salvation, the doctrine of the Trinity, the proper role of women in faith communities, and the nature of earthly religious authority, to name only a few of the most prominent points of divergence. The moral: Don't assume that, because Christian A believes one thing about doctrine, scriptural interpretation, or history and pronounces the opinion with authority, Christian B necessarily agrees.

SPIRITUAL SIGNPOST

It is common even for some Christians to repeat popular myths about Christianity. Many Christians "know," for instance, that the Church of England was "founded" to secure a divorce for King Henry VIII in the fifteenth century. This is at best an oversimplification and at worst a misrepresentation. English Christians had taken part in a long series of conflicts and disagreements with the Roman Catholic Church for many years before the king's request for a divorce. The disagreement over the king's marital status was an event that helped precipitate the formal break, but it was not the "cause" of the Church of England.

Myth #2: Only Catholics practice confession.

Non-Christians, or Christians unfamiliar with the practices of fellow believers, sometimes suggest that the practice of confessing one's sins to an individual member of the clergy, in private, is limited to Catholics. In fact, one-on-one confession is an important part of a number of Christian faith traditions. It is optional within the Episcopalian and Lutheran denominations, and required within the Orthodox Church, as it is within Catholicism. (Orthodox practitioners are required to perform confession at least once a year.)

The Methodists—among many Protestant groups—promote one-on-one "pastoral counseling" meetings that are in some respects analogous to confession in other Christian denominations.

Group confession of sins, of course, has been an important component of virtually all Christian worship throughout the history of the faith.

Myth #3: Christianity condemns homosexuals.

The role of homosexuals in contemporary Christian faith communities is a controversial topic. The promotion of gay members of the clergy to the rank of bishop within the Episcopal Church in the United States, for instance, caused a great deal of debate.

Although individual Christians have widely varying opinions on the issue of whether homosexuality is an acceptable lifestyle, and although there are clear Biblical strictures against the practice of homosexuality, the injunction to share the Gospel of Jesus Christ with all of humanity is just as clear-cut, and it omits no group or faction. Most Christian denominations teach that the practice of homosexuality is wrong. Equally indisputable is Jesus Christ's personal example of tirelessly sharing a message of atonement and forgiveness to all people, particularly those who have fallen into disfavor with religious authorities. Thus, the idea that Christianity itself "condemns" members of any unpopular or controversial group is problematic.

As for the largest Christian denomination, the Roman Catholic Church, its official teachings on the matter are as follows:

> *The human person, made in the image and likeness of God, can hardly be adequately described by a reductionist reference to his or her sexual orientation, talents, and gifts …. Today, the Church provides a badly needed context for the care of the human person when she refuses to consider the person as a "heterosexual" or a "homosexual"* and insists that every person has a fundamental identity: the creature of God, and by grace, His child and heir to eternal life …. The Church … celebrates the divine plan of the loving and life-giving union of men and women in the sacrament of marriage. It is only in the marital relationship that the use of the sexual faculty can be morally good. A person engaging in homosexual behavior therefore acts immorally …. This does not mean that homosexual persons are not often generous and giving of themselves, but when they engage in homosexual activity they confirm within themselves a disordered sexual inclination ….
>
> *However, any form of disrespect for the person is wrong.*
>
> *It is deplorable that homosexual persons have been and are the object of violent malice in speech and action. Such treatment deserves condemnation from the Church's pastors wherever it occurs. It reveals a kind of disregard for others which endangers the most fundamental principles of a healthy society. The intrinsic dignity of each person must always be respected in word, in action, and in law.*

—On the Pastoral Care of Homosexual Persona and Non-Discrimination Against Homosexual Persons (May 30, 1992)

With respect to these teachings, the most recent letter from the Roman Catholic bishops of the United States, *"Between Man and Woman: Questions and Answers About Marriage and Same-Sex Unions,"* has this to say:

> To uphold God's intent for marriage, in which sexual relations have their proper and exclusive place, is not to offend the dignity of homosexual persons. Christians must give witness to the whole moral truth and oppose as immoral both homosexual acts and unjust discrimination against homosexual persons.

So what is the church saying? First, each person has a fundamental dignity as a child of God, a dignity that reaches far deeper than individual sexual orientation; second, the full and right context for the expression of genital sexuality is within the covenant of marriage, and any other expression is morally objectionable; and third, any act of discrimination or verbal or physical abuse against any person on the basis of sexual orientation is contrary to the teaching of the Gospels.

The Catholic position has parallels in most Christian faith communities (such as the Orthodox Eastern Church and the many American Baptist churches). In recent years, however, some denominations (such as the Unitarian Universalists and certain elements of the Episcopal Church) have staked out other positions. The discussion has been heated at times, and it is likely to continue to be interesting.

Myth #4: All Christians believe that their version of Christianity is the only true religion.

This point of view is sometimes put forward by media figures, as though Christianity were a community with only intolerance as a common bond. There are certainly intolerant Christians (just as there are intolerant practitioners of every faith), but the position that only one version of Christianity is pleasing to God is increasingly rare.

Myth #5: Catholics believe the pope to be infallible in all his pronouncements.

As discussed in Chapter 9, the Catholic doctrine of papal infallibility applies only to formal statements of religious instruction in matters of faith and morals when he is speaking with the authority given to him as universal pastor to all the faithful. It has been used very rarely indeed. As far as individual Catholics are concerned, the doctrine of papal infallibility is the religious equivalent of stating that the Supreme

Court's decision in a given legal case is binding. This is a position few people would dispute.

Myth #6: The modern Mormon Church permits or encourages polygamy.

As a matter of formal church policy, the Mormon Church regards the practice of plural marriage as grounds for excommunication from the Church of Jesus Christ of Latter-Day Saints.

At one point in its history the church sanctioned polygamy, but the practice was common only among a comparatively small portion of the faithful. In 1890, following the failure of a challenge of Federal anti-polygamy laws, the president of the church announced that polygamy was no longer permitted within the Mormon faith. There have been attempts to circumvent official teachings on this point. The phenomenon of individual members of a religious community disobeying religious and ethical teachings, however, is hardly unique to the Mormons.

The Least You Need to Know

- Beyond issues of basic doctrine, Christians hold a remarkable diversity of beliefs about their faith.
- Other Christians besides Catholics take part in confession.
- Homosexuality is a controversial issue; the Gospels themselves, however, do not promote the public condemnation of homosexuals or any other group.
- Catholics do not believe the pope to be infallible in all his pronouncements.

Islam

The mission of the Prophet Muhammad has had an enduring influence on human affairs. To understand it, we must look both at his life and at the specifics of the Islamic way of life, which has retained its extraordinary appeal and power from Muhammad's day to ours. Today Islam boasts more than one billion adherents, of whom fewer than 20 percent are Arabs. In this part of the book, you learn about the history, development, and legacy of this major world religion.

The Early History of Islam

In This Chapter

- How Islam emerged in Arabia
- Muhammad, whom Muslims regard as the final prophet
- The Qur'an and the Sunnah
- The Five Pillars: the principles and obligations observed by every Muslim

The word Islam is usually translated as "submission" (that is, submission to God); the word also carries the meaning of "peace." The Arabic root from which it is derived means "whole," "safe," and "intact." Linguistically, the word Islam is closely related to the Hebrew word "Shalom," which is generally rendered as "peace," but which carries a similarly large range of meanings, including "completeness" and "welfare."

Islam is the third great monotheistic faith we'll examine in this book. Like Judaism and Christianity, it arose in the Middle East. It can be traced to the mission of the Prophet Muhammad in seventh-century Arabia, although its adherents believe it to be the faith actually practiced by Abraham, Moses, Noah, and Jesus, and many other people mentioned in the Bible. (Indeed, Muslims believe Islam to be the faith followed by Adam.)

Islam is a powerful cultural force that has shaped human civilization for more than 1,400 years. Today, it is practiced by a steadily growing number of Americans (somewhere between five and seven million, according to the best estimates) and a huge community of believers worldwide (roughly one and one-half billion). Yet for all the faith's global visibility, it remains, for many outsiders, something of a mystery.

In this chapter, you learn the basics of this much-discussed, but often misunderstood, faith system.

The Deen of the Prophet

The central document of the Islamic faith is the Qur'an, or "recitation." This document is regarded by Muslims as authoritative and divine in nature and the literal word of God. It offers a system of faithful living—or *"deen"*—guiding all spheres of human behavior.

We'll be looking at the Qur'an in a little more detail in just a moment. For now, you'll want to remember that the Qur'an is, for a Muslim, the ultimate authority.

Islam has many parallels with Judaism and Christianity. It also incorporates a number of traditions in existence in Arabia at the time of Muhammad.

Although there are major differences in worldview among the three major monotheistic faiths, the fundamental revelation of Muhammad does not conflict with core Jewish or Christian religious principles: it states that there is one God, a God who requires of human beings both moral behavior (action, not simply belief) and pious devotion.

Those who follow Islam are known as Muslims. The word is closely related to "Islam": Muslim means simply "one who submits."

Islam teaches social and personal codes of conduct that affect both men and women. This is in keeping with the dictates of the Shariah, or Law, which is rooted in the Qur'an and in the *Sunnah.*

DEFINITION

The Arabic word **deen** is often translated as "religion," but that English word hardly captures the vast scope of the Islamic social, legal, and ethical system. A more illuminating translation would be "way of life."

The **Sunnah** is a vast assembly of traditions (collected in *hadith,* a word that refers, literally, to particular individual traditions) recounting the acts and sayings of the Prophet Muhammad and those close to him.

The Sunnah includes thousands of sayings attributed to Muhammad and observations of his behavior. Like the Qur'an, these traditions have been the subject of careful study and interpretation by Islamic scholars for centuries. Unlike the Qur'an, they pose significant challenges in the realm of textual authenticity, because many, though certainly not all, of the traditions connected to Muhammad are indisputable forgeries. Hadith that convey the Prophet's rulings carry the force of law in Islamic jurisprudence; they also clarify important points of daily observance that aren't resolved definitively in the Qur'an (such as when and how to pray). That means their reliability is a big issue.

Muslim scholars have exerted tremendous energy over the centuries in their efforts to distinguish authentic hadith from inauthentic ones. In the Sunni Islamic tradition (which you'll learn about in the next chapter), the most important and legally influential hadith collections are those of Bukhari and Muslim, each containing only hadith that were considered by the scholar in question to be authentic. (Modern non-Muslim scholars, for their part, continue the long debate over the authenticity of these traditions, but not with the intention of making a legal point!)

West or East?

It is ironic that so many people in Europe, Australia, and North America should today look on Muslims as followers of something strange and inaccessible. Islam is intimately related to Judaism and Christianity, and is far closer to those faiths in its theological outlook than it is to, say, Hinduism or Buddhism.

Far from being a challenge to "Western" culture, Islamic civilizations have produced literary, scholarly, and scientific works that had a profound impact on the development of "Western" ideas, ideals, and institutions. Algebra, for instance, is derived from the work of Islamic mathematicians, and the Greek legacies of philosophy, science, and medicine—considered the pillars of the European Renaissance—only reached Europe because of the Islamic scholars who preserved and expanded upon them during Europe's so-called Dark Ages!

The belief that Islam is somehow different from, unconnected to, or even historically distinguishable from the West, is simply inaccurate. Islam has been a vital part of European history since the early seventh century, with vigorous communities in modern-day Spain (711 onward) and Sicily (827 onward). The social, intellectual, and artistic influence of Muslim communities in these areas persisted long after the Muslim polities that ruled these parts of the world fell; and these lands are located not in the East, but in the West.

Muslims were part of the American story long before there was an American republic. According to Dr. Jerald F. Dirks's book *Muslims in American History* (Amana Publications, 2006), Muslims took part in many of the Spanish voyages to the New World. Dirks and other scholars have estimated that something in the neighborhood of 20 percent of the kidnapped slaves brought to North America from Africa were

Muslims. Dirks also concludes that at least one Muslim fought for American independence during the Revolutionary War.

Although major cultural and theological differences certainly exist among the faithful of different lands, there is no good reason for anyone to view Islam or Muslims as anything other than fellow members of the human family. In fact, media stereotypes notwithstanding, most non-Muslims who pursue monotheism have far more in common with Muslims than they might realize.

SPIRITUAL SIGNPOST

Islam regards the Hebrew scriptures and the New Testament as deriving from early divine revelations. (Muslims believe, however, that these texts have been compromised over time.) The Qur'an, Islam's holy scripture, is regarded by Muslims as the definitive word of God. Similarly, practitioners of the faith view Muhammad, a merchant born in Mecca around 570 C.E., as the final prophet of God, the last in a long series of prophets that includes both Moses and Jesus.

Who Was Muhammad?

Non-Muslims often think of Muhammad, who lived in the seventh century C.E., as the founder of Islam. This is not what Muslims believe. Although Muhammad is known within the Islamic tradition as God's final prophet, he is not considered by Muslims to have "invented" the Islamic faith, nor do Muslims worship him. Nonetheless, any attempt to understand Islam must eventually come to terms with a question that has resonated through the centuries: Who was its prophet?

To say that Muhammad's historical impact has been immense is a vast understatement. The man whose mission consolidated the Islamic faith has directly affected social and religious institutions through his teachings for more than 14 centuries. Few, if any, historical figures have left such a clear and recognizable mark on human affairs.

SPIRITUAL SIGNPOST

Although Muslims do not believe in the divinity of Jesus, they honor him as a major prophet. They also recognize the angels Gabriel and Michael, familiar to both Jews and Christians. The Islamic conception of devils involves the jinn, creatures possessing free will who are, like human beings, destined to be judged by God for their deeds.

Before we go any further, a brief note is in order about the contemporary sources that tell us about Muhammad's life and times. A vast number of such sources exist. While it is true that some of these sources are obviously faulty, and while it is also true that scholars will probably be debating the status of the sources that *aren't* clearly forgeries for the foreseeable future, it is also true that the body of sources as a whole gives us a better and clearer sense of the day-to-day realities of Muhammad's life than we have about, say, the daily routine of Moses, or Siddhartha Gautama (the Buddha), or Jesus.

In this chapter of the book, you will get what amounts to a historical "close-up" on Muhammad. This is not because we want to emphasize his story over that of Moses, Buddha, Jesus, or anyone else, but because there is broadly credible reporting about what actually took place during Muhammad's life, and because some of that detail is important for people who want to understand the theology and history of Islam. We should note, too, that some scholars have arrived at revisionist understandings of Islamic origins, just as scholars have raised questions about the authenticity of the Christian Gospels. (For a recent example, see Fred Donner's *From Believers to Muslims*, Harvard University Press, 2010.)

Muhammad was born in Mecca, site of the ancient shrine known as the Ka'ba, which is traditionally associated with Abraham. Muhammad's family was part of the Hashim clan of the powerful Kuraish federation. His mother and father died shortly after his birth, and the future prophet was raised by his uncle. At 24, he married a wealthy widow and became a prosperous merchant in his community.

At the age of 40, Muhammad began to perceive a powerful force in his life. A series of mystical experiences, believed by Muslims to include a series of visitations from the Angel Gabriel (Jibreel), led Muhammad to conclude that he was being summoned to proclaim the word of the supreme and single God, Allah.

"*The* God"

Allah is an Arabic word meaning simply "The God." That word "The" is important, because Arabian culture in Muhammad's time was built around the worship of multiple deities. This practice of offering sincere devotion to any entity other than the One God was and is regarded by Muslims as a major sin.

Allah is simply the Arabic name for the same God worshipped by Jews and Christians. If you look at the Christian communities who were active in the Arabian peninsula before the time of Muhammad, you find that the name of the deity they worshipped was Allah. (See Marshall G. S. Hodgson, *The Venture of Islam: Conscience and History in a World Civilization*, University of Chicago Press, p. 156.)

It has been written in many accounts that Muhammad's message—there is only the One God, and rendering sincere worship to anything else is an abomination—was the subject of ridicule when he first delivered it in the streets of Mecca. It would probably be more accurate to say that his message was, at first, completely ignored. Only his own family members and a few close friends accepted his call to Islam in the early days. As he attracted more and more followers, however, his message eventually gained enough prominence to earn ridicule from the powerful chiefs of Mecca.

But the number of Muslims kept growing, and Muhammad eventually came to represent a serious threat to the prevailing social order in Mecca, a city whose economic prosperity then depended on drawing pilgrims to the Ka'ba. (Pilgrims from all over the region regularly came to Mecca to worship one or more of the 360 idols housed in the ancient Shrine.)

The Man Who Wouldn't Go Away

Representatives of the Meccan authorities offered Muhammad bribes to quiet him, which he briskly turned down. He simply refused to stop preaching and reciting the Qur'an. He kept up a steady barrage of attacks upon the prevailing lifestyle in Mecca, a lifestyle that embraced idol worship, seemingly endless striving for material wealth, and (among those who weren't destitute) a steadfast refusal to give assistance to the needy.

Muhammad's insistence on monotheism, and his egalitarian ideas, met with trial and opposition. His efforts to establish the faith in Mecca were met by setback after setback. Eventually, the chiefs of the Quraysh resolved to wipe out his movement. Adherents of the faith proclaimed by Muhammad were persecuted, and his family broke off relations with him.

SPIRITUAL SIGNPOST

Five major articles of faith are contained within the Muslim creed:

1. Belief in a single God
2. Belief in angels
3. Belief in the revealed books
4. Belief in the prophets
5. Belief in the Day of Judgment

With the death of his beloved uncle, a prominent figure in the Quraysh social hierarchy, Muhammad lost his most important protector. He was vulnerable as never before, and soon found himself the target of an assassination plot.

The Migration

Roughly 13 years after he first proclaimed the unity of God in the streets of Mecca, Muhammad's movement appeared to be in shambles. With his own people violently rejecting his message, his movement stalled, and his life in grave danger, Muhammad planned an escape from the city and began an extraordinary ascent in political, military, social, and religious influence.

In Yathrib (later known as Medina, or "the "City" for "the City of the Prophet"), Muhammad was to find shelter from the persecution of his faith. In the summer of 622, he organized an exodus (the word in Arabic is *Hijra*) of his followers at Mecca to go to Medina. His own exit from Mecca took the form of a narrow escape from the assassins of the Kuraish, but there was reason to hope for a better welcome in the new city. Warring chieftains in Yathrib agreed to put an end to their bloody struggles for supremacy by appointing Muhammad as their leader.

The year of the Hijra (622) is celebrated by Muslims as the first year of the Muslim era. The year is significant because it marks the point in Muhammad's mission when he stopped being the leader of a persecuted and powerless minority, and started being the leader of a community governed by Islamic law.

SPIRITUAL SIGNPOST

Muhammad's ban on idolatry forms one of the cornerstones of Muslim belief. Within the Islamic community, artistic representation of the image of Allah is forbidden.

Over the next few years, as Muhammad attracted more followers, there were a series of military conflicts between Medina and Mecca. After agreeing to a truce to aid pilgrims, Muhammad repudiated it in 630 when he concluded that the treaty had been violated. He roused his forces, captured Mecca with little effort, proclaimed the end of idolatry, and saw to the destruction of all the idols housed in the Ka'ba. Muhammad also extended a blanket amnesty to his enemies, which was remarkably lenient, considering the wartime tensions of the past years and the tradition for vengeance among Arabian tribes. Four men were executed, but pardons were extended to all others, including some bitter enemies.

Muhammad's capture of Mecca—and the Ka'ba—was a momentous event, and the Islamic state was suddenly a reality in Arabia. Shortly after this consolidation, in 632, Muhammad died in Medina.

The Qur'an

Muhammad's initial vision is said to have occurred around the year 610 in a cave near Mecca, where Muslims believe the angel Gabriel appeared to him and told him to "recite."

> *Recite! In the name of your Lord, who has created (all that exists)!* (Surah 96:1)

The revelations received during this encounter are regarded as the earliest lines of the *Qur'an.* Muslims believe that Muhammad's many divine encounters during his years in Mecca and Medina also revealed the remainder of the Qur'an, which, nearly 14 centuries later, remains the Arabic language's preeminent masterpiece. Its eloquence, rhetorical power, and enduring influence are acknowledged even by non-Muslims. That said, Jews and Christians (among others) dispute its claim to reflect the final and authoritative word of God.

Countless people of all faiths—and plenty of people rejecting faith entirely—have devoted intense scholarly attention to the Qur'an. Like the Torah, the Gospels, and the Tao te Ching, the Qur'an stands as one of the world's enduring religious scriptures.

DEFINITION

The **Qur'an,** which is held by Muslims to consolidate and fulfill all past revelations from God, sets out a rigorous monotheism. For Muslims, it is the Word of God, whose instrument was the Prophet Muhammad. A *surah* is a chapter within the Qur'an.

Here is one of the most famous passages of the Qur'an, known as the "Throne Verse":

> *Allah—there is no God but He, the Ever-Living, the Self-Subsisting, by Whom all subsist. Slumber overtakes Him not, nor sleep. To Him belongs whatever is in the heavens and whatever is in the earth. Who is he that can intercede with Him but by His permission? He knows what is before them and what is behind them. And they encompass nothing of His knowledge except what He pleases. His Throne extends over the heavens and the earth, and preservation of both of them tires Him not, and He is the Most High, the Great.* (Surah 2:255)

A Verbal Scripture

During Muhammad's life, the Qur'an was regarded primarily as a verbal message to be memorized and recited out loud by the prophet and his followers. Muslim sources tell us that there were numerous written versions, some dating to the time of Muhammad, and some of lesser authority. The authoritative collection of the surahs, or chapters, of the Qur'an was compiled by Muhammad's secretary Zaid in Thabit. The final sequence of the Qur'an was determined by the Caliph Uthman, nearly 20 years after Muhammad's death. Uthman pronounced in favor of Zaid's collection and ordered that all other versions be destroyed.

The Qur'an is written in Arabic and considered authoritative only in that language. It consists of 114 chapters, the first of which (beginning "Praise be to Allah") is universally incorporated in the daily prayers of Muslims. This first surah is sometimes referred to as the "Seven Oft-Repeated Verses."

> *In the name of Allah, the Most Beneficent, the Most Merciful. All praises and thanks be to Allah, the Lord of the Worlds, The Most Beneficent, the Most Merciful, the Only Owner of the Day of Recompense. You (alone) we worship, and You (alone) we ask for help. Guide us to the Straight Way, the Way of those on whom you have bestowed your Grace, not (the way) of those who have earned your anger, nor of those who went astray.* (Surah 1:1–7)

This surah has been compared to the Lord's Prayer of the New Testament, but such comparisons between religious texts are useful only up to a point. The parallel is helpful, though, if it helps non-Muslims understand that the first surah of the Qur'an occupies a position of great influence and centrality within Islam.

What It Teaches

The Qur'an contains three kinds of teachings: direct doctrinal messages, historical accounts that also resonate with metaphorical meaning, and mystical expressions of sublime beauty. These expressions are hard to summarize in rigid formulaic terms but nevertheless inform and support a broadly stated divine message.

The Qur'an also contains a number of stories that parallel events familiar from Jewish and Christian traditions. It calls for faith in Allah, warns of the consequences of unbelief, and outlines specific moral duties. The Qur'an emphasizes Allah's unity ("There is no God but God"). It encourages the faithful to acknowledge their complete dependence upon Allah in all situations.

SPIRITUAL SIGNPOST

In the Hebrew Book of Genesis, God made an everlasting covenant with Abraham. According to this book, Abraham's first child, Ishmael—whose mother was not Abraham's wife Sarah but Sarah's maid, Hagar—was ordered out of the tribe after Sarah gave birth to Isaac. Muslims believe that Ishmael then came to Mecca and settled there. The descendants of Abraham's son Isaac, according to both Islamic tradition and the Hebrew Bible, formed the tribes of Israel.

The Qur'an teaches that human life, which lasts only a short while, is a test. We will be rewarded or punished for our actions in a life after this one. There will also be a Day of Judgment and a resurrection.

The Five Pillars

The Qur'an outlines five obligations, or pillars, as essential to the lives of Muslims:

- **Confession of one's faith in God and in his prophet Muhammad:** "There is no God but God; Muhammad is the Prophet of God" is the basic confession of faith in Islam, and it infuses Islamic culture.

- **Ritual worship:** Formal periods of worship are observed five times every day: before sunrise, after midday, at midafternoon, shortly after sunset, and in the fullness of night. Muslims direct their recitations and petitions toward the city of Mecca, where stands the ancient and supremely holy shrine known as the Ka'ba.

- **Almsgiving:** The Zakat, or "purification" tax on property, is paid by all Muslims for the benefit of the poor, who include one's kin, the needy, and at times, the wayfarer. The amount of the Zakat is fixed. It is usually about 2½ percent of one's wealth, but in some circumstances it may be more.

- **Fasting:** Fasting is observed during the holy month of Ramadan (see Chapter 16).

- **Pilgrimage:** Every Muslim who is of sound body, sane, and able to afford the journey is expected to make a pilgrimage, or *Hajj*, to the holy city of Mecca at least once in his or her lifetime. Other pilgrimage traditions are associated with the ancient Ka'ba.

In addition to carrying out the commitments outlined in the Five Pillars, Muslims observe a general obligation to "commend good and reprimand evil." They also forswear gambling, usury, and the consumption of alcohol and pork.

DEFINITION

The **Hajj** is the pilgrimage to Mecca, required of Muslims at least once, although many exceptions are made for special cases. Those who fulfill the obligation are entitled to add "al-Hajj" (pilgrim) to their name.

Expansion and Evolution

Today Islam claims adherents in the Middle East, Africa, India, Central Asia, and in many other regions of the world. Despite invariable differences in emphasis from region to region, Muslims have shown a remarkable sense of shared community and purpose.

In Chapter 13, you'll learn about the development of the Islamic faith after Muhammad's death and the complex relationship between the Sunni and Shiite sects. You'll also find out about the important role played by separate Muslim traditions like Sufism.

The Least You Need to Know

- The fundamental monotheism of Muhammad is not out of keeping with Jewish or Christian religious principles.
- Practitioners of Islam are known as Muslims: "Those who submit" to God's will.
- Muhammad's mission was a momentous event in human history.
- Muslims believe in a single God who requires of human beings both moral behavior and devotion.
- The Qur'an is held by Muslims to consolidate and fulfill all past revelations from God.
- The Five Pillars constitute the heart of Muslim observance and practice.

After Muhammad

In This Chapter

* The early history of the Islamic empire
* The Sunni sect, the largest movement within Islam
* The origins and practices of the Shia sect
* The differences between the different groups
* The guiding ideas behind the multifaceted, mystical, and ascetic Sufi movement

Over the centuries, a number of schools, factions, and scholarly movements have shaped Islamic thought. Islam in turn has enriched other faiths, including Judaism and Christianity.

Like those of Judaism and Christianity, the practitioners of Islam have experienced division and disagreement at various points in their faith's history. In this chapter, you learn about some of the sects and schools of thought that have emerged.

The Islamic Empire

The period following the death of Muhammad saw Islam consolidate its transformation from "fringe movement" (which is how it must have been perceived by the Quraysh in Mecca in the early years of Muhammad's mission) to the moral and legal foundation of a great empire. The Islamic way of life eventually held sway from Spain to the Chinese border.

The men who followed in Muhammad's footsteps and oversaw the consolidation and expansion of this empire were known as *caliphs*. The first four caliphs were close associates (and, in two cases, relatives) of the Prophet himself. They are pivotal figures in Islamic history, and are popularly known as the "Rightly Guided Caliphs."

> **DEFINITION**
>
> **Caliph** (from the Arabic Khalifa, meaning "deputy" or "successor") was a title bestowed on the designated successor to Muhammad in leading the Islamic faith. The caliph emerged as both political leader and defender of the faith within the Islamic theocracy. Eventually political machination came to define the institution of the caliphate, which was important in a number of empires. Ottoman sultans assumed control of the last caliphate after their conquest of Egypt in 1517; the title was abolished in 1924.

Four Caliphs

The first caliph, Abu Bakr, was the father-in-law of the Prophet and one of the very earliest converts to Islam. He was elected to lead the Muslims immediately following Muhammad's death. He consolidated Islam's authority and put down several rebellious tribal movements.

The second caliph, Umar, led a series of successful military campaigns that dramatically extended the new empire's reach beyond Arabia.

The third caliph, Uthman, continued the extraordinary expansion of the empire. It was under Uthman, as we saw in the previous chapter, that the authoritative written text of the Qur'an was set down, based (we are told) on written records and the memorized recitations of those who had learned it from Muhammad. The first six years of Uthman's caliphate were marked by unity among the Muslims, but the six years that followed that were chaotic and violent, and factions arose in the empire. He was killed by rebels in the year 656.

Muhammad's cousin and son-in-law Ali emerged as Uthman's successor, and was the fourth caliph. It is important to note that Ali had, at the time of his father-in-law's death, sought to be the first caliph, only to be passed over in favor of Abu Bakr. Some Muslims insisted that Ali had been designated by the Prophet as his rightful successor, and that the choice of Abu Bakr to lead the empire was a grievous error. The controversy, as we will see, was a fateful one.

Although Ali was able to implement a number of important internal initiatives when he finally did become caliph, he was unable to maintain his own authority in the face of military opposition, and the Islamic empire descended into chaos and rebellion during his rule. He was assassinated and succeeded by an ambitious politician named Muawiya, whose claim to the caliphate was bitterly disputed, but who served as the first caliph in the line that would come to be known as the Umayyad dynasty.

The teachings of the Qur'an had laid out the goal of a peaceful, devout, and united Islamic community. Yet the second half of Uthman's caliphate, and all of Ali's, had been marked by extraordinary discord, division, and bloodshed.

Dissent and Controversy

Deep divisions within the assembly of Muslim believers had led to a number of serious disputes about the future of the empire. For instance, a militant group known as the Kharajis found a host of reasons to rebel against centralized authority. During the early years, they faced constant opposition from recognized Islamic leaders. The group was eventually marginalized, but other internal conflicts developed.

One of these conflicts was the result of an influential theological movement that arose in the eighth and ninth centuries. Its leaders held that the rational faculty of man, without benefit of revelation, was capable of determining moral issues definitively. This group saw the Qur'an as having been developed in time and not eternal in nature, as other schools believed. (As you will see, this so-called "rational" approach to matters of faith was eventually discredited in Islam.)

SPIRITUAL SIGNPOST

The argument within early Islam about whether the Qur'an was created in time or was somehow eternal can be compared to early Christian debates about the temporality or eternity of Christ. In fact, as many Muslim scholars have pointed out, the text of the Qur'an is to Muslims very much as Christ is to Christians: an embodiment of the Divine.

The outcome of these and other debates were deeply important to the Islamic community because of the profound centrality the Qur'an, a scripture that Muslims consider to be inspired only in its original Arabic, in the very words Muhammad received from heaven and then passed along to his followers. For Muslims, what is lost in any translation of the Qur'an is the authenticity of a direct quotation from God.

From a theological point of view, nothing eclipses the authority of the Qur'an for a Muslim. Yet the Qur'an did not (and does not) explicitly resolve all the community's practical questions about daily life. As we have seen, the Qur'an was supplemented by the Sunnah to address this problem. The traditions found in the Sunnah offered Muslims insights on correct behavior in a vast array of situations. Not surprisingly, though, differing scholarly lineages and competing interpretations of the various accounts of Muhammad's personal instructions and examples persisted, and these debates, too, became points of division within the community. The two most rigorously researched collections of hadith—Bukhari's and Muslim's—have, for centuries, held a kind of canonical status. These collections still serve as authoritative "argument-settlers" for the huge group of Muslims now known as the Sunnis.

The Sunni Muslims

The Sunnah, then, is the tradition or established practice of Muhammad. Sunni Muslims came to be called *Sunnis* because they were part of a scholarly movement founded on the principle of looking to the *Sunnah* of the Prophet for authority. Shiite Muslims, by contrast, believed that Allah had sent the community another source of guidance after Muhammad's death, namely the divinely guided imams from the family of the Prophet himself.

As these and other disputes played themselves out in the centuries following the death of the Prophet, yet another fateful conflict emerged: the debate between the scholars and the political establishment over who had the last word on interpreting the Islamic tradition.

The Sunni (or "Traditionalist") scholars eventually overcame the political establishment and emerged as the dominant force within Islam. This movement formalized the scholarly and intellectual tools used by most of the world's Muslims to resolve questions related to deen. Today, about 85 percent of all Muslims worship within the Sunni tradition.

It's important to understand that the Sunni group's emphasis on fundamentals—its opposition to schisms and its intolerance of dissent—did not lead to a single narrowly defined doctrine. Today, those known as Sunnis are culturally and religiously diverse. Rather than try to achieve unanimity on all questions of doctrine, Sunni Islam has opted for a broadly accepted set of theological principles. It has no structured religious hierarchy, which is one reason why statements about the "doctrines" of Sunni Muslims must be made with great care. This school of Islam has extended into many parts of the world without requiring uniformity on every question of faith and practice. A distinctive emphasis on the individual's direct relationship with Allah is one of the features of the Sunni school, but this emphasis has not prevented individual Sunnis from exercising religious influence.

For centuries, Sunni scholars have played a vital role in defining and consolidating the Islamic tradition. They have elaborated the Shari'a and given countless rulings on the religious and legal issues faced by Muslims, both in the form of *fatwas* (far-reaching legal opinions) and through judicial decisions in specific cases.

DEFINITION

A **fatwa** is a religious opinion related to Islamic law, conduct, or ritual, issued by an Islamic scholar.

Sunni Muslims can be found in many lands and cultures, from Indonesia to Africa and from Asia to the Arab communities of the Middle East.

The Shiite Muslims

Only one major school distinct from the Sunnis has survived in Islam. It is the *Shiite* school, and it is of even more distant origin than the Sunni. This group places a heavy emphasis on the role of individual clerics, and is likelier to consider their legal opinions binding upon those involved.

DEFINITION

Shia means "follower." The Shia school of Islam began as a political movement for the "followers" of Ali, the son-in-law of Muhammad.

Early Shias emerged in opposition to the central government, supporting the claim of Ali, the son-in-law of Muhammad, as the first caliph. They lost. They based their claim on the belief that Muhammad had named Ali as his heir at *Ghadir Khumm*.

DEFINITION

Ghadir Khumm, the Pool of Khumm, is where Shias believe Muhammad designated his cousin and son-in-law Ali as his heir.

The Shiite Muslim's view of the early history of the Islamic faith differs sharply from that of the Sunni Muslim. Sunnis accept all four of the first caliphs as legitimate successors to Muhammad. Shias, who believe Ali to have been wrongfully passed over, dispute this.

The genealogy here becomes important. Ali was understood to be the first Muslim *imam* (leader) after the Prophet himself, followed by Ali's son (and Muhammad's grandson) Hasan, followed by Hasan's brother Husayn, and so on. These figures are understood by Shiites not only as political leaders, but as divinely guided successors to the Prophet Muhammad, and as important figures in shaping any Islamic response to social and political issues. (Shiite hadith, for instance, often go back to an imam, rather than to Muhammad.)

SPIRITUAL SIGNPOST

Shiite Islam is the official religion of Iran, and the form of worship observed by large communities of Muslim believers in India, Pakistan, Iraq, Lebanon, and other areas. It accounts for perhaps 15 percent of the world's Muslims.

Shiites reject the claims of the first three Islamic caliphs. This point of division with the Sunnis reflects much more than an ancient political dispute. To understand why, you have to understand what happened at a place called Karbala, 13 centuries ago.

Karbala and Beyond

Eventually, the religious orientation of the Shia movement fused with its political goals. How did that happen? The critical moment in the Shia movement's development came with the martyrdom of Ali's younger son, Husayn, in 680 C.E., at the hands of the Umayyad clan, which had assumed political power, and with whom Husayn was at war.

When Husayn engaged the Umayyad forces at Karbala, he was hoping to topple their regime and install himself both as temporal ruler *and* as the Prophet's rightful successor. (At that point, Muhammad, Ali, and Hasan had all died.)

For the Shia, the failure of Husayn's campaign, and his own death, had far-reaching theological implications. Every year during Ashura, Shiites reenact the battle and the death of Husayn and his followers at the hands of the Umayyads; his death is seen by many Shiites as an atonement for the sins of all Shiites.

With Husayn's martyrdom, the political and religious dimensions of the Shia movement became indistinguishable. The right of members of Ali's family to succeed as leaders of the new Islamic nation was now a critical, and permanent, component of Shia observance.

Most Shiite Muslims belong to a group known as Imamites, or the Twelve-Imam division. The *imam* is a religious leader, regarded as sinless, with a direct lineage to Ali, the son-in-law of Muhammad. Imamites hold that there were Twelve Imams, beginning with Ali and proceeding in a direct line to Muhammad al-Muntazar, who is considered to have disappeared from human view in 878 C.E. The Twelfth Imam is regarded by believers as the only legitimate source of leadership, and is expected to return to lead the Muslims at the end of time.

The Twelve-Imam Shiites are not the only component of the Shiite sect. Another, considerably smaller branch is that of the Ismailites, who acknowledge seven Imams.

The Imam

Shiite Muslims, as we have seen, accept a doctrine focused upon a figure known as the Imam, whose leadership allows a full understanding of the truths of the Qur'an. Shia clerics in the Twelve-Imam division derive their considerable authority from their role as the deputies of this Twelfth Imam. They are considered to possess complete knowledge of the Qur'an and its implementation. Clerics may be referred to as mullahs or mujtahids. Individual members of the Shiite clergy benefit from a religious tax (khums) on Muslims; as in Sunni Islam, however, there is no formal hierarchy.

Shia Muslims incorporate distinct approaches to ritual and practice. They differ from Sunni Muslims on the important question of what ancient accounts should be accepted as constituting the Sunnah, for instance. They also acknowledge temporary marriages, unions that may be established for a specific, predetermined period of time.

SPIRITUAL SIGNPOST

The role of women in various Islamic societies is complex, more so than outsiders may think. Westerners tend to assume that Islam itself limits the rights of women. Actually, apart from certain stipulations about inheritance and laws concerning witnesses, Islamic rights and duties apply to both sexes. Ancient cultural traditions have done much more to shape the status of women than religion and doctrine. That is why Muslim societies can differ so dramatically in their approaches to this issue. For more on the role of women in this faith, see Chapter 15.

Other Important Movements

Islam is a remarkably vigorous and diverse global faith tradition. Today, it encompasses a seemingly endless series of movements and countermovements, inspires countless competing and complementary schools of thought, and encompasses many points of view. Although an understanding of the similarities and differences of the two main modern groups of worshippers, Sunni and Shia, is certainly important, we also have to understand that these two labels, on their own, don't convey the breadth, depth, and dynamism of the entire Muslim world.

There are many important movements that have been embraced by large numbers of present-day Muslims—more, in fact, than can be discussed in a book like this. Let's look at three of the most influential of them now.

The Sufis

The Sufis are the mystics of Islam. Every faith has its mystics—men and women who seek union with God through contemplation, *asceticism*, and prayer. Mystics are usually both inside and outside their religious tradition: inside because they approach God through the forms of that tradition; outside because their personal revelations cannot be confirmed and are not always condoned by the rest of the community. Mystics both enrich and threaten their religious establishment. Revered by some and suspected by others, they often symbolize the prophetic voice of the faith.

DEFINITION

Asceticism is a practice or set of practices such as fasting, going without sleep, and tolerating rough conditions, that disciplines the body so that the **ascetic** can concentrate on achieving spiritual perfection and union with God.

Early Islamic figures revered by the Sufis include Ali (the son-in-law of Muhammad whose claim to the caliphate caused such controversy) and Hallaj, a tenth-century figure who shocked some of his contemporaries by claiming unity with God.

Rabia al-Adawiyya, an influential early Sufi figure, condemned religious devotion that was motivated by a desire for heaven or a fear of punishment. For her, love for God was the sole valid expression of devotion to the Divine.

Historically, the Sufi emphasis on dissolution into the Divine has sometimes resulted in conflicts with religious authorities. Hallaj's proclamation "I am the Truth" earned him crucifixion in 922 C.E.

SPIRITUAL SIGNPOST

Sufism has made significant literary and theological contributions to Islam over the years. Conservative Muslims, however, have often viewed the movement with skepticism. You'll learn more about the Sufi movement in Chapter 30.

Still, the Sufi movement mostly developed inside the lines of orthodox Islamic practice. By rejecting the worldliness of Muslim life, early Sufism did much to reinvigorate the faith, and to reinforce notions of an individual believer's progression toward the Divine through continuous personal devotion.

Sufi orders have emerged in various parts of the world. Their flexibility and sensitivity to local tradition and custom have helped them to flourish and endure for centuries. These orders played an important role in extending Islam to new parts of the world, as well as in solidifying cultural and commercial ties.

The Salafi

"Salaf" means "predecessor" or "forefather." The word "Salafi" may refer either to a specific historical community—the first three generations of believers operating under the teachings of the Prophet Muhammad—or to later groups who appealed to the practices and examples of those early Muslims as their primary role models. A common English rendering of the Arabic phrase "Salaf as-Saaleh" is "Pious Predecessors." Thus, a modern Salafi is someone whose practice is primarily influenced by the examples and methodologies of the Pious Predecessors, the three earliest generations of Islamic believers.

Today, many people consider self-described Salafis a "sect" within Sunni Islam, but this is inaccurate; the Salafi movement is perhaps better understood as an ongoing theological discussion within Islam. The movement's scholarly and practical emphasis on the examples, teachings, and analytical methods of the Pious Predecessors is now ancient and pervasive. Salafism has expressed itself in at least three historically important revival movements within the Sunni tradition: those led by Ahmad ibn Hanbal (780–855 C.E.), Taqi ad-Deen ibn Taimiyyah (1263–1328 C.E.), and Muhammad ibn Abd al-Wahhab (1703–1792 C.E.). Each of these eminent scholars strove to revive the Salafi creed and methodology.

Wahabbism

The third of those Salafi revivals, the eighteenth-century campaign led by the brilliant Arabian scholar Muhammad Ibn Abd-al-Wahhab, came to be known as the Wahabbi movement.

Wahabbism is today the dominant form of Islam in Saudi Arabia. There, as in many other parts of the Islamic world, religious scholars play an extremely important, and often controversial, sociopolitical role.

In line with Abd-al-Wahhab's rigorous condemnation of practices he considered un-Islamic (such as cults that worshipped Muslim saints), the Wahabbis have taken a dim view of much medieval Islamic scholarship, and of various perceived innovations in the faith. Wahabbi scholars also reject the notion that they are a "sect" within Islam. They are likely to respond to such descriptions by emphasizing the universal importance to Muslims of a return to the core values expressed in the Qur'an and the Sunnah.

Many Wahabbi scholars condemn, as Abd-al-Wahhab did, a perceived moral and political decline in the Islamic world in general, and in the Arabian peninsula specifically.

The Least You Need to Know

- There are two main divisions within Islam: the Shiite sect and the Sunni sect.
- The Sunni sect is by far the larger of the two groups. Its broad platform of essential doctrines has won adherents in many geographic and cultural settings.
- The main group within the Shiite sect, dominant in Iran and elsewhere, places a heavy emphasis on the lineage of the Imams (regarded as the successors to Muhammad) and on the authority of clerical representatives acting as deputies of the unseen twelfth Imam.
- The mystical and ascetic Sufi movements, which seek direct contact with God, have been highly influential over the centuries.

Ramadan and Other Observances

In This Chapter

- Daily Muslim observances
- Important requirements and traditions that affect non-Muslims attending services
- Key facts about Ramadan
- Other important Islamic holy days

In this chapter, you learn about daily worship rituals, the settings for Muslim worship, and Ramadan, the holy ninth month of the Muslim calendar. You also learn about a number of other significant annual observances within Islam.

Day by Day

Sunni Muslims pray five prayers, with particular prayer rituals connected to particular times of day: before dawn, just after noon, midafternoon, just after sunset, and in the evening. Shia Muslims perform five prayer rituals with the same names and the same durations as their Sunni counterparts, but do so within three daily time slots: before dawn, just after noon, and just after sunset.

Although these prayers, which are typically not more than 10 minutes in duration, may be undertaken in a *mosque*, they are considered valid when offered in other settings. Additional prayers bring additional merit. Muslims believe there is more reward for prayers offered as part of a group than for prayers offered as an individual.

> **DEFINITION**
>
> A **mosque** is a building used by Muslims for worship and prayer. The mosque features a niche or other central point that orients the worshipper toward the *qibla,* or direction toward Mecca. Mosque, by the way, is an English word; the Arabic word for the same building is *masjid,* which means "place where prostration takes place."

Although there are some exceptions in practice made for travelers and sick persons, these prayers must be rendered faithfully and with full attention, regardless of one's physical location. Those engaging in the prayer must be ritually clean. The worshipper removes his or her shoes and performs a cleansing ritual, called the *wudhu,* for the hands, face, mouth, and feet. This literal physical cleansing reflects a symbolic spiritual purification.

Intricate detail is a hallmark of Islamic religious art and design.

At noon on Friday, the Islamic Sabbath day, the Islamic community gathers in the mosque for a service of prayer lasting 30 minutes to an hour. Shoes are not worn in the mosque, and men and women pray separately so as not to distract each other (local arrangements for this differ from place to place). The Friday gathering is an important time of coming together for the local community, a time to renew relationships and share community concerns. For males, attendance at the Friday prayers is compulsory. Skipping services without cause is regarded as a sin.

Once the wudhu is complete, believers face Mecca and begin a series of rituals that involve bowing, prostration, and the recitation of established prayers. During prayers, Muslims always orient themselves toward the holy shrine of Mecca. (It is important to remember, however, that their prayers are directed to God, and not to any physical structure.) In the United States, Muslim worshippers turn toward Mecca during prayers by facing to the northeast.

Islamic prayer makes use of memorized recitations and involves a repeated sequence of bowing and standing postures. The number of prayers will depend on the point in the day at which the prayers take place. Each such sequence begins with the recitation of the first Surah of the Qur'an. No prayer delivered without the recitation of this surah is valid.

Those who have recently joined the faith take part in group prayer and proceed under the guidance of a member of the clergy until the appropriate prayers are committed to memory. If you are not a practicing Muslim, you should not attempt to join the prayer line. There will usually be a separate area in the mosque for non-Muslim guests who wish to observe prayer services.

Important Islamic Life Rituals

Like most other major religions, Islam has special observances for major life events. Following is a brief summary of some of the most important customs.

Welcoming Ritual

The birth ceremony is known as an *akikah*. This informal observance can take many forms, depending on the nation or culture in which the family lives. (Many Muslims do not celebrate any form of akikah because birthdays are not celebrated in the Islamic system.)

Initiation

Initiation, or *shahada*, marks a young Muslim's formal entry into the faith. There is no set age for this rite; it commonly takes place during one's middle teens.

The ceremony must by witnessed by a prescribed number of adult Muslims. During the shahada, the individual making his or her formal proclamation of faith repeats, in Arabic, the sentence "There is no God but God; Muhammad is the Prophet of God." The ceremony is held either in a private home or in a mosque. It may follow a regularly scheduled prayer service.

The Marriage Ritual

This ceremony, seen as a sacred contract between the parties, takes place in the mosque's main sanctuary. By Western standards, the Islamic wedding rite may seem brisk and even lacking in formality. Witnesses simply observe the groom's formal offer of marriage and the bride's formal acceptance of it. An *officiant* will offer a sermon on the subject of marriage. There is no elaborate ceremony associated with the event.

After the marriage comes the *waleemah*, or reception. This can take place virtually anywhere, including the mosque where the marriage occurred. There may be music and dancing, but, needless to say, there will be no alcohol.

Funerals and Mourning Periods

An Islamic funeral service, like the marriage ritual, is straightforward. It may incorporate a service at a funeral home, and it will include the recitation of *janazah*, prayers for the dead, at the gravesite. Islamic practice does not sanction cremation, and burial takes place within 24 hours.

Islam limits the official period of mourning of the death of a family member to 40 days. No other rules are laid down regarding how long the bereaved should mourn. In practice, Muslims can be expected to assume regular work duties a few days after the funeral. When in doubt, call the family directly.

Most female Muslims do not engage in social activities for 40 days following the death of an immediate family member. Males may follow less stringent guidelines.

BARRIER ALERT!

Non-Muslim women attending religious services in mosques should respect Islamic custom by wearing a headscarf. For reasons of modesty, Muslim girls and women cover their hair and neck. And although there are no hard-and-fast rules on the subject, it is best to remember that less jewelry is definitely more in this setting. Be especially careful to avoid jewelry that incorporates people, animals, Jewish or Christian religious imagery, astrological symbols, or other potentially offensive depictions. (This goes for men as well as women.)

Ramadan

The holy festival of Ramadan occupies the whole of the ninth month of the Islamic calendar. (Because this calendar is lunar, the corresponding Ramadan dates in the solar Western calendar system change from year to year.) Ramadan is a time of daily repentance and fasting. Adults embark on a rigidly observed period of abstention, reflection, and purification. Muslims are expected to forgo all indulgences, to reflect on their past misdeeds, to reinforce basic personal discipline, and to express gratitude to Allah for his continued direction and daily presence in the life of the believer. The very young, those who are physically ill, and members of certain specially designated groups (such as soldiers), are excused from Ramadan obligations.

Between sunrise and sunset during Ramadan, adult Muslims do not smoke, eat, drink, or have sex. They are encouraged to read the Qur'an from beginning to end during the holy month, which celebrates the first revelation of the Islamic scriptures.

Other Important Islamic Holy Days

Ramadan is the most widely known observance in Islam, but other holy days are also celebrated. Each of the following is reckoned according to the lunar Islamic calendar, so Western calendar dates cannot be given.

SPIRITUAL SIGNPOST

The night of Muhammad's first revelation is known as Lailatul-Qadr, the "Night of Power."

Lailatul-Qadr

Lailatul-Qadr is celebrated on a night falling during the final portion of the month of Ramadan. During this period, Muslims commemorate Muhammad's first experience of divine revelation, which is regarded as having occurred on a single night sometime during the final ten days of the month. The actual date of the Prophet's first revelation is not known, so believers *seek* Lailatul-Qadr during the final 10 days of the month, rather than celebrate it on a specific day.

Muslims may choose to spend most of their time in a mosque during this final portion of Ramadan.

Eid al-Fitr

Eid al-Fitr is the feast period that follows the conclusion of the month-long fast. It takes place at the end of Ramadan and lasts for three days. It is typically observed with banquets and the exchange of gifts. Eid al-Fitr is also the time when alms are given, as mandated under Islamic law.

Eid ul-Adha

Eid ul-Adha, a great celebration held at the conclusion of the Hajj period, is marked by the sacrifice of a goat, sheep, or other animal. The feast and party that follows celebrates the faithfulness and obedience of the patriarch Abraham.

> **SPIRITUAL SIGNPOST**
>
> Two important celebrations observed by Shia Muslims, but not by Sunnis, are `Ashura, the 10 days of mourning for the martyrdom of Husayn, and Eid al-Ghadeer, which commemorates the sermon believed to signal Muhammad's designation of Ali as his heir.

The Least You Need to Know

- The daily life of a Muslim incorporates regular prayer to Allah.
- A mosque is a building used by Muslims for worship and prayer.
- Prayer may take place in any setting, but the person praying must be physically oriented toward Mecca if possible.
- The holy month of Ramadan, which falls in no fixed season because of the lunar Muslim calendar, is a time of daily repentance and fasting.
- Between sunrise and sunset during Ramadan, adult Muslims do not smoke, eat, drink, or have sex.

Breaking Down Barriers to Islam

In This Chapter

- The global faith community
- The reason Islam spread
- The role of women
- The Qur'an and non-Muslims

Of the three great monotheistic faiths—Judaism, Christianity, and Islam—it is fair to say that Islam is, at least in North America and Europe, the least understood. This is ironic, given that there are significant numbers of Muslims in both of these regions of the world, and have been for some time.

At last count, there were approximately eight million Muslims in the United States. Proportionally larger Muslim populations also exist in the United Kingdom and France, and have begun to emerge as major cultural and political forces there.

With Islamic communities in Europe, Australia, and North America becoming not only larger but more vocal and more politically engaged than they were, say, 10 years ago, a more comprehensive understanding of Islam is bound to emerge in those parts of the world. Conversions and immigration continue to swell the ranks of the faith's adherents in these and other countries not historically considered "Muslim."

A Global Phenomenon

Islam, like Judaism and Christianity, traces its roots to the Middle East. It is, however, a global phenomenon, and its practice has no relationship whatsoever to one's nationality. This one simple fact, so frequently ignored or glossed over in news reports and discussions about Islam, may well be the most obvious barrier to a meaningful approach to the faith.

That's why misunderstandings about the global appeal of Islam are the first of the five obstacles to understanding Islam that we'll examine in this chapter. The others are: stereotypes related to the role of the so-called "sword of Islam" in propagating the faith; misunderstanding of the term *jihad;* oversimplifications about gender relations and the role of women; and misconceptions regarding the Qur'an's teachings on warfare.

There are other barriers to understanding the faith, of course. For one thing, there are seemingly countless internal divisions of opinion, expressed in many narrow, scholarly interpretations of the faith's core texts. Outsiders can initially feel some confusion when trying to sort out the various scholarly voices. Understanding the many areas of intricate doctrinal controversy is a daunting task. (And not a task we're going to take on in this book.)

But on the major issues—the unity of God, the reality of the afterlife, the certainty of a reckoning for each of us, the special mission of the Prophet—Islam speaks with one voice. It is a voice that many people of goodwill in non-Muslim countries are now striving to understand without prejudice. An interesting pattern emerges among those people of goodwill: after they have direct personal contact with Muslims—as neighbors, as colleagues, as fellow citizens—they are less likely to accept or reinforce negative media-driven stereotypes about Islam.

ON THE PATH

"I have been on the (Senate) floor before, speaking about Islam and what a great religion it is. I have said before … that my wife's primary physicians are two members of the Islamic faith …. I know them well. I have been in their homes. I have socialized with them. I have talked about very serious things with them. We have helped each other with family problems. I have been to the new mosque with them in Las Vegas. They are wonderful people with great families. I have come to realize Islam is a good religion, it is a good way of life. Muslims maintain a good health code as their religion dictates, and they have great spiritual values as their religion dictates. It is too bad there are some people— evil people around the world—who would target the innocent in the name of Islam. I believe that the strength of Islam and the faith and fortitude of more than one billion Muslims around the world will overcome these evil people and their evil deeds."

—Senator Harry Reid, Democrat (Nevada), October 18, 2001

Myth #1: Muslim equals Arab.

If you say the single word "Muslim," you are, as a matter of statistical fact, probably talking about a non-Arab. This point is, perhaps, worth repeating. When you say that one word, "Muslim," you are probably talking about someone who is not from the Middle East and does not speak Arabic. And, given the percentage of Muslims who are converts from other faiths, there's a very good chance that you are talking about someone who grew up without any cultural connection whatsoever with Arab culture, language, or traditions.

It is certainly true that Arabic-speaking peoples—those from countries such as Iraq, Qatar, Egypt, and Jordan—are overwhelmingly Muslim, even though there are small numbers of non-Muslim Arabs in many Arabic-speaking lands. (The Coptic Christians, for instance, have been practicing their faith in Egypt for centuries, and indeed were practicing it long before the time of Muhammad.)

But Muslims from Arabic lands are easily outnumbered worldwide by Muslims who do not live in Arabic-speaking regions. So when you say the single word "Muslim," you could be talking about any one of the following people:

- Hakeem Olajuwan, the NBA superstar. He was born in Africa.

- Yusuf Islam, the singer formerly known as Cat Stevens. He was born in England.

- Muhammad Ali, the legendary professional boxer, formerly known as Cassius Clay. He was born in the United States.

Notice that each of these people has an Arabic name, even though each comes from someplace other than the Middle East. Many—but not all—Muslims are given, or adopt, Islamic names. The assumption of an Arabic name, however, does not make someone an Arab.

Assuming that all Muslims come from the Middle East, or that the religion is a regional phenomenon, is a common but major mistake among Westerners. This mistake tends to make Islam seem smaller than it actually is (it has more than a billion adherents worldwide) and more narrowly accepted than it actually is.

Muslims believe that the Prophet Muhammad, unlike all previous prophets, came to deliver his message of salvation to humanity as a whole. In keeping with Muhammad's global mission, Islam offers an international, rather than a localized, set of living standards and religious beliefs. But, as a practical matter, a Muslim in Djakarta, Indonesia, is likely to have a very different set of life experiences from a Muslim in New York City, who is in turn likely to have a very different set of life experiences from a Muslim in Lagos, Nigeria. To treat all these people as though they came from the Middle East would be to ignore the diversity, reach, and historical influence of the Islamic faith.

Myth #2: Stereotypes concerning the "Sword of Islam."

One of the most persistent obstacles to a balanced understanding of Islam is a common misconception concerning how it spread. In the century following the death of the Prophet Muhammad in 632, a great Islamic empire arose—an empire that rivaled or exceeded the previous empires of Rome or Persia in its reach. There is a common notion in the West that Islamic armies systematically eradicated the belief systems of all non-Muslims they encountered—using the so-called "Sword of Islam." This is, however, a historical fiction.

ON THE PATH

"The sword of Islam is not the sword of steel. I know this by experience, because the sword of Islam struck deep into my own heart. It didn't bring death, but it brought a new life; it brought an awareness and it brought an awakening—as to who am I and what am I and for what am I here?"

—Ahmed Holt, British civil contractor who embraced Islam in 1975

The prevailing philosophy of the Islamic state was not one of forcible imposition of Islamic beliefs (indeed, the Qur'an prohibits this), but rather the imposition of a special tax upon religious communities choosing to pursue their own faiths. In exchange for payment of this tax, followers of other faiths received military protection and enjoyed other benefits of community life in the Islamic empire.

The religion of Islam spread with great speed because people in many lands chose to embrace it, not because military or governmental authorities decreed other faiths forbidden. Islam later gathered adherents in areas of the world where no Islamic armies had ever set foot, notably Indonesia and Western Africa.

Nevertheless, the preconception remains that Islam's worldwide reach arose because of military adventurism and a history of religious intolerance. This is quite the opposite of what took place. Islam's days as an empire were marked by a remarkable tolerance for religious minorities—a tolerance that can still be found in nations such as Qatar today. (Other Islamic countries, such as Saudi Arabia, don't have an impressive record of tolerance in the modern period.)

> **ON THE PATH**
>
> "There shall be no harm for harm, no revenge for revenge."
>
> —The Prophet Muhammad

Exasperated by the "Sword of Islam" myth, Muslims sometimes ask non-Muslims whether sheer military dominance *could* bring about such broad acceptance of any religion. Could the "sword" really compel mass acceptance and endure for more than a millennium *after* an empire's period of military dominance? If military strength alone did carry this force, they argue, most of the nations of Europe would today be worshipping at the shrines of Roman gods!

Myth #3: Jihad.

Another significant obstacle to an accurate understanding of Islam has to do with the common—but frequently misused—word *jihad*. To judge by the newspaper headlines, televised news bulletins, and magazine articles, jihad means one thing and one thing only: holy war against those who do not accept Islam.

The modern association of military action with the word jihad misses a deeper concept of central importance to the faith—a concept that still drives the meaning of the word today.

Jihad means struggle—and it means struggle against the self first and foremost. To abandon oneself to lust, greed, anger, cynicism, or to forget one's ultimate accountability to God, is to abandon jihad; to make a conscious effort to develop temperance, generosity, and trust in Providence, and to remember one's eventual reckoning, is to wage jihad.

For a Muslim, jihad is the work of a lifetime, but the first and most important enemies are self-centeredness and the willingness to build one's life around material comforts and pleasures.

The teachings of Islam specifically forbid sneak attacks, assaults upon noncombatants, and the unnecessary destruction of property. Muslims also emphasize that Islam is, first and foremost, a religion of peace, one that explicitly forbids the returning of harm for harm. The September 11, 2001, suicide attacks on the United States have made many non-Muslims skeptical of the claim that Islam is a religion of peace. Muslims, for their part, counter that religious extremists exist in all religions, and that their acts should not be the standard by which any religion's precepts are judged.

There is a famous story about an Islamic warrior of the seventh century, a story that may help to put the concept of jihad in perspective for Muslims and non-Muslims alike. This warrior found himself in bloody, hand-to-hand combat with an opponent of the Islamic state. The fight was fierce, but the Islamic warrior was eventually able to disarm his opponent. They grappled with each other on the floor. Eventually, the Muslim gained the upper hand. His opponent, knowing he was about to die, spit in the Muslim's face as a final gesture of contempt.

At this, the Muslim warrior froze. Then he let his opponent go, stood up, took a deep breath, and ordered that the hand-to-hand combat begin again from the beginning. His stunned adversary backed away, retrieved the weapon he had lost, and then looked long and hard at the Muslim warrior in utter disbelief. "Why," he asked, "have you given me another chance? You had won the fight! I was yours to kill!"

Patiently, the warrior explained his reasoning. "If I had killed you just now, I would have committed a sin, because I am forbidden to kill in anger. When you spit in my face, I felt a great rage rise within me. So we should begin again, and if it passes that you kill me this time around, at least I will be able to pass without obstruction to Paradise."

Hearing this, the warrior's opponent dropped his weapon, fell to his knees, and asked to become a Muslim. As it happened, neither man died; to the contrary, they were allies for the rest of their days.

The moral: A committed Muslim is always working on himself first. That is the highest jihad.

Myth #4: Islam degrades and oppresses women.

A common belief about Islam is that it degrades and oppresses women. The vast majority of Muslim women, however, reject this notion. And that is reason enough to set it aside.

There is a great deal to be said about the subject of gender relations in Islam, and a full examination of this question is beyond the scope of this book. It does seem appropriate, however, to quote a few lines from a poem on the subject by an American *Muslimah*, and to note that she expresses the sentiments of many women who have made the conscious choice to observe her faith.

> **DEFINITION**
>
> A **Muslimah** is a female Muslim.

What do you see when you look at me?
Do you see someone limited or someone free?
All some people can do is just look and stare
Simply because they can't see my hair.
Others think I am controlled and uneducated;
They think that I am limited and unliberated.
They are so thankful that they are not me
Because they would like to remain "free."
Well, "free" isn't exactly the word I would've used
Describing women who are cheated on and abused …
See, I have declined from being a guy's toy,
Because I won't let myself be controlled by a boy.

—Author Unknown

Whether or not non-Muslims embrace such sentiments, the fact remains that most Muslimahs do. That fact should, perhaps, be a starting point for any dialogue on gender relations in Islam.

If you think Islam oppresses women, ask a Muslimah about Islam.

Myth #5: The Qur'an advocates the slaughter of unbelievers.

Two myths about Islam deserve discussion here. The first is the product of non-Muslims; the second is the product of Muslims.

"Slay the Unbelievers"?

For reasons known best to themselves, some non-Muslim commentators have insisted that the Qur'an, the holy book of Islam, advocates hunting down civilian unbelievers and killing them wherever they may be found. This is false.

Simply reading the context of the verses in question will demonstrate that they explicitly set out instructions for Muslims who were at war with a particular, clearly identified military opponent.

Here is the short passage so often quoted, with the most critical word rendered (misleadingly) as "unbelievers":

> *Slay the unbelievers wherever you find them, and take them captives and besiege them and lie in wait for them in every ambush.* (The Qur'an 9:5)

And here is the entire passage, with the same word rendered, more accurately, as "idolaters." Context shows that the passage concerns a specific pagan group who had violated a treaty with the Muslims.

> 9:1 (This is a declaration of) immunity by Allah and His Apostle towards those of the idolaters with whom you made an agreement.

> 9:2 So go about in the land for four months (i.e., the four sacred months when battle was prohibited) and know that you cannot weaken Allah and that Allah will bring disgrace to the unbelievers.

> 9:3 And an announcement from Allah and His Apostle to the people on the day of the greater pilgrimage that Allah and His Apostle are free from liability to the idolaters; therefore if you repent, it will be better for you, and if you turn back, then know that you will not weaken Allah; and announce painful punishment to those who disbelieve.

> 9:4 Except those of the idolaters with whom you made an agreement, (and) then they have not failed you in anything and have not backed up any one against you; so fulfill their agreement to the end of their term; surely Allah loves those who are careful (of their duty).

> 9:5 So when the sacred months have passed away, then slay the idolaters wherever you find them, and take them captives and besiege them and lie in wait for them in every ambush, then if they repent and keep up prayer and pay the poor-rate, leave their way free to them; surely Allah is Forgiving, Merciful.

> 9:6 And if one of the idolaters seek protection from you, grant him protection till he hears the word of Allah, then make him attain his place of safety; this is because they are a people who do not know.

It is, perhaps, worth reiterating that the subject of this portion of the Qur'an is, as a matter of historical fact, a specific tribe of pagan warriors who had broken a treaty with the Prophet Muhammad. The verses in question warned the members of this tribe that warfare was imminent. Notice that a four-month warning is given regarding the forthcoming conflict. Notice, too, that the Qur'an requires Muslim warriors to *protect* any pagan military opponents who renounce the fight and seek help, and that conversion to Islam is not a precondition of this help!

Seventy-Two Virgins?

An equally extravagant, and perhaps equally common, claim is that the Qur'an promises 72 virgins to any suicide attacker fighting on behalf of Allah.

Not only does this promise not appear in the Qur'an, it also flatly contradicts the Qur'an. The sacred text of Islam explicitly (and without exception) forbids suicide in all situations. This "urban legend" derives, not from the Qur'an, but from a Muslim saying attributed dubiously to the Prophet Muhammad, a saying that has nothing whatsoever to do with suicide attacks. Its authenticity is highly suspect, and it is not regarded as binding or obligatory by responsible scholars.

The Least You Need to Know

- Islam is a global faith tradition; it is not a regional or Middle Eastern phenomenon.
- Most Muslims are not Arabs.
- The Qur'an forbids compulsion in religion.
- Jihad is, first and foremost, the struggle with one's own faults and worldly desires.
- Muslimahs (female Muslims) are likely to resent the implication that they are abused or victimized by their faith.
- Islam does not justify suicide attacks or the slaughter of non-Muslim civilians; to the contrary, it prohibits these activities.

Hinduism

The absence of a single founder is only one of several fascinating "gaps" outsiders may encounter in examining this faith. (Another "gap": formal doctrine!) These "missing pieces" result from our preconceptions, not from a deficiency within Hinduism. Someone who is unfamiliar with the traditional religious practices of India might expect them to look more like other great religions. But Hinduism, a label that incorporates countless sects and practices, is, as it has always been, unique and sufficient within itself.

That Old Time Religion

In This Chapter

- The ancient early forms of Hinduism, a religion with no precise beginning
- The most important Hindu holy texts
- How Hinduism expanded and developed
- The common elements that define this diverse religion

In this part of the book, you learn about the mysterious early centuries of Hinduism, its development over perhaps 4,000 years, and the close association of its many rituals, practices, and texts (such as the *Bhagavad Gita*) with the people of India.

As you are about to learn, Hinduism is missing something most of the other major world religions consider absolutely essential: a beginning.

No Founder

Hinduism, which claims about 800 million practitioners worldwide (most originating in India or of Indian descent), is unique among humanity's major religions in that it cannot be traced to any specific individual or historical event. Because Hinduism arose from no single person or institution, it is seen as eternal and unchanging in its essence. Believers regard it as having existed forever. Scholars believe it arose about 3,500 years ago out of interactions between conquering Aryans and traditions already present on the Indian subcontinent.

The faith, which is as diverse as India itself, is an extraordinary collection of variations and expansions—some ancient, some more recent. This profoundly varied religion places a heavy emphasis on attaining freedom from the perceived world and on eliminating ties to the material plane of existence, eventually including one's personal identity. For all Hinduism's complexity, interconnection, and continuing development, this distinctive mystical core endures.

> **SPIRITUAL SIGNPOST**
>
> A kind of inspired pragmatism supports the Hindu faith, unlike the history-based approach of many other world religions. Loosely connected beliefs and principles are combined with techniques such as meditation and formal study to bring about personal spiritual development.

Hindu means "Indian." The diverse religious practices included under this name make up the dominant (though by no means the only) religious tradition in India, but practitioners themselves do not describe their faith in a limited or nationalistic way.

It's a mistake to try to extract one "belief system" from Hinduism's vast array of traditions and rituals. That's why some people prefer not to use the word Hinduism at all but to speak of "the religions of India." Although it is possible to identify broad elements within the faith, Hinduism in its structure expresses the profound diversity of humanity's experience of the Divine. Free of absolute or formal doctrines, Hinduism has shown remarkable adaptability in its approach to the cultivation of mystic and transcendental experiences.

"Those who see all beings in the Self, and the Self in all beings, will never shrink from it." So reads a passage in the *Upanishads*, a holy text that seeks to reconcile the (apparent) discord and profusion of physical existence into a single entrancing harmony. The lines are relevant both to the spiritual journey of the individual and to the countless tools Hinduism provides to help expedite that journey.

A Westerner seeking to compare his or her faith's religious doctrines to those of Hinduism is likely to come away shaking his or her head. Precise doctrines are hard to come by in this faith. Still, there are a few broadly accepted principles. The best way to get at these may be to take a quick look at the roots of the Hindu faith.

The Indus Valley Civilization

The story of Hinduism begins about 1,500 years before the birth of Jesus. In the Indus Valley in modern-day Pakistan, a sophisticated urban people had lived for perhaps a millennium. This still-mysterious agricultural and mercantile culture is now known as the Indus Valley Civilization. It used a form of pictorial writing that contemporary scholars have not been able to decode completely.

The Indus Valley Civilization in its heyday exceeded, at least in geographical terms, the influence of two other ancient civilizations—Egypt and Mesopotamia. It is possible that this ancient civilization, which may have been centrally governed, was in a period of decline around 1500 B.C.E., when a wave of Aryan invaders from the northwest conquered the region. The term "Aryan" as it relates to the Indus Valley has nothing at all to do with Nazi pseudo-science about a "master race." It is an unrelated archeological term.

The Aryans propagated their own language and practices in the Indus Valley, but they did not wipe out the cultural heritage of the Indus people. Modern science is not entirely sure whether the Aryan warrior bands consciously incorporated existing Indus Valley rituals, or simply failed to secure total control of the valley, allowing small pockets of indigenous religious worship to thrive. Either way, they assimilated many local practices and beliefs and combined them with existing Aryan rites. These rites involved the celebration of *Brahman*, a word now taken to describe an eternal, absolute reality beyond the multiplicity of forms. Other Aryan worship centered on fires, on the singing of hymns, and on the veneration of ancestors.

SPIRITUAL SIGNPOST

Among the many images discovered by twentieth-century archaeologists in the remains of the Indus Valley Civilization are what seem to be depictions of Shiva, one of the greatest deities in today's Hindu pantheon. In contemporary Hinduism, Shiva has various aspects. This deity's depiction in the symbolic form of a phallus (Shiva appears to have been regarded as a fertility figure by the Indus people) is balanced by the deity's role as the great cosmic destroyer.

So an ancient union of utterly different religious practices formed the first of many adaptations associated with Hinduism. What could better illustrate the richness and elasticity of the Hindu faith?

Did Hinduism emerge as the gradual result of contact between the two traditions over the centuries? Or did it develop from an intentional set of decisions to combine forms? We don't know. It is always dangerous to use modern language to describe an ancient process, but the very earliest Hinduism on record suggests what could cautiously be called an "inclusive" approach to competing cultural and religious claims. As Hinduism developed, it would continue to stress convergence rather than suppression in its encounter with other faiths. A hallmark of today's Hinduism is the reconciliation of tensions and differences between religious structures. This character seems to have been essential to the development and growth of the faith.

One and Many

Hinduism is an ongoing, pragmatic, and inspired synthesis, not the product of any strict ideology or doctrine. This is both its distinction and its greatness. Although it is not a religion that can be traced to a single revelation, neither is it a random "patchwork quilt" of fragmented ideas.

The earliest historical data shows Hinduism expanding and synthesizing the ancient practices of "competing" cultures. These practices became more meaningful and coherent because of their contact with one another, resulting in important new tools for self-discovery that extended the faith to its next phase of development.

The same features are in place to this very day. The most vigorous recent revivals of Hinduism, for instance, reflect its contacts with Christian morality, introduced by colonialism and missionaries in the nineteenth century, and with the twentieth-century movement for Indian independence from Britain.

But back to our story ....

The Vedic Period

The Rig *Veda*, the earliest and among the most revered of the holy scriptures of Hinduism, was developed between 1500 and 1200 B.C.E. Legends associated with the Aryan warrior aristocracy and the adapted Indus Valley traditions influenced this collection of hymns.

There are 1,028 hymns in the Rig Veda. These make up the first portion of the Veda, and are one of the world's oldest religious scriptures. Three other collections—the Samaveda, the Yajurveda, and the Atharaveda —were assembled during the first millennium before the beginning of the common era. Together with the Rig Veda, these make up the Samhitas, or basic Vedas.

Between perhaps 800 and 300 B.C.E. (scholars are unclear about the dates), further writings were appended to the Vedas. These included the Brahmanas (including an explanation of ceremonies discussed in earlier Vedas), the Aranyakas, and the

Upanishads. This last collection proved to be one of the most influential in the development of Hinduism.

> **DEFINITION**
>
> **Veda**, a Sanskrit word meaning "knowledge," refers to the great collection of early Hindu religious scriptures. The Vedas outline spiritual principles accepted by Hindus as fundamental to their religion. Vedic teachings emphasize the notion of a single supporting reality, manifested in Brahman, or eternal reality. All Hindus embrace the authority of the Vedas.

The name Upanishads means "sitting near," that is, near the feet of a sage or master. The texts are presented as direct accounts of advice from spiritually advanced mystics. They mark the final phase of development of the sacred Vedas and the beginning of elements of Hindu philosophy familiar to believers today.

The Upanishads, for instance, set out the principle of *reincarnation*. In this sacred book emerged mystical disciplines designed to help the believer escape the cycle of death and rebirth. Believers are reminded that clinging to faith in one's own separate identity is like assuming an alias, making recognition of the true Self impossible.

The hymns of the Rig Veda appear to incorporate notions of heaven and hell, with the virtuous proceeding to heaven upon death. But around 600 B.C.E., a new trend of thought emerged, one that accepted the principle that a human spirit, in an ongoing quest for perfection, returns again and again in varying forms after the death of each physical body. Freedom from this cycle was seen as a preeminent spiritual goal. This is the doctrine of reincarnation.

> **DEFINITION**
>
> The Hindu doctrine of **reincarnation** holds that one is trapped by the cycle of life and death until one attains true realization.

The Faith Develops: Circles of Life

The emergence of the doctrine of reincarnation had several striking effects on Hinduism. For one thing, it placed an emphasis on individual spiritual development, the better to attain release from the cycle of birth and death. For another, a reverence for all forms of life began to emerge, and sacrifices meant to impress or pacify the various gods became less and less common.

Teachings arising out of the notion of reincarnation allowed Hinduism, over time, to transfer primary focus from one set of gods (Brahma, Indra, Agni, and Varuna, the first of whom is a progenitor figure, and the rest of whom seem to be personifications of natural forces) to another (Vishnu, Shiva, and Shakti, all of whom present spiritual themes of greater complexity and subtlety than their Vedic counterparts). For many faiths this kind of transition would have been traumatic, possibly leading to a major schism or bloody religious wars. Under the conception of divine incarnation (gods assuming flesh), however, Hinduism was able to establish a more or less seamless succession of teachings that allowed believers to accept one god as incarnate within another!

The multitiered system that is so pronounced within Hinduism has given it certain unique advantages. The ancient, flexible structure of the faith and its tolerance for widely divergent elements has allowed it to extend across a huge social and geographic landscape. As it did so, it focused on distinctive and enduring spiritual ideas, and cultivated, over time, acceptance of such distinctive elements as the *mantra* and the principle of *karma*.

> **DEFINITION**
>
> **Karma** is the doctrine embodying an impartial principle of moral cause and effect, under which actions have unavoidable implications and even affect one's future incarnations. Only those who escape the cycle of birth and death may be said to go beyond the reach of karma. A **mantra** is a word or phrase repeated in meditation and religious ritual.

This is the symbol for AUM, the Hindu "syllable of supreme reality." This vitally important mantra (incantation or prayer) symbolizes, in its three sounds, the Hindu triad of Brahma, Vishnu, and Shiva. Buddhists and Sikhs also attach great significance to the utterance.

Hindu Philosophy

The influence of the Upanishads and the later emergence of Buddhism pointed Hinduism toward a formal enunciation of philosophical principles. Six ancient schools of Indian philosophy acknowledge the Vedas as a religious authority. All have played important roles in the development of the religion, but they should not be misconstrued as "dogma" that is universally accepted and promoted by Hindus.

The following is a list of classical schools of Indian philosophy:

- **Nyaya** was a logical school that emerged in the sixth century B.C.E., and sees clear thinking and analysis as essential means on the path to higher realities.

- **Vaisheshika** examined physical reality and offered a six-tiered system for categorizing it. This school emerged in the sixth century B.C.E.

- **Samkhya** emphasized the principles of matter and soul and is perhaps the oldest of these six methods. It stresses the evolution of the cosmos and of "the person."

- **Yoga** was built on the Samkhya model, and developed patterns meant to help instill personal, physical, and spiritual discipline. It developed in the second century B.C.E.

- **Purva Mimamsa,** which emerged in the second century B.C.E., offers guidance in interpreting the Vedas.

- **Vedanta,** perhaps the best known of these schools, gave rise to a number of disciplines, each placing emphasis on the transcendent messages of the Upanishads, the final portion of the Veda. This school came into existence around the first century C.E.

In addition to forming the platform for the various schools of Indian philosophy, the Upanishads gave rise to one of the masterpieces of human religious thought, the *Bhagavad Gita.* This Sanskrit classic is usually elevated to the level of the Upanishads when authoritative Hindu scriptures are discussed. It is not, technically at least, a formal part of the Hindu canon, but its influence over the centuries has been so immense that it might as well be. In a nation with many "Bibles," it has emerged as the most popularly revered of them all.

The *Bhagavad Gita* is an epic poem relating the dialogue between the human Prince Arjuna and the beloved Lord Krishna (one of the most important Hindu deities) on the eve of a great battle. In it, Krishna imparts spiritual wisdom that reinvigorates the faltering Arjuna. The text emphasizes union with God by means of love, selflessness, and total devotion.

Social Realities

The system of *castes* has been a distinctive part of Indian religious and social life for centuries. There are thousands of castes, each one differentiated from the others by its religious practices, among many other factors.

Operating simultaneously with a caste system has been a broader method of caste-related social ranking. The major classes in this system are: *Brahmins* (a scholarly elite long associated with the priesthood), *Kshatriyas* (the ruling and military class), *Vaisyas* (merchants and farmers), *Sudras* (the peasantry), and, beneath the other four designations, the so-called *untouchables*, assigned the most menial jobs. Although twentieth-century reforms began to address some of the most glaring inequities of the system, rendering untouchability illegal, entrenched distinctions among social castes have persisted.

DEFINITION

The **caste** system is a social hierarchy ordering marriage and social roles. Over the centuries, Hindu India has developed a complex and rigid social structure incorporating thousands of individual castes.

The words "Brahma," "Brahman," and "Brahmin" can be intimidating for those encountering Hinduism for the first time. Use great care when using them; these frequently confused expressions can cause unintended offense.

Brahma is a specific creator god who, despite a decline in popularity since the sixth century C.E., is still regarded as one of the supreme deities in the Hindu pantheon. *Brahman* is a Hindu term for ultimate reality without change, or eternity, and may be conceived as the Supreme Being or single God. (Just to keep things confusing, this word is sometimes rendered as Brahma, but the two concepts are nevertheless distinct.) A *Brahmin* is a member of the prestigious priestly class (caste) in India; to this day, only members of this group are allowed to read from the Veda. (Continuing to keep things confusing, the word Brahmin is sometimes rendered as Brahman.)

Contemporary Brahmins are likely to work in careers having nothing at all to do with religion, but they are still situated in positions of high status in India.

Hindu Beliefs

Hinduism is a massive religious system with a glorious profusion of entry points. Can any devotional practice on this large a scale support specific propositions of faith? The surprising answer is yes.

The following core beliefs are broad enough to support the activities of, for instance, both the devotees of the sun god Surya and the Vedantist celebration of an ultimate and impersonal Reality. Although they should not be mistaken for a religious creed or catechism, they do represent shared positions commonly accepted by Hindu believers.

Hindus believe that ...

- The Vedas present authoritative and divinely inspired teachings.

- Brahman (or the Absolute) is both essentially impersonal and, at the same time, personal; it is made manifest in a variety of forms, which are best understood as symbols of divine truth.

- Brahman may be reached through many different paths.

- What is commonly considered to be reality—the physical world—is actually temporal, illusory, and capable of concealing the divine truth from all but the wisest people.

- The doctrine of karma ensures full accountability for every thought, action, and word. Hardships and inequalities in this life may be explained by actions and decisions undertaken in previous lives.

- The doctrine of reincarnation holds that one is trapped by the cycle of life and death until one attains true realization.

- A devotee may embrace any number of revealed forms of the Absolute, and he or she may do so in any number of ways.

- Family life and social interaction are marked by four stages: the student, the householder, the seeker, and the ascetic. Believers in the last category improve the lot of the world at large through the process of their renunciation.

- Life has four goals: righteousness, earthly prosperity and success, pleasure, and spiritual liberation.

> **SPIRITUAL SIGNPOST**
>
> Hinduism is rare among major religions in that it promotes the worship of animals. The homage paid to particular animals is best understood as part of the worship directed toward the particular deities regarded as riding on them. For example, Orthodox Hindus regard cattle and peacocks as sacred, and will not permit their slaughter under any circumstances.

In the next chapter, you'll learn more about the complex, many-faceted approach that Hinduism takes to God (with a capital "G"), and to its many gods (with a lowercase "g").

The Least You Need to Know

- Hinduism, which is as diverse as India itself (the nation with which it is strongly associated), is an extraordinary collection of variations and expansions—some ancient, some more recent.

- Hinduism is regarded as having existed forever; it has no founder or point of origin.

- Specific, universally held doctrines do not play a major role in the Hindu faith.

- A series of loosely connected beliefs, such as a common acceptance of authoritative scripture, combined with a huge number of techniques for personal spiritual development within Hinduism.

- Hinduism's many forms of religious worship are meant to help believers move toward the direct experience of the Absolute.

God's Many Faces

Chapter

17

In This Chapter

- The single guiding idea behind the Hindu faith and its innumerable expressions
- The one God/many gods question as it relates to Hinduism
- The Hindu understanding of the transcendent reality
- Some of the principal Hindu deities

In this chapter, you learn about the principal deities of Hinduism (which claims thousands of gods), and about the unique blend of diversity and unanimity that supports this faith's many sects and practitioners.

One God, Many Gods

Hinduism can be as simple or as complex as any particular believer (or explorer) chooses to make it. Because this is a book for beginners, the best way to begin a chapter on the Hindu conception of God (and gods) may be to take the simple approach first.

Here it comes—don't blink!

There is something eternal and inherently divine within the human heart, and that "something" is not different from that which is eternal and inherently divine and permeates all of creation. The purpose of human existence is to discover a path that will lead to a direct experience of this "something."

That's the principle at the heart of the Hindu faith, which accepts God as both a grounding, absolute reality and as the exponent of innumerable changing processes. All the same, an important issue arises …: does Hinduism celebrate a single god or a profusion of gods?

It's a fair question. The answer from the vast and ancient Hindu tradition can sound strangely ambivalent, maybe even flippant, to a newcomer to the faith. It is, however, an ancient and quite profound response that has been worked out with exquisite care over a period of centuries. The answer is: "Yes!"

Monotheists—those who believe, as Christians, Muslims, and Jews do, in a single, *personal* God—are quite likely feeling the Hindu tradition is sending mixed signals, with its inspiring principle of Ultimate Reality, and its occasionally bewildering profusion of specific deities.

The complex question of whether Hinduism is or isn't a "polytheistic" religion can be illuminated briefly by an imaginary dialogue:

> **Newcomer:** *So, which is it? One God, Brahman, or a whole bunch of gods?*
>
> **Hindu:** *Absolutely. Or, if you prefer, not so absolutely.*
>
> **Newcomer:** *This is a pretty important issue. Doesn't Hinduism address it directly somewhere?*
>
> **Hindu:** *Of course.*
>
> **Newcomer:** *And how is it resolved?*
>
> **Hindu:** *You know, it's funny. Someone came in here just a millennium or so ago asking basically the same question. "How many gods are there?" he asked.*
>
> **Newcomer:** *What was the answer?*
>
> **Hindu:** *How many do you want?*
>
> **Newcomer:** *Suppose I were to tell you that it still sounds like fence-straddling?*
>
> **Hindu:** *Suppose I were to ask you where human beings get off trying to tell the Brahman, the Eternal, and the Ultimate, what forms are off-limits?*
>
> **Newcomer:** *But it has to be one way or the other, doesn't it?*
>
> **Hindu:** *If labeling the Divine is the thing that's really limited, what difference does it make what forms are acknowledged?*
>
> **Newcomer:** *I'm getting confused. What do the Vedas have to say about this?*
>
> **Hindu:** *This Self, what can you say of it but "no, no"?*
>
> **Newcomer:** *No, no?*
>
> **Hindu:** *No real description of Brahman is possible; but direct experience, through whatever method, discipline, or form of devotion, is.*

Newcomer: *So there's one God.*

Hindu: *From a certain point of view.*

Newcomer: *And there are lots of gods.*

Hindu: *From a certain point of view.*

Newcomer: *I'm still feeling just the tiniest bit woozy …*

Hindu: *Don't worry. That doesn't last long. Keep practicing.*

The members of the various Hindu sects worship a dizzying number of specific deities and follow innumerable rituals in honor of specific gods. Because this is Hinduism, however, its practitioners see the profusion of forms and practices as expressions of the same unchanging reality.

The panoply of deities are understood by believers as symbols for a single transcendent reality. The earliest Hindu holy texts, which focus on matters of ritual sacrifice and are clearly polytheistic, envision the various gods in an extraordinary way: as manifestations of an inborn, singular governing force or principle, regarded as ultimate in nature and capable of taking on particular forms.

Is Hinduism polytheistic or isn't it? The best way to approach the issue may be to avoid the temptation to resolve the matter definitively. Put the question aside and simply consider that this grouping of faiths accepts both infinite and single expressions of the Divine.

Having It Both Ways

It is not at all accurate to say that Hinduism *rejects* the concept of monotheism as it is understood within Judaism, Christianity, and Islam. Hinduism's monotheism simply chooses not to *exclude* specific concepts and incarnations of the Divine—including personifications that some people would probably call polytheistic.

These two ideas are not seen as incompatible with one another in Hindu thought, as they are in the other faiths just named.

In the Brihadaranayaka Upanishad, Vigadha, son of Shakala, asks Yajnavalyaka, "How many gods are there?" After an appropriate citation of scripture, the answer comes: "Three hundred and thirty three." Yajnavalyaka is praised for the perceptiveness of his answer, and is then asked again: "How many gods are there?" This time the answer is thirty-three, and the response is once again praised. The process continues until Yajnavalyaka answers that there is a single God, an answer for which he is praised; but each of the preceding answers is also acknowledged as inspired and correct!

The Big Picture

The vast implications of the varied theologies of Hinduism, which regard revealed forms as inherently limited, illusory, and, ultimately, exceeded by Brahman, can be quite far-reaching. Consider the subject of human history.

Western ideas of clear, divinely inspired historical progression, for instance, are in contrast to the Hindu conception of cyclic action, which acknowledges both creation and destruction as forces governing human history. This is a far cry from the Christian idea of the final deliverance of humanity via the Second Coming (to take just one example).

Instead of a single (and perhaps vengeful) God judging the entire human race, Hinduism emphasizes a divinely appointed drama that must be played out repeatedly over an inconceivably long time frame.

A Brief Introduction

A book like this cannot begin to describe the vast grouping of Hindu deities in a responsible way. Following, however, are some short descriptions of a few of the most important deities in Hinduism as they have emerged over the centuries.

As you read on, please keep two things in mind:

1. Hinduism is an evolving religion, one that has constantly incorporated new practices and outlooks as spiritual needs have demanded. As a result …

2. Its panoply of gods is a shifting phenomenon, one that is constantly being transformed. The most important deities may engage in rivalries before being reconciled, or may even combine with one another.

Tracing the lineage, incarnations, and convoluted histories of a particular deity can be a daunting task indeed!

The Big Three

Brahma is a personification of the Absolute, the creator of the world, which is perpetually destined to last for 2,160,000,000 years before it falls to ruin, at which time Brahma recreates it. The passage of one such cycle represents a single day in Brahma's life. One of the three supreme gods in the *Hindu triad*, Brahma is revered as the Creator within that grouping.

Vishnu has many incarnations, of which two are worthy of note here: as *Krishna* and as *Rama*. In the Hindu triad, he is the Preserver. Vishnu is seen as a force of transcendent love.

Shiva symbolizes the various potent forms of the energy of the Ultimate. Usually depicted with four arms and surrounded by fire, Shiva is the third supreme god in the Hindu triad. Shiva embodies both the creative force (he is closely associated with a symbolic phallus) and the idea of destruction. This is his role within the Hindu triad, but Shiva represents an ancient and complex figure whose most important attributes are not easily summarized.

Vishnu and Shiva were initially depicted as rivals. True to form, the Hindu faith reconciled them and eventually merged them, as elements of the triad that also includes Brahma.

DEFINITION

The worship of **Vishnu**, the preserver and protector, is known as Vainavism.

Some Other Important Deities

Krishna, an enormously popular Hindu deity, is an incarnation of Vishnu. He is seen variously as lover, trickster, cowherd, and military hero. First and foremost, however, he is the object (and source!) of extraordinarily devoted and unfailing love. Krishna's sexuality is often startling to Westerners; he is frequently depicted as a seducer of wives and daughters—metaphorical expressions of the human soul's union with the Divine.

Rama is another incarnation of Vishnu; his story is told in the epic known as the *Ramayana*. Rama's tale celebrates the commitments of family life and the supreme value of virtue and right living; it also illustrates the shortcomings of worldly possessions and authority. Rama has been described as "God incarnate as morality."

Shakti, consort to Shiva, goes by many other names as well, including Parvati, Kali, Uma, and Durga. She represents the creative force but may take the terrifying form of the destroyer-goddess. This seemingly paradoxical figure is sometimes worshipped in Shiva's place. This happens at times when Shiva is regarded as having entered a trance that makes him unable to heed the requirements of humanity. As you can see, Hindu forms of worship are remarkably fluid and adaptable.

There is a great deal more that could be said of Hinduism's conceptions of the Divine, but these will serve as an introduction to this multifaceted and remarkably adaptable faith system.

Mahatma Gandhi, who spoke so powerfully and so eloquently on behalf of those injured by the caste system, may well have captured the true essence of this faith when he frankly refused to follow certain scriptural dictates. "My belief in the Hindu Scriptures," Ghandi said, "does not require me to accept every word and every verse as divinely inspired …. I decline to be bound by any interpretation, however learned it may be, if it is repugnant to reason and common sense."

SPIRITUAL SIGNPOST

Worship of Shakti gave rise to Tantric devotion, a practice that employs supremely disciplined and focused sexuality as a pathway to unity with the Absolute.

Gandhi could expand "abstract" spiritual values into the real world. By adapting what could be used and transcending what could not, he modeled the most exciting and vigorous elements of Hinduism.

The Least You Need to Know

- Hinduism features many, *many* individual deities.
- Although some religions regard monotheism (worship of one god) and polytheism (worship of many gods) as incompatible, Hinduism is not one of them.
- Each of the many Hindu deities is regarded as a particular and useful form of the Ultimate.
- The Hindu triad includes the gods Brahma, Vishnu, and Shiva. Other important deities include Krishna, Rama, and Shakti.

Respect for Life and Personal Growth

In This Chapter

- The straight scoop on reincarnation
- The cycle of *samsara*
- The sanctity of life within the Hindu tradition
- The important patterns of Hindu worship

In this chapter, you find out more about the principle of reincarnation and about Hinduism's emphasis on personal spiritual purification, rather than regular worship within a congregation.

Life and Death

The Hindu view of life and death is essential to the day-to-day observances of this faith. Hindus believe that humanity is cast into a long cycle of repetitive incarnation, known as *samsara*. Hindus also accept as a transcendent goal one's ultimate escape from that cycle. Everyday life—our day-to-day experience of existence—is seen as a burden, very often a very painful one, thanks to the working-out of karma from our current lives and past incarnations. This process is seen as an intrinsic part of the human condition.

Spiritual progress, according to Hinduism, is all about avoiding rebirth. This notion can be a misleading one, however, especially for outsiders.

Asceticism

These theological principles explain Hinduism's emphasis on asceticism (practices of self-denial that discipline the body) but exclude nihilism, a distaste for life itself. Nihilists deny that human existence has any meaning or purpose. This has no place in Hinduism.

Instead of dismissing existence as meaningless, committed Hindu practitioners seek, in countless ways, to cultivate a profound joy and celebration of the process of working out past karma. Their joy exists side by side with a pious desire to transcend the physical world.

SPIRITUAL SIGNPOST

Recent Hindu leaders such as Swami Vivekenanda and Mahatma Ghandi have upheld spiritual movements within Hinduism that stress social awareness and compassion toward others, de-emphasizing the ascetic disciplines of the individual. Nevertheless, asceticism is likely to continue to represent an important current of belief and practice within Hinduism.

Some extraordinary ascetic disciplines can be found in Hinduism. Familiar images of the lean-boned penitent; the holy person meditating alone on a remote hilltop; the guru who demands full rigor, attention, and devotion from his followers—these do indeed reflect a strand running through this complex faith, but they are also easily misunderstood and overemphasized. And they are certainly not the only paths for spiritual development within Hinduism!

Some schools within Hindu practice teach an intense, solitary self-mortification. Others promote the pursuit of one's spiritual destiny through home celebrations, sexual discipline, everyday life with one's family, service to others, and countless other methods. Hinduism makes room for an exhilarating array of disciplines, each of which reveres life as a profound gift and many of which are incorporated into everyday life.

BARRIER ALERT!

The law of karma should not be mistaken as a system of divine reward or punishment. Karma is an impartial force, almost like the physical law of cause and effect. It takes no sides and is not filtered through a supreme entity. It affects even the minutest aspects of the human experience.

Religion, Religion Everywhere

For Hindus, each new incarnation offers the opportunity for growth. Believers pursue four life aspirations, each one recognized as spiritually valid: pleasure, development of wealth, righteousness, and liberation from the cycle of birth, death, and rebirth.

Life is seen as a sacred opportunity for a particular believer to embrace a particular, appropriate discipline at a particular time and hasten his or her journey toward union with Brahman. For this reason, the line separating "religion" and "everyday life" in Hindu practice can be difficult to make out.

> **SPIRITUAL SIGNPOST**
>
> When Hinduism came to embrace the concept of reincarnation, larger questions of purpose and destiny became easier to address—though not necessarily easier to resolve. The idea of each person being reborn into suffering to attain purity and freedom from rebirth is one element of a massive drama, a drama that cannot be separated from the larger human task of acknowledging the divine presence in all forms.

Where's the Sabbath?

Many non-Hindus expect religious life to take the form of regular weekly observance of established rituals, with congregations of fellow believers.

A Hindu practitioner, however, is perfectly at home in a situation in which such expressions of group devotion are comparatively rare. Hinduism has no formal, universally acknowledged Sabbath. It would also, of course, be accurate to say that Hinduism sees every day as the Sabbath, because absolute reverence for life, or *ahimsa*, is fundamental to the everyday experience of Hinduism.

> **DEFINITION**
>
> **Ahimsa** is the Hindu principle of reverence for life. The idea arose around 600 B.C.E. and led to the rapid growth of vegetarianism.

In recent years, some American Hindu believers have formed groups that practice Western-style traditions of worship—like weekly congregational gatherings on Sundays. Most, however, still practice the traditional forms.

"Purify us from all sides," reads the Atharva Veda in a hymn to the earth. Later, it reads, "May Earth, clad in her fiery mantle, dark-kneed, make me aflame; may she sharpen me bright ...." An ancient emphasis on purification within Hinduism presupposes a unity with all created forms. This is the unity the dance of life is meant to express and uncover.

Temples and Homes

Celebration of life in all its kaleidoscopic glory is an essential element of Hinduism. For this reason, temple worship and private worship rituals in the home are important Hindu disciplines. Some believers practice no external worship whatsoever, choosing to cultivate awareness of the divine presence in other ways.

Hindu worship and religious observances may take place either in a temple dedicated to a particular deity, or in the worshipper's home, at small shrines that incorporate images of a god or goddess. Prayers are directed to the god or goddess, who is regarded as an honored guest. During worship, or *puja*, the consumption of sacramental food known as *prasad* may take place. It is blessed before it is eaten.

For those attending Hindu worship services for the first time, a gentle reminder may be in order. Chanting before an image or statue of a particular god, or offering that figure flowers, incense, or special oils, is not regarded as "idolatry" by Hindus. Outsiders often have a difficult time understanding such forms of worship, but it may help to remember that in the Hindu tradition, devotion to a particular form of the nameless, formless, and ultimate reality is a way of honoring the one essential divine principle.

Hinduism acknowledges any and every depiction of the Absolute as both valid and inherently limited. It holds the eventual transcendence of such forms to be an important spiritual goal.

SPIRITUAL SIGNPOST

Hindu males born within the priestly class take part in a private initiation ceremony between their eighth and twelfth birthdays to mark their formal entry to the priesthood. This rite is known as the "sacred thread ceremony."

Individual devotees may conduct particular worship rituals at whatever speed is comfortable to them. When more than one person is engaged in worship, group chanting may take place.

Outsiders will never be expected to take part in rituals that make them uncomfortable. Neither will they be excluded from any part of the service in which they wish to participate. Unless you are taking part in chanting, you should expect to maintain silence during Hindu religious ceremonies. When in doubt about what will happen, ask before the services begin. The order of rituals can usually be confirmed ahead of time by talking directly with the celebrant.

> **SPIRITUAL SIGNPOST**
>
> Although Hindus regard one's physical body as transitory, the soul, or atman, is seen as neither beginning nor ending.

Celebrations

Following is a brief review of some of the most holy days within the Hindu faith. Needless to say, this is not a comprehensive list!

- **Duhsehra/Durga Puja:** Generally observed in early autumn, an observance of the triumph of good over evil.

- **Rama Navami:** Generally observed in springtime, an important holiday centered on the god Rama.

- **Krishna Janmashtami**: The birthday of Krishna, generally celebrated in late summer.

- **Shiva Ratri:** An all-night celebration of the Divine as manifested in the god Shiva. Shiva Ratri usually occurs in the latter part of the winter season.

> **SPIRITUAL SIGNPOST**
>
> For centuries the Ganges River in India has been revered as holy within the Hindu faith. Containers of holy water drawn from the Ganges often play a part in Hindu religious services.

Life Rituals

Following is a brief summary of some of the most important life rituals within the Hindu faith.

- **Infant welcoming ritual:** Hindus place great importance on the point at which a child first consumes solid food. This is an occasion for group celebration and a formal "rice-eating ceremony." It takes place about six to eight months after birth and is accompanied by religious rituals. It is often preceded and followed by a reception.

- **Marriages:** In the Hindu tradition marriages are usually arranged, a contract between two families. Each incorporates five ceremonies: a verbal contract between the male parents or guardians of the bride and groom, the giving-away of the bride by her father or guardian, a welcoming ceremony for the new couple, a hand-holding ritual, and a walking rite. Hindu marriages generally take place after sunset.

- **Funerals:** Funerals center on the cremation ritual known as *nukhagni*. After a predetermined period of days, depending on the caste of the deceased, a ceremony known as *shradda* marks the end of the family's mourning period and the journey of the soul of the departed.

The Least You Need to Know

- Understanding Hinduism begins with understanding the concept of reincarnation.
- The cycle of *samsara* reflects the Hindu belief in an extended pattern of reincarnation.
- Although Hindus make deliverance from the process of rebirth their highest spiritual goal, they view life itself as sacred.
- Hinduism's many patterns of home and temple worship focus on particular deities within the Hindu tradition.

Breaking Down Barriers to Hinduism

In This Chapter

- Hinduism as a comprehensive system of living
- Polytheism
- Idol worship
- Social concerns

Hindus sometimes say that the biggest misconception about their religion is that it is a religion in the first place. They prefer to think of it as a comprehensive system of living with principles that are applicable to all aspects of human existence, one that transcends the narrow label of "religion." The vastness of Hinduism is certainly hard to dispute, and the claim that the tradition carries teachings that qualify it as a "way of life" is persuasive, but the world at large certainly *thinks* of it as a religion.

Here are some of the most common obstacles to developing a meaningful understanding of this rich and ancient faith system.

Myth #1: Hinduism is a polytheistic religion.

The question of whether Hinduism worships many gods or a single god is complicated, and no brief summary can do it justice. As a practical matter, however, it is worth quoting the Vedas, which tell us, in translation, "What is whole? This is whole. What has come out of the whole is also whole. When the whole is taken out of the whole, the whole still remains whole."

This verse envisions a source of infinite intelligence that is impossible to quantify, and that is clearly analogous with the single god promoted by such faiths as Judaism, Christianity, and Islam. Why then, is there so much controversy over whether Hinduism is a monotheistic religion? Why is it not more frequently described as such a religion?

The answer is to be found in the Hindu trinity, an essential component of worship and practice that takes the form of three specific, identifiable deities. The three gods, you will recall, are Brahma, Vishnu, and Shiva. Brahma is the creator, Vishnu is the sustainer, and Shiva is the destroyer and/or consummator. For many people, including a fair number of Hindus, the "monotheism" label is inadequate to describe the importance of each individual god within the trinity.

Hindus believe that infinite intelligence can be worshipped and glorified in any form. This approach is distinctive to the faith, and is seen by Hindus as a testament to the power and might of that entity frequently described by non-Hindus as a single god. Presently, monotheists, such as Christians, Muslims, and Jews, take exception to this component of Hindu belief.

Myth #2: Hindus are idol worshippers.

The label "idol worshipper" is an emotionally barbed one that should be avoided in discussions of Hinduism. "Idol worship" is simply not how a Hindu practitioner describes his or her religious activities. A Hindu is more likely to regard a physical object's use in religious worship as a starting point in a long journey toward communion with divinely revealed principles.

Hindus hold that they are worshipping not an idol but a divine reminder of God—or perhaps a manifestation of God that has taken the form of a particular physical object. These ways of looking at worship are, taken together, distinct to the faith. They may give pause to followers of other traditions, but they are nevertheless established elements of Hindu religious practice that mirror similar modes of worship in, for instance, Catholicism and Orthodox Christianity. At any rate, they're unlikely to change.

"The use of an image—whether we call it an icon or an idol—did not imply belief in the reality of the image. That we keep a photograph of our wife and children at our work desk does not mean that we think that our wife and children are the photograph. It is a reminder, not a false reality …. The use of the term 'idol' inflames the sentiments of anti-idolatry religions like Christianity and Islam, as both the Bible and the Qur'an, at least in places, expect their followers to oppose idolatry …. The use of the term 'idol' in excess, particularly in the Indian Press, is thus careless, insensitive, inflammatory, and communal. It should be removed in an effort to promote greater understanding and goodwill between religious groups."

—David Frawley (Vamadeva Shaftri), from the article "The Misrepresentation of Hinduism in the Press," 1994.

Myth #3: Hinduism promotes social discrimination and the exploitation of the poor.

Many people identify Hinduism strongly with the caste system of religiously mandated social classes. As a matter of history, members of various elite groups within Indian society encouraged the development of literally thousands of groups in an elaborate social hierarchy that features strong distinctions between "upper" and "lower" castes (religiously mandated social classes).

This system, which has been in transition thanks to developments in Indian political and social life in the modern period, has its roots in the scriptures of the Vedas. Those scriptures, however, mention only four social groups, and are related to an ordering of human society that Hindus believe is not without compassion, elegance, and beauty.

The degree to which the noble principles of the Vedas are actually carried out in the day-to-day life of Hindu society is, of course, a matter of debate. The same, however, could be said about any human society's ability to implement the noblest goals of its religious scriptures.

The Least You Need to Know

- Many Hindus feel that the label "religion" is insufficient to describe their faith; yet this is how most of the world looks at this system of belief.
- To say that Hinduism is polytheistic is to oversimplify a complex subject.
- Use of the term "idol worship" in relation to Hinduism should be avoided.
- The caste system has its roots in four social categories described in the Vedas, but is, in its actual form, the result of ancient social practice.

Buddhism

Buddhism has translated its teaching of divine love and transcendent purpose into a pacifism capable of shaping human actions on a large scale. Indeed, pacifism and nonviolence have significantly shaped the destinies of countries where Buddhism has predominated. This part will tell you what you need to know about this enduring and influential world religion.

Buddhist Origins and Doctrine

In This Chapter

- Buddhism and Hinduism
- The story of the Buddha
- The Four Noble Truths
- The most important ideas within Buddhism

Buddhism developed in India as a nonconforming system outside of Hinduism. Buddhists explicitly rejected the usefulness of the elaborate Vedic rites and refused to accept the caste system as authoritative. Despite these differences, however, Buddhism shares many fundamental beliefs with Hinduism, including the concepts of reincarnation, karma, and entering Nirvana, or absolute liberation.

Discover the origins of Buddhism in the momentous decision of Prince Gautama to disobey his royal father's orders and explore the real world on his own.

The Legend of the Buddha

In the sixth century B.C.E. (we think), Siddhartha Gautama was born, the son of the wealthy and powerful ruler of a small kingdom. At his birth, the legend holds, an old sage foretold that the prince would become either an ascetic or a supreme monarch.

The boy's father, eager to ensure that his son would become the leader of his kingdom and a great warrior, sought to protect Prince Gautama from fulfilling the prophecy as an ascetic. He kept his son isolated in the kingdom, allowing him to live a life of supreme luxury. He was determined that the prince should never want for anything—and never desire any other life than that of a monarch.

As a young man, Gautama married and became a father. It is said that during his
twenty-ninth year he finally made his way out of the palace. Buddhism holds that the
sheltered prince Gautama had never encountered old age, illness, or death until he
ventured outside the royal estate. That journey brought shattering revelations about
human suffering. Eventually he encountered a man whose knowing smile reflected contentment and peace. Gautama asked his chariot-driver how the man could be happy in
such a world, and was informed that he had just seen a holy man, one who had obtained
complete liberation. The journey shocked him and forever changed his life.

On to Asceticism

After this experience, Gautama reacted radically against the luxurious lifestyle that
had brought him what he now recognized as an empty and useless existence. Vowing
to become a holy man himself, he pursued a life of deprivation and asceticism. He
forsook the palace and his family in search of liberation and a solution to the problem
of human suffering. Years of intense spiritual searching followed.

During this period, Gautama became an itinerant ascetic, subjecting himself to
intense physical disciplines. Yet spiritual progress remained elusive.

After one rigorous fast, he accepted a meal of rice cooked in milk from a local woman.
This was a breach of established religious practice within the ascetic discipline
Gautama was pursuing, and is usually seen as a rejection of asceticism for its own sake.
Having thus compromised the ascetic "war" against his own body, the Buddha sat on a
straw mat beneath a Bodhi tree and made a vow not to move until he had attained true
liberation.

On the morning of the seventh day, he opened his eyes and looked out to the morning star. At that moment, he became enlightened.

The Awakening

Tradition holds that, upon attaining this awakening, Gautama/Buddha exclaimed that
all beings possess enlightenment, but that some are blinded to this fact.

Buddhism, the faith that developed as a result of this realization, places a heavy emphasis on liberation from delusion—and by extension, from three habits that give rise to distorted human perceptions. Those habits are desire, anger, and ignorance.

Attaining True Knowledge

By charting a path between extreme self-indulgence and rigorous self-denial, Siddhartha Gautama had attained true knowledge. His embrace of this path was a defining moment that led to his designation as the Buddha, or Enlightened One.

The Buddha was tempted to remain in seclusion for the rest of his life, but before long he encountered some of his earlier companions, fellow seekers who had pursued the ascetic path with him. They ostracized him at first because of his decision to violate the ascetic lifestyle. Eventually, however, they acknowledged the depth of his realization and decided to follow him. The Buddha's ministry had begun.

Having directly experienced ultimate awakening, he spent the rest of his life traveling the countryside, preaching, and organizing a monastic community, the *sangha*.

 DEFINITION

In Buddhism, a **sangha** is a community of monks, much like a Western monastery.

Nirvana (Before It Was a Rock Band)

Nirvana, the state of final liberation from the cycle of birth and death (recognized in both Hinduism and Buddhism) is held to be beyond definition. Rather, there are steps one must take to gain direct experience of ultimate reality—Nirvana—just as the Buddha had.

The Buddha's very first discourse, which he gave in a place called Deer Park, was known as "the setting into motion the wheel of the dharma." It revealed the basic doctrines of Buddhism.

Dharma in Buddhism refers to sublime religious truth. It also serves to describe, on a technical level, any particular facet of experience or existence. Hindus also use the word *dharma*, but for them it has to do with a religious obligation, social convention, or individual virtue.

The Buddha accepted the principle of reincarnation. He believed that living beings are trapped within the physical cycle of birth and death under the law of karma until complete release is attained. His teaching mission was to enable disciples to attain a clear, deep, direct understanding of the obstacles they faced in their own spiritual lives.

The Deer Park sermon laid out the basic road map by which believers could avoid the obstacles that prevent people from understanding their true nature. In this talk, the Buddha laid out the Four Noble Truths that are still the bedrock of the faith two and a half millennia later. Although Buddhism has evolved in many ways over the centuries, expressed itself in a great many sects, and developed an extremely broad system of philosophical thought, these fundamental beliefs of Buddhism have remained unchanged since the Buddha's time.

ON THE PATH

In the Surangama, Buddha describes Nirvana as the place "where it is recognized that there is nothing but what is seen of the mind itself; where, recognizing the nature of the self-mind, one no longer cherishes the dualisms of discrimination; where there is no more thirst nor grasping; where there is no more attachment to external things."

Even many non-Buddhists have acknowledged the purity of the Buddha's revelation and the profundity of his religion's basic principles. The simplicity and clarity of the core ideas of Buddhism have moved ancient Chinese philosophers, twentieth-century Beat poets, and contemplative Catholic monks, to name just a few. In the Four Noble Truths, the Buddha taught that …

1. **Life is suffering.** The very nature of human existence is inherently painful. Because of the cyclical nature of death and rebirth, death does not bring an end to suffering.

2. **Suffering has a cause: craving and attachment.** Suffering is the result of our selfish craving and clinging. This in turn reflects our ignorance of reality.

3. **Craving and attachment can be overcome.** When one completely transcends selfish craving, one enters the state of Nirvana, and suffering ceases.

4. **The path toward the cessation of craving and attachment is an Eightfold Path:**

Right understanding

Right purpose

Right speech

Right conduct

Right livelihood

Right effort

Right alertness

Right concentration

The Buddha also taught that the abiding self is illusory. Physical form, sensations, perceptions, psychic exertions, and even consciousness itself, do not yield an unchanging, independent self. And the human tendency to view the self as an independent, controlling entity is not merely a benign delusion, but a significant barrier to spiritual progress.

Beyond Substance

The notion of "non-self," emphasized in the teachings of the Buddha, has frequently been misinterpreted. In fact, many Westerners have dismissed Buddhism as "atheistic" or "nihilistic" because of it. Such labels may build barriers to understanding the faith. The limitation probably lies with familiar conceptions of what is and is not "God," and not with Buddhism.

The Buddha taught that any conception dividing one phenomenon from another—a blade of grass from a meditating woman, for instance, or a meditating woman from her own Buddha-nature—is illusory. Nothing exists independently or eternally. According to Buddhist philosophy, a blade of grass, examined closely enough, is simply a transitory collection of processes. Indeed, the very label "a blade of grass" is misleading. Why? Because the lines dividing the smallest possible components of the blade of grass from the rest of creation are imposed by our own perceptions. They do not actually separate that (transitory) blade of grass from anything.

Buddhism sees all manifested forms as subject to decay and division. Fixating on particular forms (even spiritual ones) is regarded as a form of delusion. Nothing is permanent. No form endures forever. No single perceived manifestation fully expresses the supreme reality. The line between "a blade of grass" and "not a blade of grass" is illusory, in the end. Although it may be convenient in certain situations for the woman to use the term "blade of grass" to describe what is next to her as she meditates, or the term "enlightenment" or "Buddha-nature" to describe the eventual result of her sustained, disciplined practice, Buddhism reminds us not to take such labels too seriously—even (especially) when that meditation appears to be promising, or incorporates the experience of *samadhi*.

DEFINITION

Samadhi, in Buddhism, is understood as a state of single-minded concentration. Along with morality and wisdom, samadhi is seen as an essential tool for pursuing a path of self-awakening. (In Hinduism, this word describes the point at which an individual's consciousness merges with the Godhead.)

For the Buddhist, developing the right kind of self-discipline offers a pathway out of delusion and toward true awareness. Holding on to what does not actually exist will only lead to suffering.

The same principle of continuity between the meditating woman and the blade of grass is also applied to the God or distinct Supreme Being a non-Buddhist might think is guiding the woman's meditation. All imagined separateness between perceived entities is, as it were, a hallucination.

It is as a result of this philosophy, and not out of cynicism or any lack of piety, that Buddhists reject the notion of a separate God that is somehow set apart from everyday experience.

Gods

Buddha's path focuses on the single-minded pursuit of an individual's spiritual goals, not on the establishment of new conceptions of the Deity. With such a doctrine, it is no surprise that Buddha taught that one should not seek divine intervention in this life. The familiar Hindu gods do indeed exist, he taught, but they do not hold dominion over daily human life. Instead they are subject to the same universal laws that human beings must observe.

The emphasis of the religion he founded is on meditation and the observance of important moral precepts, seen as expressions of one's own actual nature rather than as standards derived from external divine authority.

Both lay and monastic Buddhists commit to the following precepts:

- Not to kill.

- Not to steal.

- Not to act in an unchaste manner.

- Not to speak falsely.

- Not to take intoxicants.

In addition, monks vow the following:

- Not to eat at times not appointed.

- Not to view entertainments deemed as "secular."

- Not to wear perfumes or bodily ornaments.

- Not to sleep in beds that are too high or too wide.

- Not to accept money.

In addition, many other vows may accompany the pursuit of a monastic lifestyle.

SPIRITUAL SIGNPOST

In Buddhism, the realization that the self has no true reality is more important than devotion to ascetic practices. Indeed, if such practices lead to pride, they do more harm than good. In the Buddhist tradition, the deities named in Hinduism are spirits who have not yet attained the final liberation.

Teaching, Living, Dying

The Buddha is said to have spent 45 years teaching, ordaining monks and nuns, and promoting a solitary, secluded style of spiritual discipline. This method of self-discovery would profoundly affect the religious lives of millions of followers through-out Asia and around the world in the centuries to come.

The Buddha appears to have shown no interest in assembling a written record of his own teachings. His disciples transmitted the most important sermons orally. Hundreds of years after his death, they were finally committed to paper. (Even these early scriptures, initially written in Sanskrit, are not extant; the earliest surviving accounts of the Buddha's teachings are in Pali, an ancient northwestern Indian dialect.)

Tradition tells us that the Buddha died at the age of 80 without naming a successor. His final words, passed along for centuries, form the perfect encapsulation of the faith he founded.

"All composite things decay. Diligently work out your salvation."

The Least You Need to Know

- The traditional accounts of the life of the Buddha show him turning away from both a life of indulgence and the ascetic excesses sometimes associated with Hinduism.
- The Buddha's enlightenment beneath a Bodhi tree in India marked the beginning of Buddhism, a new religious tradition outside of Hinduism.
- The Four Noble Truths form the most important principles of the Buddhist faith.
- Buddhism sees all manifested forms as subject to decay and division, and acknowledges liberation only by overcoming selfish desire and craving.

Buddhism After Buddha

In This Chapter

- Buddhism after the Buddha
- The history and development of the Theravada school
- The history and development of the Mahayana school
- Important Buddhist scriptures

In this part of the book, you learn about the two great divisions of the Buddhist faith, their differing approaches to spiritual life, and the many movements and trends within each. You will also get an idea of the most unusual and influential scriptures within the various Buddhist traditions.

After the Buddha

The Buddha chose not to appoint a formal successor before he died, preferring to allow each of his followers to choose a path and to search within themselves for enlightenment. Soon after his death, however, a council convened to settle the growing differences among Buddhist followers.

This council, led by the monk Mahakasyapa, was the first of many such attempts to resolve differing views on the direction of the faith. Doctrinal disputes within the new religion were common in the centuries following the Buddha's death, and these disputes were not easily resolved. Many sects of Buddhism emerged, in part because of disputes over the details of monastic disciplines.

Eventually, 18 schools or disciplines were acknowledged. Of these, only one, the Theravada ("doctrine of the elders") school, still exists today.

The lotus is a sacred symbol in both Buddhism and Hinduism.

The Two Schools of Buddhism

There are no written records on the early development of Buddhism. The earliest Buddhist scriptures were written about 400 years after the Buddha's ministry. Thus it is hard to be certain just what the Buddha said or taught. (This is one of the interesting features of the major religious traditions; most of them embrace scriptures that were finalized many years after the figure who inspired them.)

The Theravada school, which views its most sacred teachings as those of the Buddha himself, emphasizes a solitary life of personal religious discipline. Around 100 C.E., however, a very different conception of Buddhism began to emerge as a powerful movement within the faith. This was known as the *Mahayana* school.

This view of Buddhism focused less on the supreme virtues of a life of seclusion and more on the importance of compassion and service to others. The ideal of this wing of the faith was not the *arhat*, or perfected sage, but the *bodhisattva* —the advanced soul who deserves Nirvana but vows to postpone entry to it until all sentient beings are rescued from the wheel of rebirth and suffering. This became known as the Mahayana school of Buddhism.

SPIRITUAL SIGNPOST

Although Buddhism arose and developed in India in its early phase, it is now almost completely absent from that country. Of the few living in India who practice Buddhism today, many are from other countries.

An important early figure in Mahayana Buddhism was the revered philosopher Nagarjuna. Nagarjuna taught that Buddha-hood can be obtained without necessarily renouncing the world. According to this view, Nirvana is a reality that can be brought into existence in the present moment.

His movement has exceeded the influence of the earlier Theravada path, with its emphasis on individual discipline and solitary practice. Because of its reliance on these points, the Theravada school has been labeled the *Hinayana* school, although some consider this term to be inappropriately pejorative.

Theravada/Hinayana Buddhism survives today in Sri Lanka and Southeast Asia, while Mahayana Buddhism is likely to be found in Japan, Korea, Mongolia, and China. (Tibet, as you will learn later in this chapter, follows a distinctive Buddhist path of its own.)

> **DEFINITION**
>
> **Mahayana** means "Greater Vehicle." **Hinayana** means "Lesser Vehicle." An **arhat** is a holy person who attains enlightenment through solitude and ascetic practices. In Mahayana Buddhism, a **bodhisattva** is one who deserves Nirvana but postpones entry to it until all sentient beings are rescued from rebirth and suffering.

Theravada Buddhism

The Theravada school, with its emphasis on detachment and seclusion, reveres the way of renunciation—the pursuit of a rigorous, purifying lifestyle for the sake of spiritual goals. Of course, lay believers are apt to pursue a less ambitious spiritual regimen, following a generally ethical way of life and perhaps helping to support the monastic orders.

Theravada Scriptures

Theravada scriptures are in three parts, known as the Tipitaka, or Three Baskets. The three parts are the *Vinaya Pitaka* (monastic regulations), the *Sutta Pitaka* (discourses and discussions attributed to the Buddha), and the *Abhidamma Pitaka* (discussions and classifications relating to philosophy, psychology, and doctrine). Within the *Sutta Pitaka* is the *Dhammapada*, a summary of the Buddha's teachings on a variety of mental disciplines and moral issues.

The following is a list of five more things you should know about the Theravada school:

- As one of the 18 major early schools of Buddhism, the practices and beliefs of the Theravada School are believed to reflect the essential early doctrines of Buddhism.

- The arhat, or worthy one, is sometimes known as the "solitary saint" within the Theravada tradition.

- Besides those already discussed, important texts within Theravada Buddhism include the Milindapanha (Questions of King Milinda), a dialogue about common problems in Buddhist thought …

- … and the somewhat later Visuddhimagga (Path of Purification), which is a brilliant summary of Buddhist thought and meditative practices.

- A third-century B.C.E. council resulted in the expulsion of members of the sangha (monastic community) who were considered to have joined monastic orders for political rather than spiritual reasons.

The Mahayana School

Around the first century B.C.E., the movement that would become known as the Mahayana school of Buddhism first emerged with the circulation of a new body of scriptures, the Mahayana sutras. In addition to promoting a new spiritual ideal, we find the idea of the bodhisattva, an Enlightened being who postpones union with the Ultimate for the benefit of all beings. Mahayana Buddhism also formulated an important spiritual principle: *sunyata*. This Sanskrit word for "emptiness" states that all ultimate entities, including the Buddha and the state of Nirvana, are empty—that is, completely undivided from the rest of the Supreme Reality.

The idea of Sunyata arose in the first century B.C.E. as a radical reassertion and expansion of the doctrine of non-self. Mahayana Buddhists argued that all ultimate entities—including the Buddha and the state of Nirvana—are empty. This view undercuts the common perception that the Ultimate is somehow separate or independent from direct experience. Does "emptiness" mean the same thing as "nihilism"? Not at all. Rather, it has to do with interconnection. When a Mahayana Buddhist holds that "all dharmas are empty," what is really being rejected is duality, division.

This rejection of *dualism* carries a number of tricky implications. Chief among them, perhaps, is the classic Mahayana belief that *dualistic thinking*—which is another phrase for the (common!) shared assumption that the world is made up of separate entities—is fundamentally delusional. Establishing formal guidelines for Mahayana Buddhism's practice therefore presents something of a challenge.

That's because all language—including, for instance, this sentence—is built on principles of metaphor (the word "language" comes from the Latin word for "tongue") and distinction (one way to understand the word "all" is as the opposite of the word "none").

In other words, the Buddhists noticed that human language ultimately reflects some form of dualistic thinking. Not surprisingly, language is considered by Mahayana Buddhists (and, interestingly, by the great Taoist teachers) to be of limited use in illuminating spiritual truths. Nagarjuna was of the opinion that nothing conclusive could be said in words concerning ultimate reality.

 DEFINITION

Dualism is the attempt to explain phenomena by means of opposite poles: good and evil, black and white, old and new, "I" and "other," "God" and "creation," and so on.

Duality is any example of this way of seeing. Buddhism considers all expressions of duality to be heretical—that is, contrary to the fundamental principles of the religion. This insistence on the unity of all things has distinguished Buddhism from religions that have historically emphasized the separateness of the Creator and the Created, notably the great monotheistic faiths: Judaism, Christianity, and Islam.

The doctrine of emptiness rejects as inadequate any conception of separate, independent existence, whether of individuals, objects, spiritual states, or anything else. Empty things are seen as transcending existence and nonexistence; such things simply merge.

The Heart Sutra advises that "form is emptiness, emptiness is form." Interpreting these words could take a lifetime, and we will not presume to begin a meaningful interpretation here. Consider, however, that, in the Mahayana view, emptiness is *not* different from the universe in which we live. All forms and processes, including true realization, are relative and interconnected. This fact, for the Mahayana Buddhist, does not describe emptiness; it *is* emptiness.

Mahayana in Black and White

The Mahayana division of Buddhism is divided into a large number of sects, each with a particular scriptural tradition. The many variations reflect centuries of teaching traditions and evolved points of emphasis. The variety can be daunting to the outsider, but in fact there is a great deal of overlap among the various holy texts. Even the Pali writings of Theravada Buddhism are accepted by most Mahayanists as inspired.

The diverse Mahayana division of Buddhism differs from the Theravada school in placing a greater emphasis on the idea of assistance from the bodhisattvas. Many Mahayanists also accept the notion of Tathata, or Suchness, a governing principle of the universe that manifests itself as the pure Mind, or absolute and enduring Buddha-nature. Mahayana Buddhism places a special emphasis on the study of the *prajnaparamita* (perfection of wisdom) sutras.

Among the many movements and sects of Mahayana Buddhism still active today are the nonacademic movements of Zen and the Pure Land sects, each of which is discussed in detail in the next chapter. One influential belief within Mahayana Buddhism is that the Buddha is eternal and absolute. This view regards the historical Buddha as a temporal form of the eternal Buddha-nature.

SPIRITUAL SIGNPOST

Among the most widely studied of the (many) Mahayana scriptures are the Lotus Sutra, which emphasizes the grace of the eternal Buddha and counsels enduring faith; the Diamond Sutra, which arrests normal logical processes and focuses on the nature of emptiness; and the Heart Sutra, regarded by many Buddhists as the essence of true wisdom.

Tibetan Buddhism

Tibetan Buddhists revere the most important Mahayana teachers as bodhisattvas. They also incorporate an important tradition independent of both the Mahayana and Theravada traditions, *Vajrayana*.

Among the best-known Tibetan Buddhist scriptures is the *Bardo Thodol*, popularly known as the *Tibetan Book of the Dead*, an extraordinary book of instruction for the dying and for their spiritual guides. This complex work is neither easy to read, nor easy to forget after it has been read.

For many believers, the Bardo Thodol is an essential companion to the principle expounded by the Buddha in the opening lines of the Dhammapada: "All that we are is the result of what we have thought; it is founded on our thoughts, it is made up of our thoughts."

DEFINITION

Vajrayana is a strand of Buddhism with ties to Hindu Tantric practice. It uses yogic discipline to transcend and redirect desire, the better to attain union with the Ultimate Reality.

The Least You Need to Know

- After the Buddha's death, 18 formal schools or disciplines were acknowledged within Buddhism.
- Theravada Buddhism is the oldest surviving school of Buddhism, and the only one of the ancient grouping of 18 to endure.
- Mahayana Buddhism, which emphasizes compassion, service, and the notion of emptiness, has been an important trend in Buddhism since the first century B.C.E.
- Tibetan Buddhism incorporates both Mahayana traditions and Vajrayana, an esoteric strand of Buddhism associated with Hindu Tantric practice.

Zen and Other Buddhist Schools Popular in the West

In This Chapter

- Zen's early history and development
- Various Zen approaches
- Zen in the West
- Other Buddhist schools

In this part of the book, you learn about the history and development of Zen, one of the most notable and widely studied Buddhist schools in America. You also learn about other modern Buddhist schools.

What Is the Sound of Zen Beginning?

The word "Zen" derives from the Sanskrit word *dhyana*, meaning meditation. It's a little strange that the name of this much-analyzed sect of Buddhism has become a kind of catchword for all that is elusive, vague, and baffling in Oriental thought. In fact, the derivation of the word "Zen" describes this school, and its outlook, perfectly. Zen's central tenet is not a particular rule, idea, or stated philosophy, but rather the personal practice of various forms of meditation. In other words (a Zen student might ask), why bother with words?

Explanations, scriptures, and dogma are viewed with deep suspicion in the Zen tradition. The direct personal experience of meditation—and all aspects of everyday life—is of paramount importance. Only through this personal commitment to actual, engaged presence, Zen students believe, can human delusion arising from greed, anger, and ignorance be overcome. Transcending this delusion demands not only the experience of meditation, but the direct grasping of our true nature in everyday life. This breakthrough goes by various names: Satori or Kensho in the Japanese tradition, or enlightenment in English. Whatever the language we use to describe the experience, Zen holds that it must be experienced directly. Reciting dogma, instructions, or other people's conclusions just won't cut it.

> **DEFINITION**
>
> **Satori,** within the Zen Buddhist tradition, is an experience of sudden awareness of one's true nature. It is believed to be the first step toward nirvana, which is the extinguishing of desire, anger, and ignorance.

Zen is the Japanese name for this school. In China where it was founded, it's called "Chan." It is said that Zen was brought from India by a figure known as Bodhidharma ("Enlightened Tradition"). Because the Japanese term is most widely used in the West, we will use it in this chapter.

An American once asked Zen Master Suzuki Roshi to define the term "zazen" (sitting meditation). Rather than engage in a long-winded discussion of technique or terminology, the teacher answered by assuming the cross-legged meditation position on a nearby table and sitting quietly for half an hour!

Suzuki Roshi had given a perfect object lesson in "beginner's mind"—the state of openness and innocence that renders secondhand words and concepts obsolete.

> **SPIRITUAL SIGNPOST**
>
> Although Zen Buddhism is not the most popular Buddhist denomination in the West, it is among the most influential. Americans eager to explore new social and religious perspectives have been especially interested in Zen since the second half of the twentieth century.

Bodhidharma Gets Things Started

Zen traces its origin to the legendary figure Bodhidharma of the Mahayana school of Buddhism. Bodhidharma is said to have arrived in China from India near the end of the fifth century C.E.

The earliest development of Bodhidharma's school is hard to trace. We know that he is said to have meditated for nine straight years in search of direct insight into the ways of enlightenment. Eventually Bodhidharma took on the role of teacher to a group of disciples and passed his teachings on to a successor, Hui-k'o, known as the Second Patriarch. Under the Third Patriarch, Seng-ts'an, Zen came under the influence of Taoism, which emphasizes an open, noninterfering approach to the processes of nature.

Seng-ts'an observed:

> *The Way is perfect like vast space, Where nothing is missing and nothing is in oversupply. Indeed, it is because of our choosing to accept or reject that we do not see the true nature of things.*

"Original Mind"

Bodhidharma's teaching lineage eventually extended to Hui-Neng, the Sixth Patriarch, who emphasized the importance of discovering one's own "original mind" and "true nature." These teachings have remained staples of Zen practice to this day.

In the eighth and ninth centuries C.E., Zen strengthened and developed its traditions of one-on-one instruction and direct experience of the enlightened way. While other schools of Buddhism were enduring a period of intense persecution in China, Zen continued to flourish—in part because of its lack of dependence on written texts, which could be (and often were) destroyed by those seeking to eradicate Buddhism.

Zen Buddhism survived because of its willingness to transcend standard forms, rituals, and written instructions. Today, it continues to teach practitioners to move beyond dependence on such trappings, even beyond dependence on standard forms of thought, into the direct experience of enlightened consciousness. This detached approach has allowed Zen to adapt well to social and cultural challenges over the centuries.

ON THE PATH

Bodhidharma is said to have described Zen as "a special transmission outside of the scriptures. There was no need for dependence on words and letters; direct pointing to the real person; seeing into one's nature, which was identical with all reality, justified Buddha-life and led to attainment of Buddhahood."

Two Schools

Two distinct approaches to Zen practice occurred in China. One focused on "sudden enlightenment" through such tools as *koans*, or anti-rational teaching riddles. The other school preferred to encourage its students to pursue zazen practice (cross-legged meditation) with no expectation of enlightenment, sudden or otherwise. This second school also rejected the method of the sudden enlightenment school, in which masters engaged in constant questioning—and occasionally even physical violence!

When Zen made its way to Japan, the "hard" and "soft" schools became known as the Rinzai and Soto schools, respectively. These two schools have profoundly influenced the development of Zen teaching, and are active to this day.

Next Stop: Japan

Although Zen eventually declined in China, it assumed a vigorous new life in Japan, especially among the medieval military class. As a result, it profoundly influenced the art, literature, and aesthetics of the country. The influences went both ways: the style of Zen with which most Westerners are familiar has a distinctly Japanese flavor.

SPIRITUAL SIGNPOST

Don't expect to find a lot of explanation in Zen training or practice. In this tradition, even the words of a revered teacher are suspect. Master Rinzai said, "Rather than attaching yourselves to my words, it is better to calm down and seek nothing further. Do not cling to the past or long for the future. This is better than a pilgrimage of 10 years' duration." Having broken Rinzai's own rule by quoting him, we now venture a second violation of Zen spirit by passing along an old and well-worn story.

Master Tung-shan was weighing some flax one day when a monk walked up and asked him, "What is Buddha-nature?" (Or in other words, "What is the nature of enlightenment?") Without hesitation, Tung-shan answered, "Three pounds of flax."

The moral: Committed Zen students strive to stay completely involved in the present moment, because that's the only place true enlightenment can ever be found!

The Zen school has been the object of particularly strong interest in the United States, where its purity and clarity have had an enduring impact on religious movements, literary works, and even media culture. Prominent Americans who have embraced, directly or indirectly, the teachings of Zen Buddhism include poet Allen Ginsberg, actor Peter Coyote, author Robert Pirsig, and professional basketball coach Phil Jackson. There have probably been more words written in the West about this school of Buddhism than about any other—which is ironic, given Zen's insistence that its fundamental message defies any verbal summary!

Whatever culture it has occupied, Zen's first objective has always been to encourage direct personal experience on a moment-to-moment basis. Typically, this is accomplished (or at least attempted) by means of hours of solitary meditation under the guidance of a teacher. But periods outside of formal meditation, in the Zen model, are just as important as opportunities for direct experience and honest perception.

Zen Buddhism's insistence on every-minute awareness and full participation in the moment have important parallels with other religious traditions. Among these is the Islamic doctrine of *taqwa* (right action guided, moment to moment, by the fear of God).

BARRIER ALERT!

The point of Zen practice is not to become withdrawn or self-absorbed, but to discover the authentic self, capable of participating in the world fully. Zen emphasizes not elite remoteness, but 100 percent involvement, with no distraction, in whatever one is doing. One American Zen school has adopted the slogan of a sneaker manufacturer: "Just do it."

Other Buddhist Sects

There are, of course, many other sects within Buddhism. Two notable sects are the Pure Land School and Nichiren Buddhism. We will explore these sects more fully in the next section.

The Pure Land School

Pure Land Buddhists appeal to the grace of Buddha Amitabha (Amida), who, according to tradition, vowed in the second century C.E. to save all sentient beings. This redemption, believers hold, is brought about by invoking Amitabha's name, and results in rebirth into the Western Paradise, a transcendent domain in which miraculous surroundings abound. From the Western Paradise, it is believed, entry to Nirvana is assured.

Pure Land Buddhism is an extremely influential, devotional expression of Mahayana Buddhism, particularly in Japan.

Absolute reliance on the Buddha of Infinite Light is a central tenet of this expression of Buddhism, which enjoins believers to cultivate supreme and unwavering faith in the Buddha Amitabha. Believers within the various Pure Land schools pursue a spiritual path whose means of union with the Ultimate is an absolute reliance on the Buddha's grace. Individual exertion along paths of internal spiritual development is rejected as self-centered, or even insulting, to the Buddha Amitabha insofar as they reflect a lack of faith in his grace.

From its earliest days, Pure Land Buddhism was notable for its occasional evangelical fervor, and for contrasting the bliss that awaited true believers with the torments of hell that were reserved for others. This doctrine, combined with the Pure Land Buddhists' rejection of human works as a means of spiritual salvation, has led this sect to be compared to Protestant Calvinism.

There are a number of branches within Pure Land Buddhism. Among the most notable is the Jodo Shinshu, the largest Buddhist denomination in Japan.

Nichiren Buddhism

Nichiren Buddism (named after the Japanese Buddhist Nichiren, 1222–1282 C.E.) covers a number of different schools within Japanese Buddhism. Nichiren Buddhism's most notable expression in recent years has probably been the lay Buddhist movement known as Soka Gakkai, which claimed more than a million Japanese adherents in 1993. Today, the various forms of Nichiren Buddhism play an important role in American Buddhist life, both in and out of the Japanese American community.

Celebrations

There are so many denominations and varying traditions within Buddhism that we can only touch on the most common here.

Nirvana Day

This is observed on February 15; the date on which the Buddha's passing is observed.

Buddha Day

April 8 is the date on which the Buddha's birth is celebrated.

> **SPIRITUAL SIGNPOST**
>
> The Buddhist Churches of America, whose followers numbered 500,000 in a recent count, is the most numerous American Buddhist denomination. It is an outgrowth of the Japanese Jodo Shinshu school.

Bodhi Day

Buddhists celebrate December 8 as the day on which Prince Gautama took his place under the Bodhi Tree, vowing to remain there until he attained the supreme enlightenment.

The Least You Need to Know

- Zen is one of the best-known Buddhist schools in America.
- Zen Buddhism is rooted in direct experience and rejects scholarly abstractions.
- Other important contemporary Buddhist movements include the Pure Land and Nichiren sects.
- The three most important holidays in Buddhist tradition are Nirvana Day, Buddha Day, and Bodhi Day.

Breaking Down Barriers to Buddhism

In This Chapter

- Buddha and Jesus
- Reincarnation
- Meditation
- The joy of life

There are a number of common misunderstandings and misconceptions concerning Buddhism. Even as Buddhism has grown in popularity in the West, the likelihood of encountering one or more of these inaccurate ideas about the faith has remained high.

In this chapter, the facts behind some of the most common misunderstandings are addressed.

Myth #1: Buddhists worship Buddha as Christians worship Jesus.

Buddhism is sometimes described as being structured around a "savior" figure. The whole notion of a "savior" in Buddhism is problematic because of the word's overlap with the theology of Christianity. It's important to take any religious faith on its own terms, and not on those of its counterparts.

Theravada Buddhists are likely to emphasize the aid of the Buddha as an important component of their faith practice, and this emphasis is sometimes expressed by means of the word "savior." The notion of "savior" is also closely related to the Mahayana conception of the bodhisattva, a saintlike figure who takes a personal commitment to bring all sentient beings to enlightenment. Ultimately, however, both Theravada and

Mahayana Buddhism require the understanding that no Buddha or bodhisattva can possibly be separate from the believer, or indeed from the observable universe.

To understand why this is so, consider an example from the world of sports. There is an old habit among American baseball fans of comparing any prominent Japanese baseball player to any familiar American one. Thus, in his heyday, the great home run hitter Sadaharu Oh was continually described in America as "the Japanese Hank Aaron." Sadaharu Oh was not the Japanese Hank Aaron; he was, in fact, the Japanese Sadaharu Oh! Similarly, the Buddhist attitude toward the Buddha simply is what it is; it is not a variation on the Christian attitude toward Jesus.

Myth #2: Overemphasizing reincarnation.

Contrary to popular belief, a number of Buddhist schools *de-emphasize* or *omit* the doctrine of reincarnation to such a point that it is not a meaningful feature of the religious practice. (Among these are the Shin Buddhists.)

In particular, the emphasis of Tibetan Buddhism upon reincarnation has given many non-Buddhists the impression that the concept is central to the contemporary practice of the faith. In fact, many Buddhists, particularly in America, categorize the question of reincarnation in the same way they categorize the question of the belief in a deity: they choose not to distract themselves with it. (See also Chapter 33.)

Myth #3: Buddhism is masochistic.

Because of the Buddhist's emphasis on the enduring role of suffering as a component of human experience, some outsiders have concluded that Buddhists rejoice in suffering or seek it out. No responsible summary of the Buddhist faith, however, can embrace such an idea.

The idea that suffering is an inescapable fact of human existence has parallels in many other religions, notably Judaism and Christianity, both of which accept as divine revelation the Book of Ecclesiastics, which makes much the same points. The Buddhist idea of suffering requires not that one embrace it as something "desirable," nor that one flee from it, because it is a central element of humanity's path. It is an inescapable feature of humanity's lot on earth. Rather, Buddhists attempt to come to terms with the pervasive suffering that they see by treating suffering as a chance to nurture spiritual maturity.

Myth #4: All Buddhists look at meditation in the same way.

The prominence of the Zen school has encouraged many non-Buddhists to conclude that long hours of meditation are a required component of Buddhist practice. In fact, certain Buddhist schools de-emphasize meditation, and only practice it glancingly, during periods of communal worship and chanting.

The importance of meditation in the history of the Buddhist faith is, of course, immense—given that its practice was so very important a component of the Buddha's own practice and teaching. All the same, there are different approaches to the faith and to its points of necessary emphasis, just as there are in Judaism and Christianity and Hinduism.

ON THE PATH

"There are two main branches in Buddhist meditation: samatha (calmness, concentration) and vipassana (insight), which stresses mindfulness. This doesn't mean that the two are entirely separate, since you cannot be mindful unless you have at least some level of concentration. The techniques of samatha meditation are many, some older than Buddhism, others developed after the time of the Buddha."

—From *Buddhist Meditation* www.sawadee.com/thailand/meditation/index. htm

Myth #5: Buddhists hate life.

"All that talk about delusion and transcendence ... doesn't it really boil down to the Buddhists hating life itself?"

No. Buddhist teachings do relentlessly emphasize that life is impermanent and not something to cling to. But the same teachings also emphasize that human beings should experience it fully in each moment.

Emphasizing the first point at the expense of the second, however tempting it may be to those unfamiliar with the faith, is an error. The Buddha did not want his followers to become mindless automatons, and Buddhists are not life-haters. In fact, the Buddha advocated a persistent, pragmatic approach to spiritual questions, an approach that Buddhists believe yield both spiritual benefits and a long, happy life.

"Listen, householder, these five conditions are desirable, worthy of favor, worthy of pleasure, and are hard to come by in this world. They are longevity … pleasant appearance … happiness … status … heaven. These five conditions, I say, are not to be had by mere supplication or aspiration. If these five conditions were obtainable through mere supplication or aspiration, then who in this world would not have them? Listen, householder, the Noble Disciple, desiring long life, should not waste his time supplicating or merely indulging in the wish for longevity. The Noble Disciple desiring longevity should maintain the practice which produces longevity. Only the practice which produces longevity is capable of procuring longevity. That Noble Disciple will thus be one who has longevity, both divine and human … he who desires pleasant appearance … happiness … status … heaven, should develop the practice which produces pleasant appearance … happiness … status … heaven …."

—The Buddha

The Least You Need to Know

- Buddhists view the Buddha in their own way; it is a mistake to assume that they adopt the approach of Christianity or followers of any other religion.
- Not all Buddhists place a heavy emphasis on the principle of reincarnation.
- Not all Buddhists place a heavy emphasis on the practice of meditation.
- Buddhists do not hate life.

Other Influential Traditions

The following categories of observance challenge assumptions about what is (and is not) "religious observance." Many consider Confucianism, for example, to be a pragmatic philosophy, not a religion. Yet the sage Confucius has had an important spiritual and ethical influence on the Chinese people. Taoism is both a philosophy and a religious system, and also claims an impressive history of medical, literary, theatrical, and artistic influence. Shinto, the former state religion of Japan, shows how an adaptive religion can be both traditional in its faith to its ancient roots, and "secular" in any number of modern expressions! And one of Sikhism's core teachings is a paradox that seems to echo through all religious traditions: "Realization of Truth is higher than all else. Higher still is truthful living."

Confucianism: Human Relations 101

In This Chapter

- What is Confucianism?
- The life and mission of Confucius
- The *Analects* and the *I Ching*
- How this school has evolved over the centuries

Religion? Philosophy? Ethical system? Social tradition? Scholarly discipline?

Confucianism has been all these things over the two and a half millennia of its existence. It endures today as a collection of diverse schools of thought closely associated with, and affected by, centuries of Chinese historical development. The school has seen its share of heady ascents and steep declines, but it has never faded completely from the scene.

Confucianism has periodically reinvented itself, introducing new strands of thought and reassessing and revising its practices, yet it continues to emphasize the harmonious way of life first expounded by the sage Confucius.

Who Was He?

The name by which the supreme philosopher of ancient China is known in the West is a Latinized form of the Chinese phrase K'ung Fu-tse, which means "Master K'ung." For the purposes of this book, we'll use the name most familiar to English-speaking Westerners.

Confucius was largely self-taught. Interestingly, although his influence has been monumental and his teachings eventually resulted in a formal and imperial Confucian orthodoxy, no Chinese ruler ever wholeheartedly embraced Confucius's doctrines during his lifetime.

SPIRITUAL SIGNPOST

The name "Confucius" is a Latinized form of the name of the ancient Chinese sage K'ung Fu-tse (Master K'ung). It was coined centuries after his death by Jesuit missionaries in China.

Confucius was born in 551 B.C.E. As an official in the state of Lu (today known as Shantung), he endeared himself to the public by advocating important reforms based on humane principles of administration. Deeply concerned about the dominant militarism of China, Confucius offered instruction for potential Chinese leaders to refine and stabilize the government according to principles of peace and equity.

Confucius was more interested in ethical and political matters than religious principles as such. The ideals of decorum and harmonious social interaction that he preached relied heavily on personal moral development and obedience to proper forms. He rejected any identification of himself as a sage, but this did not prevent a cult of honor and ritual sacrifice from arising around his name and image some centuries after his death. Confucius has been called one of the most influential thinkers in human history.

Five Interactions

Confucius's identification of six ethical relationships transformed Chinese thought and profoundly influenced social systems in China and other Asian nations for centuries.

> *Six Relationships*
>
> Parent and child
>
> Ruler and minister
>
> Government officials
>
> Husband and wife

Older sibling and younger sibling

Friend and friend

Particular importance is usually attached to the relationship between parents and children. These binding relationships are, within Confucian thought, founded upon and made possible by a compassionate, humane approach that incorporates a profound love. This broad principle requires only a single word for expression in Chinese: *jen*. Also essential to Confucianism is *li*, or seamlessly proper conduct between parties.

Jen expresses itself in *chung*, "faithfulness to oneself." But such faithfulness is not to be misunderstood as self-absorption. Confucianism depends upon attention to moral duties befitting a son or daughter (*hsiao*).

The moral ideal in Confucianism is exemplified by the *chun-tzu*, or noble individual.

DEFINITION

Jen is the compassion and humanity arising from genuine love. **Li** is correct ritualistic and etiquette-based behavior between individuals.

Opposition, Departure, Return

Confucius's reformist ideas won him the enmity of some powerful people in his home state. Eventually, he left Lu and pursued a mission he believed to be willed by heaven. Although his disciples included some highly positioned people, Confucius himself never received the prestigious royal appointment he sought. It seems his outspoken approach with high-ranking members of the hierarchy may have doomed his dream of implementing his reforms.

Nevertheless, the accomplishments of Confucius were extraordinary. According to tradition, before his death in Lu in 479 B.C.E. he edited and compiled, with his followers, a number of vitally important texts. At the same time, he developed a body of teaching that is revered to this day in Asia and elsewhere in the world. His doctrines are considered to be reflected most authoritatively in the *Analects*.

The *Analects*

The *Analects of Confucius (Lun Yu)* was not acknowledged as a classic until the second century C.E. The work records the deeds and sayings of "Master K'ung"—although this work was compiled not by Confucius himself, but by his later followers.

The bulk of the work consists of sayings and remembrances assembled not long after the death of the sage. The teachings of Confucius reflected in the *Analects* are straightforward and direct: if people pursue courtesy, correct form and etiquette, reverence, and humane benevolence within each of the six basic human relationships, harmony will exist at every level of society.

Although every individual within the social hierarchy must act righteously, in Confucian thought special emphasis is always laid on the virtuous conduct of the ruler of a state, whose deeds serve as moral patterns that affect the entire nation.

In Confucian thought, the perfect human being combines the roles of sage, noble, and scholar. To be a leader whose aims revolve solely around ideas of political power and personal aggrandizement is to be a very limited kind of leader indeed.

Confucius saw the family structure as the environment in which the virtues of a lifetime could be developed, virtues that would eventually benefit society as a whole. The teachings set out in the *Analects* view social hierarchy and correct action within it as necessities, a kind of extension of the family structure.

This emphasis on the family structure is not, however, an endorsement of rigid social roles. Rather, it sees the family as a series of constantly shifting relationships; one must be a child, for example, before one becomes a parent. Each of life's roles must be accompanied by appropriate discipline, regard for form, and ethical commitment.

Other Literary Stuff

Confucius lived during a time of tremendous philosophical activity in China. During this time he and his followers oversaw the development and formalization of a number of important writings. These books are traditionally divided into two groups: the Five Classics and the Four Books.

The Five Classics are all believed to have originated well before Confucius's time. They are the *Book of Changes (I Ching)*, the *Book of History (Shuh Ching)*, the *Book of Poetry (Shih Ching)*, the *Book of Rites (Li Chi)*, and the *Spring and Autumn Annals (Ch'un Chi)*, which chronicle major historical events.

The Four Books incorporate the works of Confucius and Mencius (372–289 B.C.E.), as well as the commentaries of their followers. They are considered by many to be the fundamental teachings of early Confucianism. They include the *Analects (Lun Yu)*, the *Great Learning (Ta Hsueh)*, *The Doctrine of the Mean (Chung Yung)*, and the *Book of Mencius (Meng-tzu)*. Together with the Five Classics, the Four Books make up the basic texts of Confucianism.

Confucius seemed to have felt particular respect for the ancient *Book of Changes*, or *I Ching*. As an old man he is said to have remarked that if he were to be granted 50 more years of life, he would devote them to the study of this book and thereby avoid mistakes in his life.

Ch-Ch-Ch-Changes

In the East, the *I Ching* is regarded as the first of the Five Classics. It is also the most popular of all the Confucian classics in the West.

People sometimes forget that this remarkable book was not "written" by Confucius. It was timeless when he first encountered it; its earliest layer of text is now at least 3,000 years old. Commentaries and appendices attributed to Confucius and members of his school would eventually be incorporated into the work.

The *I Ching* is a manual of divination for those seeking guidance. Whatever unfolding event or circumstance the reader wishes to explore, the *I Ching* has an answer. Advice is offered by means of 64 numbered, six-line figures, known as hexagrams. The lines may be broken or solid; broken lines symbolize the universal yin (female or yielding) force, while solid ones reflect the universal yang (male or active) force.

SPIRITUAL SIGNPOST

Within Chinese cosmology, *yin* and *yang* are the polar aspects of the primal energy. Interaction between these female and male, dark and light, passive and active principles is seen as a basic and observable element of cosmic development and evolution. Hexagrams within the *I Ching,* six-line figures developed by means of (seemingly) random patterns initiated by the reader, are thought to be symbolic of interactions between the yin and yang principles in the situation under examination.

To the sincere seeker, the *I Ching* is held to offer insights into the workings of any event or phenomenon. Come to the book with a question, and you will develop a hexagram that answers it. Talk about more bang for your scriptural buck!

Hexagram 30 (Fire) is a good example of how this *I Ching* process works. With this hexagram, the *I Ching* advises that "It will be advantageous to be firm and correct, and thus there will be free course and success. Let the subject nurture a docility like that of a cow, and there will be good fortune." A modern questioner might toss coins to develop the hexagram, perhaps in search of an answer to the question, "Should I ask my boss for a raise?"

Hexagram 30 (Fire), named after the trigram, or three-line pattern, that appears in both the upper and lower positions. (Notice that the top three lines are, in this hexagram, identical to the bottom three.)

"Does It, You Know ... Work?"

Whether the book really predicts the future or not, the *I Ching* has passionate adherents in both the East and the West. (The psychiatrist Carl Jung was a notable devotee.) Many supremely skeptical Westerners, in fact, find in the *I Ching* a pragmatic and accessible (if occasionally vague) source of wisdom. Its profound Confucian study and analysis can be an excellent starting place for reflecting on the elemental forces affecting human relationships.

Perhaps that is why the *Book of Changes* has been applied longer, more consistently, and more thoroughly than almost any other collection of religious scriptures.

SPIRITUAL SIGNPOST

Mencius is considered to be the author of the *Meng-tzu,* one of the Four Books of orthodox Confucianism. In it, he argued that human nature is intrinsically good, and that preexisting elements within the human character could, with practice and attentive nurturing, blossom into the mature virtues of benevolence, rightness, propriety, and wisdom.

After the Master

After the death of Confucius, his philosophy branched into two schools. One, led by Mencius, held that human intuition is inherently good and should serve as a guide to action and choice. Mencius believed in working toward a world that would enable the good of the majority to be realized. In fact, he has often been recognized as an early advocate of democracy.

Another school within Confucianism was that of Hsun-tzu (312–230 B.C.E.), who argued that people are born with innately evil natures and require ritual (*li*) to cultivate true virtue. Hsun-tzu regarded ritual as worthy in and of itself, teaching that established codes of behavior were to be observed for their own sake.

Hsun-tzu placed a heavy emphasis on the observance of ceremonial rites and the practice of civilized arts such as music. It is one's birthright, he taught, to cultivate good in oneself, and to maintain this goodness, one must be ever vigilant and work against one's own (destructive) nature. He opposed what he viewed as the rarefied idealism of Mencius.

SPIRITUAL SIGNPOST

Confucianism's vigorous emphasis on the formation of the proper society and the establishment of ethical standards stands in stark contrast to the open, formless, impersonal, and effortless Taoist path (see Chapter 25). Interestingly, however, the two schools are seen as complementary. Rather than serving as rival philosophies, the two systems are generally regarded as balancing and amplifying one another.

Confucianism Tops the Charts

Before the Han dynasty (206 B.C.E.–220 C.E.), Confucianist thought experienced a brief but precipitous decline. During the Han period, however, it experienced a powerful revival. The works associated with Confucius were canonized and once again taught by scholars in the national academies. Candidates for government positions would be appointed based on their knowledge of the classic literature. Confucianism emerged as the dominant intellectual force in China.

After the Han dynasty, however, China fell into chaos. During this period of uncertainty, Buddhism and Taoism (see Chapter 25) emerged as counterparts to Confucian thought. When stability was restored during the Tang dynasty (618–906 C.E.), high-level bureaucrats nurtured the teachings of Confucianism once again and secured its position as the official orthodoxy of the state.

Over the centuries, Confucianism served as a platform for new debates and embraced new schools of thought. In the twelfth century C.E., the renowned thinker Chu Hsi advanced the notion that one's moral development, when carried out in harmony with transitions in the exterior world, permits one to "form one body with all things." Chu was the most notable of several important figures in the Confucianist renaissance that has become known as Neo-Confucianism—a period that is considered to have extended to the end of the Ch'ing dynasty in 1911, some 800 years later!

Neo-Confucianists incorporated ideas from Buddhism (especially Zen Buddhism) and Taoism to formulate a system of metaphysics—explanations for ultimate questions of existence. Previously, Confucianism had not addressed such issues.

With the collapse of the Chinese monarchy in the early decades of the twentieth century, Confucianism was increasingly regarded as decadent and reactionary. It was reinvigorated in the modern era by the efforts of Hsiung Shih-li (1885–1968), regarded as the inspiration for the New Confucianism. This movement sought to make the Confucianist tradition a model for the development of a harmonious and tolerant world civilization.

The Changing, Changeless Way of Confucius

Twenty-five hundred years later, what is the way of Confucius? It's still hard to describe the school founded by "Master K'ung" concretely. Is it a religion or not? Although late nineteenth-century attempts to have the philosophy acknowledged as the official state religion of China were unsuccessful, there is an important and enduring religious dimension to this tradition.

Confucianism, in all its many manifestations and through all its varying accents, has contributed in an important and distinctive way to the moral and spiritual traditions of untold millions of people. Its emphasis on humaneness, tolerance, harmony, and duty are in keeping with the world's great spiritual teachings.

The continuous evolution and development of this body of teachings has never altered its central and abiding concern: the encouragement of proper relations between human beings. Relationships are seen as most perfect when they are motivated by love and an understanding of reciprocity very similar in nature to the familiar principle, "Do unto others as you would have them do unto you."

Despite its many formulations and variations over the centuries, the fundamental ideas of Confucianism remain unshakable guiding forces. Among the most important of these is that correct conduct arises, not through external force, but as a result of virtues developed internally through the observation of laudable models of behavior.

After Confucius's death, the master's emphasis on *jen*, or humane love, was eloquently taken up by Mencius, who continued the Master's work when he wrote:

> *All things are within me, and on self-examination, I find no greater joy than to be true to myself. We should do our best to treat others as we wish to be treated. Nothing is more appropriate than to seek after goodness.*—(Meng-tzu, 7a:4)

The Least You Need to Know

- Confucius developed a highly influential system of thought based on ethical principles for the proper conduct of social relationships.
- Confucianism emphasizes proper action within five primary relationships through observation of li, correct ritual, and etiquette.
- Although Confucius's focus is on moral behavior and social interaction, there is an important spiritual foundation to his teachings.

- The *Analects* are considered to be the most authoritative reflection of the teachings of Confucius.
- The *Book of Changes,* or *I Ching,* is an ancient book of divination that grew to incorporate Confucianist commentaries.
- Despite many alterations, challenges, and countermovements, Confucianism has retained its focus on the cultivation of harmonious relations between individuals as the basis of a sound social system.

Taoism: The Effortless Path

In This Chapter

- Taoism's complementary relationship with Confucianism
- The fundamental ideas of Taoism
- Establishing a working definition of "the Tao"
- Why Taoism caught on

In this chapter, you learn about the influential religious and philosophical system known as Taoism, a tradition whose name, like its guiding force, defies complete explanation. Its practitioners would maintain that this inexpressibility is completely appropriate.

In recent years, Taoism, like Buddhism (another hard-to-define belief system), has given rise to a wave of articles, books, manuals, and essays in the West. To find out what all the fascination and fuss is about, read on!

"Not to Be Impolite, but ..."

Taoism has a long and rich history that crisscrosses that of Confucianism. With Confucianism, it has served as a fundamental component of Asian spiritual and philosophical life for centuries. The fundamental doctrines of Taoism may be said to reflect a principle of action based on the natural world.

Unlike Confucianism, which advocates conformity and proper behavior within an ideal social system, Taoism illuminates a receptive approach to life. The Taoist viewpoint sounds something like this: the individual should seek the truth by means of a patient, accepting focus on natural patterns and influences worthy of emulation.

Not surprisingly, the Confucian emphasis on social hierarchy and scrupulously correct etiquette within that framework is largely rejected by Taoism. It would be a mistake, however, to view Taoism simply as a critique of Confucian thought. The teachings of this school reflect spiritual principles of great antiquity, and their expression in Taoism is part of an ongoing process of growth, development, and interaction with a wide variety of beliefs.

BARRIER ALERT!

Although rigid Confucians may sometimes regard it as such, Taoism is not a subversive or antisocial system of thought. It does not hold social forms to be meaningless or without merit. It simply believes that conscious efforts to control people and events are counterproductive.

Nature: Close to the Ground

The ideal Taoist lifestyle is that of the farmer, seeking complete harmony with the patterns of nature. If the seeker can live openly and without artifice, in touch with nature's rhythms, his or her day-to-day experience will lead directly to the power of the Tao.

Taoism elevates the principles of noncontrol and noninterference. To pursue the Tao means to abandon all restless struggling, no matter what form it may take. Under Taoism, the ideal personal situation, attainable only through prolonged observation and meditation, is one of utter simplicity, profound faith in natural processes, and true transcendence of shortsighted craving and grasping.

SPIRITUAL SIGNPOST

The differences between Taoism and Confucianism have often been exaggerated. There are similarities; for example, both Confucianism and Taoism accept a cosmology embodied in the concept of yin and yang.

Words: The *Tao Te Ching*

The ancient Chinese religious and philosophical system known as Taoism derives from the *Tao Te Ching*, ascribed to the sage Lao-Tzu (520 B.C.E.). The book is one of the most moving and sublime achievements of Chinese culture.

Here are some examples of the teachings of the *Tao Te Ching*, which has been offering influential (and deceptively simple-sounding) spiritual and social advice for the past two and a half millennia:

> *As to dwelling, live near the ground.*
> *As to thinking, hold to that which is simple.*
> *As to conflict, pursue fairness and generosity.*
> *As to governance, do not attempt to control.*
> *As to work, do that which you like doing.*
> *As to family life, be fully present.*
> —*Tao Te Ching*, Chapter 8

> *One who is filled with the Tao*
> *Is like a newborn child.*
> *The infant is protected from*
> *The stinging insects, wild beasts, and birds of prey.*
> *Its bones are soft, its muscles are weak,*
> *But its grip is firm and strong.*
> *It doesn't know about the union of male and female,*
> *Yet his member can stand erect,*
> *Because of the power of life within him.*
> *The infant can cry all day and never become hoarse.*
> *This is perfect harmony.*
> —*Tao Te Ching*, Chapter 55

> *I lack desires—and thus the people self-simplify.*
> *They become like uncarved wood.*
> —*Tao Te Ching*, Chapter 57

Words: The Chuang-Tzu

The writings of another brilliant philosopher, Chuang-Tzu (c. 369–c. 286 B.C.E.), have also become very important in Taoist practice. This challenging (and, seemingly, occasionally nonsensical) collection of satirical parables and allegories shines a light on the relative nature of all "rational" processes and assumptions. Today it is second in influence only to the *Tao Te Ching* in Taoist practice.

In recent years, in fact, there has been more and more interest in Chuang-Tzu, with some people claiming that his teachings are more directly relevant and applicable to daily life than those of Lao-Tzu. Here's a sampling—you be the judge.

"Who am I to Say?"

Who am I to say that rejoicing in life is not an illusion? Who am I to say that in despising death we do not resemble children who are lost and have no idea how to get home? Lady Li was born the daughter of a man who worked in Ai as a border guard. When she was taken into captivity by the authorities in Jin, she wept bitterly, and her clothes became drenched. Yet once she made her way to the palace, and enjoyed the favors of the king's bed, and ate sumptuous meals, she repented her weeping. Who am I to say that dead people do not repent all their graspings to maintain hold of life? Someone who has a dream of getting drunk may well weep in the morning out of regret. Someone who has a dream of weeping may decide to go out hunting the next morning. When we are dreaming, we have no idea that we dream. We may even dream that we interpret a dream! On awakening, we know to treat it as dreaming. Then there may be a Great Awakening, and we will know to treat this as a Great Dream; fools will think themselves awake, proudly knowing it and saying "I am a ruler," or "I am a shepherd." Stubborn! Confucius and you are dreaming, and I, who call you dreamers, am also dreaming. This is the saying. And it's called dangerous dangling. After ten thousand generations we may chance on a great sage who knows how to explain this. We see them every morning and evening.

(Note: Translations of the *Tao Te Ching* and the *Chuang-Tzu* come from Brandon Toropov and Chad Hansen's *The Complete Idiot's Guide to Taoism*.)

For all Chuang-Tzu's recent popularity, it is important to remember that the central text of Taoism has always been, and always will be, the *Tao Te Ching*. It has been translated into English in countless editions, and with the *I Ching*, is one of the most influential sacred Asian texts read in the West.

Brevity is the soul of wit—and of the *Tao Te Ching!* The book is one of the world's shortest primary religious texts. The entire work is less than five thousand words long. In its spare way, it describes a view of the world in which man, heaven, and earth function as interdependent entities.

SPIRITUAL SIGNPOST

Taoists, like Confucians, regard the *I Ching (Book of Changes)* as an inspired work.

The *Tao Te Ching* addresses matters of culture, emotion, nature, right action, language, and mysticism through reflections on the Tao. The term "Tao" has led scholars and translators to develop many wandering, scholarly explanations. An adequate one-word rendering of "Tao" into English remains out of reach.

Wow: The Tao!

So what is the Tao? We might as well ask: What is God? Literally, *Tao* means "path" or "way." All the same, the scriptures of this faith advise that the "eternal Tao" cannot actually be named. We'll take a calculated risk, though, and follow the lead of other commentators by describing the Tao as a sublime "Natural Order"—one marked by the effortless alternation of cycles (night and day, growth and decline) and an unconstrained, pervasive creativity that transcends impermanent expression. The Tao may best be described as "the way the universe works."

One thing is certain: The Tao is "sought" only through the most yielding approach. To reach unity with it, one must put aside all that is artificial, strained, and unnatural. Instead, one must seek to develop a personal code from the naturally arising and spontaneous impulses of one's own true nature. Such a code, Taoists believe, transcends narrow, externally imposed teachings and doctrines.

SPIRITUAL SIGNPOST

Te is a controlling power, virtue, or magical energy. Another dimension of its meaning has to do with integrity or moral rectitude. One way to translate the title of the central Taoist set of scriptures would be The Classic Text (Ching) Concerning Power/Integrity (Te) and the Way (Tao).

Emptiness is essential to Taoist thought. The enlightened person is thought to be like a hollow reed or bamboo shoot: empty within, upright and resolute without. Taoists teach inaction, but this idea must not be misunderstood. True inaction, in the Taoist sense, is the most efficient possible action, the most spontaneous possible action, and the most creative possible action.

Maintaining contact with the Tao means allowing activity to spring spontaneously, without conscious effort, from a well of nothingness accessible to all. This "doing nothing" is known as *wu-wei*. A Taoist who acts in accordance with this principle does not pursue a life of sloth or laziness, but one in which the least possible effort yields the most effective and productive outcome. This approach, the Taoists maintain, enables the believer to connect with the elemental flow of the universe itself.

A classic Taoist illustration of effortless action involves water, which naturally occupies the lowest possible position, but nevertheless exerts sufficient force over time to wear down the hardest stone.

Such unity with the mystical is known as *te*, a force that makes possible true liberation. It is taught that this power can allow the believer to overcome even death itself.

Who Founded Taoism?

Lao-Tzu, author of the *Tao Te Ching*, may have been a committee, rather than a single individual. Traditionally, he has been described as a sage living in the same period as Confucius—slightly older, we are told—who passed his teachings along to a border guard. The guard is said to have faithfully transcribed the teachings into the book with which centuries of spiritual seekers have become familiar.

There's a problem with this account, however. Confucius is known to have lived in the sixth century B.C.E., and internal evidence within the text of the *Tao Te Ching* points to a later compilation—possibly formalized around the fourth century B.C.E.

Old Voices

Today, scholars believe that the school we call Taoism arose from ancient beliefs and practices having to do with nature worship and predicting the future. Although scholarly debate continues, most regard Taoism's central scriptures as a collection of wisdom from Chinese sages over the centuries.

The person or persons who edited the *Tao Te Ching* and consolidated the various ancient teachings was probably responsible for giving Taoism the form we know today.

The *Tao Te Ching*, the central text of Taoism, is a brief and immensely influential book that uses poetic (or, if you prefer, cryptic and elusive) language to point out the futility of struggling against universal processes. It advocates instead a course of submission, flexibility, and profound self-awareness.

To believe one can somehow overcome or outwit the waxing, waning, creative natural order is held to be a great error. It is far more advisable, a Taoist would argue, to find a way to act in accordance with the unknowable, unnamable force that underlies all creation and is visible in every manifestation of it.

Western observers have tended to emphasize Taoism's serene and inscrutable side. The truth is, over the centuries, the system has expressed itself directly and pragmatically in political, military, mythological, artistic, medical, and scientific areas. Even certain doctrinal conflicts with Confucianism have yielded when the time was regarded as appropriate. The hallmarks of Taoism are flexibility and a vision of an inspired, continually reinvigorating, self-revealing path by the person of integrity.

New Voices

The Taoist tradition can be seen as a counterpart to Confucianism, but it also embraces features of Mahayana Buddhism. Today, Taoism is an independent system that incorporates the following:

- The rejection of calculated, restless, goal-oriented effort.

- Trust in the benefits of effortless, spontaneous action in accordance with the requirements of the time.

- Belief that the Tao manifests itself everywhere and in all situations.

- An understanding of the Tao as eternally new, fundamentally creative, and beyond literal expression.

- Emphasis on the importance of balance, especially on that which is communicated between the human realm, heaven, and earth.

Whether or not a single individual named Lao-Tzu articulated the principles of Taoism, these timeless teachings inspired one of the world's great spiritual traditions. If Lao-Tzu didn't actually exist, he might as well have.

Back and Forth with Buddhism

Influenced as it was by Mahayana Buddhism, Taoism in turn played an important role in the development of the well-known school of Buddhism that Westerners know as Zen.

Taoists believe that the spontaneous, creative Tao can be seen everywhere. It renews itself continually and can never be exhausted. Practitioners who remain still and silent are held to be capable of discerning its directions, and thus to act in accordance with those promptings without preconception and in full possession of their true selves. Some formulation of all these beliefs came to be reflected within Zen Buddhism.

How Has Taoism Expressed Itself?

Let us not try to count the ways—because it's pretty complicated. Detailing the "expressions" of Taoism can be elusive, because it's served as an acceptable channel for innumerable principles and movements. It has existed on many levels, too, often with rituals that "mean" one thing to its lay believers and perhaps something broader to its priests and devotees. In keeping with its own teachings, Taoism has been quite flexible in adapting to times and circumstances.

The Believers

Instead of asking what Taoism looks like in practice, we might ask to whom it appeals. Throughout history, those who have turned from worldly exploits as shallow and unrewarding, those who have become disillusioned with social agitation or military conquest, and those who have tired of the daily struggles over rank and position—have turned to Taoist teachings. In the faith, they have often discovered meaning within the unfolding dance of nature—and perhaps come closer to learning how best to perform their own roles within that dance.

The Outside World

By its very nature, Taoism generally refrains from trying to influence political or social institutions. In this way it stands as a polar opposite to Confucianism. In fact, many of the ethical and social concerns of Confucian thought were dismissed by early Taoists as excessive, restless strivings out of step with the naturally unfolding harmonies of the universe.

This is not to say that there has never been any attempt to implement a Taoist political philosophy; there has been. The political side of Taoism holds that the best model for government is the undisturbed harmony of nature. From this it is argued that the duty of the ruler is to rule according to as few restrictions and directions as possible. It is sufficient simply to guide the populace away from want and turmoil.

It Caught On!

Taoist thought and practice eventually met with widespread acceptance in Chinese society as a whole, in large measure because of interest in its relevance to medicine. One of its basic principles was the promise of eternal physical life.

What Was That About Immortality?

For many Chinese, Taoism's nature-based teaching gave rise to a profound reverence for natural processes and a desire to retreat to the natural world. At the same time, Taoism encouraged a powerful embrace of life itself, expressed in health, long life, and even immortality. Thus, knowledge concerning the Tao was held to be a pathway to superior physical health and even the transcendence of death.

For centuries, Taoism has been associated with noninvasive herbal remedies, regular breathing techniques, and deep concentration as methods of promoting longevity and reducing stress. The great advances the Taoists brought to the medical arts in China have had much to do with the enduring popularity of the faith.

SPIRITUAL SIGNPOST

Interest in alchemy as a means of attaining the Taoist goal of long (or even eternal) physical life led to the development of many curatives and elixirs. A great many of these are still widely employed in Chinese medicine today.

What Was That About Release?

Another reason for the enduring popularity of Taoism is its historical role as an ancient and reliable form of release (and, often, escape) from the cycle of historical processes and bitter political conflicts.

Taoism has served for centuries as a platform for individual spiritual growth—and as a respite from important, but perhaps ultimately unresolveable questions about social structures. Taoism's emphasis on integrity, authenticity, and relaxed, attentive engagement with the world may be the best expression of "traditionalism" within this faith.

The Least You Need to Know

- Taoism and Confucianism form complementary systems of thought.
- Taoism derives from the book *Tao Te Ching,* ascribed to the sage Lao-Tzu, but believed by scholars to be a compilation of many ancient sources.
- The fundamental doctrines of Taoism reflect a principle of action modeled on the natural world.
- Taoism elevates principles of noncontrol and noninterference to high importance.
- Although a definition for the Tao remains elusive, it may best be described as "the way the universe works."
- True inaction, in the Taoist sense, is the most efficient possible action, the most spontaneous possible action, and the most creative possible action.

Shinto: Harmony and Clarity

In This Chapter

- The history and development of Shinto
- The important role that nature plays in this tradition
- The many forms taken by kami (spirits)
- How this adaptable faith has become a vital part of the Japanese cultural heritage

In this chapter, you find out about the history, development, and practices of Shinto, a native Japanese religious tradition that can also be found in the many countries in which sizable Japanese communities exist.

Shinto: The Basics

Shinto is the indigenous, nature-focused religion of Japan. It incorporates a number of ancient Japanese mythological rites and has undergone many formulations and structural revisions over the centuries. It is related to the religions of Manchuria, Korea, and the region today known as Siberia.

Deriving as it does from ancient Japanese tradition, Shinto does without some things that most other religions consider central: a founder or central figure, a holy scripture, or a preaching tradition. It is one of the world's oldest religions; its origins extend into the far reaches of prehistory. Formal institutionalization of many of its forms did not occur until the middle of the first millennium B.C.E., when it was considered necessary to distinguish native Japanese forms from Chinese religious influences.

Eventually, diverse mythological and ritualistic elements were combined into a single accepted creation account. Although there is no deity regarded as supreme over all kami, the sun goddess Amaterasu is accorded a high rank. Within Shinto, the emperor of Japan (whose temporal power has undergone many fluctuations over the centuries) is regarded as a direct descendant of Amaterasu.

DEFINITION

The word **Shinto** is a Chinese transliteration of a phrase created in the late sixth century C.E. to distinguish native religion from others that had become widely accepted in Japan. The corresponding Japanese term, **kami-no-michi,** is commonly translated as "The Way of the Gods," or "The Way of Those Above."

First and foremost, Shinto is a form of nature worship; it took shape around the reverence of kami, or divine spirits—manifested and recognized in natural forces, objects, powerful individuals, and other entities. Today, Shinto continues to elevate established tradition and reverence over formal theological questions.

In place of rigid intellectual structures, Shinto emphasizes the harmony of natural beauty and a clear, often poetic, appreciation of perceived reality. Shinto's many rituals celebrate purity, clarity, and contact with the diverse forces of nature. Essential to the Shinto faith is the word *kami,* which describes something possessing a power that an individual believer does not.

BARRIER ALERT!

The common English translation of the word kami is "god," but don't let it mislead you. Kami has certainly been used in Shinto practice to describe supernatural beings, but not in the Western sense of an omnipotent God. A better translation may be "spirit" or "one residing above."

The word may be used to identify something that is physical, animate, and familiar (an animal or a person), spiritual (a ghost or spirit), or inanimate (rock formation or a personal computer). Believe it or not, the term kami, as applied to your Macintosh, does in fact carry a certain religious significance.

Contemporary Shinto observance reflects historical interactions with Buddhism and Confucianism. However, early forms of Shinto preceded the introduction of these faiths to Japan, perhaps by many centuries.

Shinto has historically promoted rituals that were closely linked to the seasons: to planting and harvest patterns—for instance, to the observance of the new year, and to times of ceremonial purification. For all the influence exerted upon it by other faiths, Shinto has retained its unique focus on personified natural forces. Festivals honoring kami are central to Shinto practice. Important festivals include February 11 (National Founding Day in Japan), those honoring locally recognized kami, and the first days of each season. Spring and fall festivals are particularly important.

Two Big Dates

In modern times, Shinto has undergone two major periods of abrupt change. Social forces shaped the religion at two key points, one in the nineteenth century and one in the twentieth.

1868: Drawing the Line

The intertwining of Shinto with other forms (particularly Buddhism) eventually gave rise to a counter-reaction that tried to reestablish Shinto as a separate and distinctly Japanese religious form. (Catholicism, introduced by Jesuit missionaries in the sixteenth and seventeenth centuries, also experienced this "counter-reaction.")

Beginning in the 1700s, Shinto devotees undertook an energetic campaign to identify, distinguish, and reawaken old practices within their faith. This effort reached its full expression after the Meiji Restoration of 1868, when Shinto rites were formally separated from Buddhist practices. The Meiji Restoration also transferred political power away from the warrior class and to the emperor. This movement led to the promotion of Shinto, with its emphasis on the divine nature of the emperor, as the official, state-sponsored religion of Japan.

SPIRITUAL SIGNPOST

Although Shinto priests continued to observe ancient customs of ritual purification and abstinence, the indigenous Japanese faith was practiced in (literally) close quarters with Buddhism for much of the nation's history. It was common, for instance, for Buddhist practices to extend into Shinto shrines, many of which were built adjacent to Buddhist temples and vice versa.

Shinto's emergence as an important and truly independent religious form is often traced to political events of 1868 and the years that followed. During the second half of the nineteenth century and the first 45 years of the twentieth, the Shinto religion served as a vehicle for Japanese nationalism. Elements within the society strongly encouraged the use of the ancient mythological elements to venerate the emperor, the state, and, eventually, an aggressive military policy.

1945: A New Direction

After World War II, Shinto formally disclaimed its direct ties to the state. Under the direction of the occupying Allies, a number of dramatic reforms were enacted. The provision of public funds to maintain shrines was forbidden, and in 1946 Emperor Hirohito explicitly renounced his claim to divinity.

These changes in structure and emphasis were certainly not the first to be associated with Shinto. Although the faith now operates as one of a number of coequal religious forms in Japan, its vibrancy and ritualistic tradition are as important as ever to the cultural and religious heritage of the nation. The post-1945 period has been a productive and important one for Shinto, which continues to thrive in Japan and in other countries where Japanese have formed large communities.

Day by Day

Shinto has become completely assimilated into day-to-day Japanese custom and tradition. Its rituals are accepted on so many levels as to be nearly indistinguishable from "everyday life." A new construction project, for instance, is unlikely to begin without a formal offering and ritual prayer ceremony overseen by a Shinto official at the site.

SPIRITUAL SIGNPOST

In the second half of the twentieth century, new Shinto sects that explicitly emphasize the importance of brotherhood, world peace, and harmonious relations among nations have arisen.

In the Shrine

Shinto ritual embraces much more than religious practice conducted in shrines, but many of the most important events of the faith take place within these buildings. Shinto shrines are made entirely of wood and are generally situated near sacred trees and flowing water.

When a visitor enters a Shinto shrine, he or she is regarded as having left the world of finite things and entered the realm of the infinite and immeasurable, where the powerful kami may be invoked for the purpose of the ceremony at hand. Although many kami may be honored after one passes through the tori, a special gateway in each shrine, one kami in particular is specially venerated.

The Heart of Shinto

Shinto practice nourishes local traditions and promotes an awareness of kami and the natural world. It has more to do with traditions and beliefs than dogma or morality. As one of Japan's grounding institutions, Shinto has contributed to the extraordinary fusion of ancient tradition and cutting-edge, technologically influenced life in contemporary Japan.

Anything Missing?

To an outsider, Shinto is perhaps most fascinating for what it doesn't have. Some things noticeably absent within the Shinto faith are ...

- **A founder:** Like Hinduism, Shinto claims no individual originator.

- **Written scriptures:** The closest Shinto comes to these is the mythological history known as *kojiki*, or "documents of ancient matters," completed in 712 C.E. These writings deal with the ancient "age of the spirits," as well as court proceedings, but they are not revered in the way that inspired writings are in other faiths.

- **Exclusionary patterns of worship:** Believers may practice Shinto in combination with other faiths. Most Japanese follow both Buddhism and Shinto.

- **Rigid dogma about the nature or form of that which is worshipped:** No requirement is laid on any Shinto practitioner regarding his or her belief in specific kami.

- **Strict formal doctrines or bodies of religious law:** Beyond a few important "affirmations," the beliefs of this system are basically open-ended, not seen as conflicting with other faiths.

SPIRITUAL SIGNPOST

A kami-dana is a Shelf of the Spirits in the home of a Shinto believer, a miniature depiction of the holy central section of a shrine. In its center is a mirror meant to allow kami a means of entry and exit.

Divine Power

Natural events are considered to be manifestations of heavenly energy within Shinto. Reasoning and dogma are regarded as unnecessary in the face of such forces; only the blessings of the kami are to be sought when one wishes to influence the course of natural forces and events. Accordingly, Shinto places heavy emphasis on reverence toward nature; tradition, family, and ritual; and tranquility, individual ritual purity, and cleanliness.

This last point deserves a closer look. In the West, there is a saying that "cleanliness is next to godliness," but the Japanese conception may be closer to "cleanliness is not distinct from godliness." Because the spirits are regarded as holding disorder and slovenliness in high disdain, a deep concern with bathing, personal cleanliness, and order takes on great importance in Shinto.

SPIRITUAL SIGNPOST

The doctrine of *yorozu-yomi,* or flexibility, allows Shinto to be adapted easily to the lives of many people. Under this principle, it is accepted that there are many kami—kami for every purpose, taking any number of forms. Kami may also be worshipped in any physical location, according to one's taste and inclination.

Core Beliefs

Shinto employs the word "affirmations" in talking about fundamental beliefs. The Japanese term carries the connotation of "things we agree are good." There are four affirmations in Shinto:

1. **The affirmation of family and tradition.** Shinto reveres the major life events, especially rites of birth and marriage. Because traditions are passed on generation by generation, Shinto places extraordinary importance on the central family unit.

2. **The affirmation of reverence toward nature.** The Japanese have a history of respect for physical beauty, perhaps because they live in one of the most beautiful parts of the world. Closeness to nature is a sacred component of Shinto devotion.

3. **The affirmation of physical cleanliness.** Shinto requires not merely symbolic or ritual cleanliness, but the real thing. One must be absolutely clean when one encounters the spirits, and so must one's surroundings!

4. **The affirmation of *matsuri*, or festivals held in honor of one or more kami.** Matsuri represents a chance for people to congregate, socialize, and honor the particular spirit or spirits associated with the festival.

All four of these affirmations have ancient pedigrees, and all four remain essential components of the faith to this day.

A Binding Force

Since its earliest days as a nation, Japan has employed the adaptable forms and practices of Shinto to promote a deep respect for nature and for life-affirming custom, continuity, and tradition. For centuries, in addition to reinforcing notions of sincerity, purity, and cleanliness, Shinto has celebrated divine forces and influence in a distinctively Japanese way.

Today Shinto continues to exert a powerful influence on the Japanese people, often in concert with other traditions. Its supreme adaptability and its avoidance of dogma allow it to flourish in a modern setting, where it can continue to stress the enduring harmony of nature and its relationship to daily life.

The Least You Need to Know

- Shinto is the indigenous religion of Japan; its roots are prehistoric.
- Shinto is a form of nature worship.
- Preeminent among the innumerable Shinto kami, or spirits, is Amaterasu, the sun goddess, regarded as the source of the dynastic line of Japanese emperors.
- Shinto does not promote a system of dogma or a moral code.

- Ritual and tradition are essential to Shinto, as they are to all Japanese culture.
- The four "affirmations"—tradition and family, love for nature, physical cleanliness, and matsuri (festivals honoring the spirits)—guide Shinto practice.

Sikhism: Pursuing the Path of God

27

In This Chapter

- The preaching of Nanak
- The ten gurus
- Who is a Sikh?
- How this book can help you

One day more than 500 years ago, a Punjabi man who had gone missing from his village and had been presumed drowned for some time reappeared quite unexpectedly. To those he encountered, he imparted a mystical—and provocative—pronouncement: "There is no Hindu, there is no Muslim. Whose path, then, shall I follow? I shall follow the path of God."

The man was known as Nanak, and he soon attracted a group of devoted followers. Narak was hailed as the first guru of a new and enduring religious tradition that came to be known as Sikhism. (The word "Sikh" comes from the Punjabi phrase for "student" or "disciple.") Sikhism, which originated in a region in present-day Pakistan, is today based in India.

Sikhism offers important parallels with traditions and principles found within Hinduism and Islam, the two faiths mentioned in Nanak's now-famous utterance. It also sets out a distinctive monotheistic vision, one that is unique to Narak and his successors.

The Guru Speaks

Nanak's preaching complemented the *Bhakti* movement within Hinduism, notably its rejection of heedless ritual and its insistence that God comprises a single reality. He also emphasized the familiar Hindu notion of a cycle of birth, death, and rebirth, and he embraced, as Hinduism does, the principle that release from this cycle was necessary for attaining unity with God.

In addition, Nanak followed Hinduism's emphasis on such activities as the repetition of the name of God (an area of devotional common ground he shared with many other religious traditions). He briskly rejected most other religious rites, however, as obstacles to spiritual advancement. Finally, Nanak followed Hindu tradition in emphasizing the role of the spiritual teacher, or guru, in helping the student to gain insights and, eventually, attain freedom from rebirth.

> **DEFINITION**
>
> **Bhakti** was one of several influential and enduring reform movements active within Hinduism at the time of Guru Nanak's journeys and preachings. It promotes a personal focus on devotion and practice and de-emphasizes ritual for its own sake.

Yet Nanak was, in keeping with Islamic practice and belief, deeply opposed to what he perceived as polytheistic strains within Hinduism. An uncompromising monotheist, he had no tolerance for the statues that supposedly presented multiple manifestations of the Deity—statues that absorbed the time, attention, and devotion of countless Hindu practitioners. Nanak also shared Islam's rejection of the Hindu caste system, and he embraced its fundamental emphasis on human equality in both theological and practical matters. Sikhs of widely varying social positions were, before long, eating and otherwise socializing together (as they do to this day). Last but not least, Nanak's teachings were in alignment with the mystical influence of the Islamic Sufi movement, which placed a heavy emphasis on attaining a meditative state that made a direct encounter with the Divine possible.

In accommodating elements of *both* of the dominant religious traditions prevalent in his world, Nanak beat a new spiritual path—one that reformulated many of the roles, labels, and structures of each system. What was not reformulated was left behind. Indeed, Nanak's new vision simply deleted much of what was considered to be basic, foundational, and religious practice in his era. This included fasting and other forms of asceticism central to the lives of many Hindu believers, pilgrimages to Mecca, declarations of faith, group fasting during Ramadan, structured religious almsgiving, and Qur'an-centered prayer that define the Muslim experience. His was a new (or perhaps a very old) approach to spiritual practice. Not surprisingly, it stirred up controversy and opposition.

> **SPIRITUAL SIGNPOST**
>
> "[God], since I have fallen at your feet, I do not care for anybody else. I do not follow the religious ways preached by various religions believing in Ram, Mohammed, Puran, or Qur'an. The Simritis, Shastras, and the Vedas lay down different doctrines. But I do not recognize any of these. O God, I have written these hymns with your grace and kindness. All that has been said is in fact spoken by you."—Rahras, a Sikh prayer

The Ten Gurus

Nanak was the first in a sequence of ten gurus who influenced and systematized the faith of Sikhism. All ten played important roles in the survival and propagation of the faith. Of particular interest among Nanak's successors are the third, fifth, sixth, and tenth gurus in the line:

- Amar Das, the third guru, relentlessly promoted the idea of salvation within the Sikh belief system. He also instituted distinctive ceremonies to mark the major events in the human lifecycle (birth, death, and marriage) and implemented a centralized system of oversight for local religious practice.

- Arjun, the fifth guru, compiled material from earlier gurus (as well as from Hindu and Islamic sources). This material eventually became the *Adi Granth* (First Book), now the sacred text of Sikhism. Arjun also assumed important political and military responsibilities as the Sikhs came into conflict with the Mughal Empire, the Islamic empire in India.

- Har Gobund, the sixth guru, was a central figure in the creation of an effective, authoritative decision-making process based on the gurmata (guru's decree), an order binding on all Sikhs. This system allowed Sikhs to respond in a unified way to the various challenges they faced.

- Gobind Singh, the tenth guru, formalized the final text of the *Adi Granth*, instituted a ritual of baptism, and declared that the sequence of living gurus would end with him. From this point forward, the sacred text of

Sikhism—known as Guru Granth Sahib—would itself serve as the guru, and thus became the object of devotion in all Sikh *gurdwaras*, or houses of worship.

DEFINITION

Adi Granth, also known as Guru Granth Sahib, is the holiest text of the Sikh religion. A **gurdwara** is a Sikh temple; at last count, there were more than 200 gurdwaras operating in India.

One memorable passage of the scripture the tenth guru elevated to the status of perpetual guru for all Sikhs reads as follows:

> *I observe neither Hindu fasting nor the ritual of the Muslim Ramadan month;*
>
> *Him I serve who at the last shall save.*
>
> *The Lord of universe of the Hindus, Gosain and Allah to me are one;*
>
> *From Hindus and Muslims have I broken free.*
>
> *I perform neither Kaaba pilgrimage nor at bathing spots worship;*
>
> *One sole Lord I serve, and no other.*
>
> *I perform neither the Hindu worship nor the Muslim prayer;*
>
> *To the Sole Formless Lord in my heart I bow. We neither are Hindus nor Muslims;*
>
> *Our body and life belong to the One Supreme Being who alone is both Ram and Allah for us.*
>
> —Guru Granth Sahib, Raga Bhairon

Despite Nanak's distaste for forms and rituals, Gobind Singh, the tenth guru, made a historically critical decision in 1699 to embrace the rite of baptism in a prominent way. This change marked a critical point of development for the faith.

Over time, prominent Sikh leaders were martyred in conflicts with the Islamic Moghul Empire. A long period of military opposition to Islamic rule culminated in the Sikh Empire (1799–1849), which was notable for its pluralism, its tolerance, and its respect for Islamic, Hindu, and Christian belief systems.

Sikhs who are baptized are considered to be initiated in Khalsa. The word literally means "pure," and those who earn the designation are known as Khalsa Sikhs. They are obligated to wear physical articles of faith known as the Five Ks. They are ...

- Kes (uncut hair)

- Kangha (a small comb)

- Kara (a circular iron bracelet)

- Kirpan (a dagger)

- Kaccha (a special undergarment)

These serve as personal reminders of the believer's commitment to the Sikh faith—and as an expression of faith to the outside world. Sahajdhari Sikhs—those who have not yet been baptized—do not wear all Five Ks.

So—Who Is a Sikh?

Although Sikhism is deeply rooted in the historical and cultural experience of the Indian subcontinent, it is not a "closed" faith. Conversion is accepted, and an ongoing debate about the best accommodations to surrounding (non-Sikh) culture has been unfolding for several decades.

Article 1 of the Reht Maryada—the authoritative guide to conduct within the faith—defines a Sikh as follows: Any human being who faithfully believes in

   (i)   One Immortal Being,

  (ii)   Ten Gurus, from Guru Nanak Dev to Guru Gobind Singh,

 (iii)   The Guru Granth Sahib,

 (iv)   The utterances and teachings of the ten Gurus and

  (v)   The baptism bequeathed by the tenth Guru, and who does not owe allegiance to any other religion, is a Sikh.

What Sikhs Believe, What Sikhs Practice

Sikhs believe that the purpose of human life is to overcome egoistic desires, live daily life in harmony with the will of God, behave ethically, and fight for what is good. They believe in avoiding the five cardinal vices: lust, anger, greed, attachment to the physical world, and pride. They believe that reincarnation is inevitable until the point at which one's karma is resolved by means of living a pure life; when karma is resolved, they believe, a merging with God is possible.

> **ON THE PATH**
>
> "Each individual has many reincarnations, but being born a human means the soul is nearing the end of rebirth. God judges each soul at death and may either reincarnate the soul or, if pure enough, allow it to rest with Him."—A modern-day Sikh publication, *Message of Sikhism*, explains Sikhism's stand on the afterlife

Sikhs pray several times a day and are forbidden to worship idols, images, or icons. They are also forbidden to consume alcohol, marijuana, liquor, or any intoxicant.

An interesting remnant of the faith's rejection of the Hindu caste system lies in the requirement that, upon baptism, all Sikh men share the Khalsa name "Singh" (Lion), and all Sikh women share the Khalsa name "Kaur" (Princess). Names served (and still serve) as important status indicators within the Hindu caste system. The creation of common naming elements leveled the social playing field—though of course other names are also used to distinguish individual Sikhs!

> **SPIRITUAL SIGNPOST**
>
> Major Sikh holidays include Vaisakhi Day, an ancient harvest celebration that also commemorates the establishment of the Khalsa baptism ritual in 1699; the birthday of the first Sikh guru, Nanak; and the birthday of the tenth Sikh guru, Gobind Singh.

The most important gurdwara is certainly the magnificent Harmandir Sahib, also known as the Golden Temple of Amritsar. Its four great doors, one on each side of the structure, symbolize Sikhism's openness to visits from practitioners of all faiths and from all corners of the globe. This is the chief shrine of the faith, one of the architectural wonders of the world, and one of India's major tourist destinations. The primacy of Harmandir Sahib among Sikh houses of worship is undisputed, although

Sikh belief insists on the sacredness of any place where the holy text of Sikhism has been installed.

The Sikh Turban

Probably the most noticeable element of Sikh attire is the turban worn by male Sikhs. This garment has been a central part of Sikh tradition since the days of Nanak. The turban shows a personal commitment to all 10 Sikh gurus, and demonstrates the believer's willingness to serve as an instrument of God's will.

Ironically, male Sikhs are sometimes mistaken for Muslims—a faith system that their creed explicitly rejects—because of their observance of the tradition of wearing the turban. (Although some Muslim males choose to wear turbans, their use is not mandated in Islam, nor is any form of male head covering.) In one of the most extreme contemporary examples of the destructive effects of religious intolerance, many American Sikhs were, in the days and weeks following the 9/11 attacks in 2001, assaulted by outraged vigilantes who imagined that the Sikh turbans implied some connection to terrorism. One lesson to be drawn from this sad affair: inflicting violence on total strangers is, at best, an ineffective response to incidents of people inflicting violence on total strangers.

SPIRITUAL SIGNPOST

Some essential information about Sikhism:

- There are more than 26 million practicing Sikhs.
- Roughly three quarters of all Sikhs live in India. Most live in the Punjab state.
- Large Sikh communities also live in the United States, Canada, the United Kingdom, Singapore, and Malaysia.
- Sikhs reject the ideas of a Day of Judgment, heaven, and hell. They accept the doctrine of reincarnation and see paradise as union with the Divine after the cycle of birth and death has been broken.
- Sikhs also reject the concepts of asceticism and celibacy, and view the lifestyle of the householder as the model lifestyle for all people.

The Least You Need to Know

- The first guru of Sikhism, Nanak, rejected both Hinduism and Islam—while at the same time accommodating influences from both traditions.

- Sikhism embraces Hindu beliefs about reincarnation, but condemns the caste system; it embraces Islam's rigorous monotheism and its emphasis on the egalitarianism of spiritual life, but rejects other aspects of Muslim belief and practice.

- The tenth guru, Gobind Singh, established the ritual of Khalsa baptism and installed the Adi Granth, the holiest text of the Sikh religion, as the eleventh and final guru of the Sikh faith.

- Although most Sikhs live in India, there are active Sikh communities in other countries.

Old Paths, New Paths

In this part, you learn about ancient patterns of worship that have evolved in indigenous settings; about other ancient patterns that have been revived or adapted in modern contexts; and about some of the new religious forms, movements, and ideas that have left their mark on the world in recent years. You also find out how the religious traditions you've been studying answer some of the most important human questions. Don't be surprised if you discover some common ground in the process!

Ancient Creeds

In This Chapter

- The three-millennia reign of the Egyptians
- The mythology and religious practices of the Greeks
- The kinship and genealogy of the Maya
- The nature-based religious ceremonies of the Druids
- The highly developed civilization of the Aztecs

In this chapter, we examine five important ancient faiths: those of the ancient Egyptians, Greeks, Mayans, Druids, and Aztecs. Each is fascinating not only for the light its practices and founding myths shed on current systems of belief, but also for the social, cultural, and historical insights it offers into the civilization in which it operated.

Ancient Egyptian Worship

The sheer diversity and scale of ancient Egyptian forms of religious observance are awe-inspiring. A full discussion of the subject is, unfortunately, beyond the scope of this short chapter. What follows is a summary of key points.

Ancient Egyptian Worship: The Cultural/Historical Setting

The native dynasties of ancient Egypt extended from the founding of the First Dynasty circa 3110 B.C.E. to the conquest of the final native rulers of the New Kingdom by Alexander the Great twenty-seven centuries later. Periods of foreign domination intervened at various points during that period; after Alexander, a line of monarchs descended from—and named after—Ptolemy I (previously Alexander's general) ruled the empire.

Cleopatra, queen of the Nile (and daughter of Ptolemy XI), attempted to restore Egyptian power and influence—not least by means of her complex political and personal relationships with Julius Caesar and Mark Antony. Eventually Octavian (later the emperor Augustus Caesar) secured a period of unquestioned Roman control and ended the days of the Egyptian empire. Refer to the 31 B.C.E. portion of the timeline that follows.

SPIRITUAL SIGNPOST

Mummification played an important role in ancient Egyptian religious practice. Ever more elaborate embalming practices evolved over a period of centuries, always with the goal of faithfully preserving the deceased's likeness for eternity. Royal tombs were supplied with treasures meant for enjoyment in the afterlife.

The age, duration, and vitality of the ancient Egyptian civilization, which spanned a period exceeding three millennia, simply boggles the mind. Religious worship was a constant identifying and energizing force throughout this remarkable, and exceptionally long-lived, civilization. A unifying theme of the period of ancient Egyptian empire was the divine or semi-divine nature of the pharaoh, or king. This tradition may well have had social and political origins relating to questions of national unity and identity. The condensed Ancient Egyptian dynasties timeline that follows can serve as an adequate starting point for those interested in familiarizing themselves with some of the principal events.

Old Kingdom (circa 3200–2258 B.C.E.)

- Circa 3200 B.C.E.: Tradition holds that Menes, king of Upper Egypt, subdued the forces of the Lower Delta, forming a united kingdom of Egypt.

- 2884–2780 B.C.E.: Egypt emerges as a major trading nation.

- 2780–2680 B.C.E.: Earliest practice of sun worship is believed to have occurred during this period. Mummification is initiated.

- 2680–2565 B.C.E.: Construction of the great pyramids, monuments to the monarchs whose mummified bodies they house (and to the centrally organized Egyptian nation as a whole).

- 2420–2258 B.C.E.: Period of rising commercial and military influence but steadily weaker and less effective political institutions, culminating in the collapse of the Old Kingdom.

Middle Kingdom (circa 2000–1786 B.C.E.)

- 2000–1786 B.C.E.: After an intermediate period not entirely documented, but during which centralized authority was restored, the Twelfth Dynasty presides over another flourishing Egyptian civilization. Writing standards are formalized and religious life is vibrant.

New Kingdom (circa 1570–31 B.C.E.)

- 1570–circa 1342 B.C.E.: Following a century of rule by the Hyksos, Amasis I ejects this group (which may have been Syrian) and launches the Eighteenth Dynasty, under which the Egyptian civilization ascends to its peak. The boy king Tutankhamen rules during this period.

- Circa 1342–945 B.C.E.: A series of weak rulers ensues; priests rise in influence and maintain a sort of worship-centered de facto government; period of general decline.

- 945–332 B.C.E.: Period notable for domination by outside powers, culminating in conquest under Alexander the Great.

- 323 B.C.E.: Death of Alexander the Great. His general Ptolemy eventually assumes control of Egypt and rules as Ptolemy I, founding a line of Ptolemaic kings, as well as the great library at Alexandria.

- 31 B.C.E.: Cleopatra, daughter of Ptolemy XI and regarded as a divine queen by her people, is defeated with her lover Mark Antony near Actium by the forces of Octavian (afterward the emperor Augustus Caesar). Later, they return to Egypt, but eventually fall to the Romans and commit suicide. Octavian has Cleopatra's son and (titular) joint ruler Ptolemy XIV—almost certainly the issue of Cleopatra's earlier union with Julius Caesar—put to death. The final line of divine Egyptian monarchs comes to an end.

So much for the history. Let's look next at the view of creation taken by the Egyptians.

Two Ancient Egyptian Creation Myths

One version of how the world came into existence: At the beginning, all that existed was Nu, the abyss of chaotic waters. Then the sun god arose from the waters by means of the power of thought.

Having no place to stand, the sun god fashioned a hill, and it is on that hill that the city of Heliopolis (literally, "City of the Sun") was erected. He joined with his own shadow to create a race of gods. Later, Shu and Tefnut got lost in the watery abyss of Nu. The sun god sent his own eye out to find them—and when the eye returned with his offspring, he wept tears of joy. Those tears became the first humans.

SPIRITUAL SIGNPOST

The fact that there are more than one popularly circulated "creation" myths in Egyptian practice gives some sense of the scale and diversity of this faith.

Another version of how the world came into existence: At the beginning, the sun god took on the identity of Khepri, the great scarab god. Khepri created everything—including the watery abyss from which he himself arose. He chose to breathe out air (the god Shu), and then moisture and rain (the goddess Tefnut).

Shu and Tefnut mated and produced earth (the god Geb) and sky (the goddess Nut). At this point, with air, rain, earth, and sky created, the physical universe was in place. Later, Khepri wept when his children brought him his own eye, the sun, which had been hidden from him. His joyful tears were the first humans.

Key Concepts from Ancient Egyptian Observance

Among the most important points to remember about the religious practices of the ancient Egyptians are the following:

SPIRITUAL SIGNPOST

Despite variations in Egyptian creation myths, Geb and Nut were always regarded as parents of Osiris (god of the underworld), Isis (goddess associated with nature and renewal), Seth (sun god who eventually murdered Osiris and who came to represent evil), and Nephthys (faithful comforter of Isis).

- Members of specific clans worshipped animal totems that were regarded as their ancestors. Many of these totems later emerged as gods.

- Major deities included Ra, the sun god; the inexhaustibly popular brother/ sister/husband/wife pair, Isis and Osiris (central figures of the enduring *cult of Isis and Osiris*); Horus, their son; and Thoth, the god of learning. A large number of other gods, many of them combinations of humans and animals, were part of this system of worship.

- There was no single, specific set of ancient Egyptian religious beliefs, but rather a broad collection of practices and group-specific worship systems. As the empire expanded and solidified, however, many of these rituals took on national significance.

- Originally, the Egyptians regarded an afterlife as a privilege obtainable only by mummified kings. Later, during the New Kingdom, elite wealthy Egyptians also began to be accorded preparation for the journey to the next world.

One final note: In the fourteenth century B.C.E., pharaoh Ikhnaton launched an effort to acknowledge Aton as the official national god. It didn't catch on.

DEFINITION

The **cult of Isis and Osiris** was one of the most influential and widespread religious practices of the ancient world. Worship of Isis and celebration of the mysteries related to the resurrection of her husband/brother Osiris spread to Greece, eventually becoming one of the dominant religious traditions of the Roman world. Isis remained an object of pious devotion for a remarkably long period of time; the cult associated with her was active for several centuries after Constantine I's conversion to Christianity.

Ancient Greek Worship

Roughly 4,000 years ago, scholars believe, an invasion by Aryan warriors combined Aryan civilization with that of the Aegeans and Minoans. The likely result: a synthesis that would eventually become Greek culture.

The ancient Greek city-states had an incalculable influence on Western culture, and elements of their mythology and religious practice have pervaded both ancient and modern life.

Ancient Greek Worship: The Cultural/Historical Setting

The vast Greek *pantheon* of gods suggests a combination of the religious practices and images of the Aryan victors with those of the conquered Aegean and Minoan peoples. Zeus, for instance, was the Aryan sky-god; his sister and wife Hera was a fertility goddess of the Aegeans. (These two gods fought a great deal, a situation that may be a reflection of real-life postwar social strife between the former combatants.)

DEFINITION

A **pantheon** is the entire collection of gods featured in a particular culture's mythology.

Speaking very broadly, the great flowering period of Greek civilization occurred between the eighth century B.C.E., when colonies that later emerged as city-states were formed, and 146 B.C.E., when Rome took full control of the often-unstable network of Greek polities. During the glorious interim, Greek religion was a vital shared reference point. Without a common set of religious ideas and rituals, the forever squabbling city-states would probably have had far less of a sense of shared identity and purpose.

SPIRITUAL SIGNPOST

Minor variations on the Greek creation myth are common. This may have something to do with the confluence of cultures and traditions that occurred in a murky period (1100–800 B.C.E.) about which historians still have many questions.

The ancient Greek religion—which emphasized action and the cultivation of one's own personal virtue—helped to bind together a diverse and frequently divided nation whose stunning advances in politics, literature, the arts, philosophy, and architecture echo through virtually all major cultures today.

In no small measure because of their religious values, the Greeks managed, at the right moments, to celebrate intellect, logic, open inquiry, thoughtful living, and creativity in a way that has served for centuries as a model to all humanity.

The Ancient Greek Creation Myth

In the early times, shapeless Chaos reigned over a universe without light, a place where endless night and the vast region of death were the only realities. Then Eros

(Love) sprang forth for reasons humans can never understand or explain, and with Eros arrived light and order. With the arrival of light came Gaea, the earth, daughter of Chaos.

Gaea bore Uranus, heaven-god and first king of the universe. Uranus took his mother Gaea as his wife. Their children included the three Cyclopes (huge one-eyed beings) and the three Hecatoncheires (hundred-handed ones). Later, the 12 Titans were born. The original Titans were the huge children of Uranus and Gaea. Among their number were Cronos, Rhea, Themis, and Oceanus.

> **SPIRITUAL SIGNPOST**
>
> Rhea's sister Titan Themis, symbolizing the principles of order and legality, eventually gave birth to Prometheus—who gave stolen fire to the human race and was punished for this crime by Zeus.

Uranus proved a poor father and husband, mistreating his own progeny, and Gaea fashioned a sickle out of flint and tried to incite her children to attack him. All were terrified at the thought—except Cronos, the youngest of the Titans. Cronos attacked and castrated Uranus, usurping his power. Where drops of Uranus's blood fell on the ground, the Furies sprang to life, ferocious pursuers of those who commit murder. Where Uranus's blood fell in the sea emerged Aphrodite, the exquisite goddess of love and fertility.

Cronos wed his sister Rhea and ruled as king of the Titans. Convinced that one of his own would rise up against him, Cronos swallowed his first five newborn children alive. To save the life of her sixth child, Rhea tricked Cronos into eating a stone wrapped in swaddling clothes. She hid her child among the nature goddesses known as nymphs, who raised the infant—named Zeus—secretly.

Grown to adulthood, Zeus disguised himself, returned to Cronos's domain, and tricked him with a drink. As he choked on Zeus's potion, Cronos coughed up the five children he had consumed. Zeus had thus reclaimed the lives of Hestia, Demeter, and Hera (his sisters), and Pluto and Poseidon (his brothers).

There followed a fierce battle against Cronos and the Titans loyal to him; Zeus prevailed and overthrew his father. He cast lots with his brothers, and it was determined that Pluto would rule the underworld and Poseidon would rule the sea, with Zeus exercising dominion over heaven and earth. Zeus, an amorous monarch, reigned at Mount Olympus as king of all gods.

Key Concepts from Ancient Greek Observance

Among the most important points to remember about ancient Greek worship are the following:

- The Greek pantheon included Zeus, the god of heaven; Hera, his sister/wife; Demeter, the earth mother; Apollo, who was connected with divination, the arts, medicine, and certain higher intellectual pursuits, and who watched over flocks; Hermes the war god; and many, many others.

- Greek practice emphasized mystery cults—secret groups led by a priest or other officiant that typically incorporated initiation rituals, some kind of purification ceremony, display of holy relics, dramatic recital elements, and dispersal of unique wisdom.

- The Eleusinian Mysteries were perhaps the most prominent mysteries of the period. The secrecy surrounding a number of their specific practices appears to have endured, but scholars do know that the rites involved the goddess Demeter and her daughter Persephone's return from the underworld. The Eleusinian Mysteries emphasized the immortality of the soul and the permanence of divine renewal.

- The Dionysian and Orphic Mysteries were also important to the Ancient Greeks. Dionysius was the god of wine and of sensual revelry; Orphic observance incorporated hymns and aimed at a final triumph over death.

- *Oracles*, such as the one at Delphi, were vital locations of Greek worship; so were the specific temples of gods associated with particular city-states and the healing centers dedicated to Aesculapius, the god of medicine.

- The philosopher Plato (427–347 B.C.E.) strongly influenced Greek religious practice. In the centuries following his teaching, Greek worship moved away from the idea (frequently expressed in Homer's writings) that the trials of humans served as amusements for the often-capricious gods of Olympus—and toward a devotional conception of ultimate underlying reality and the perfection of form.

DEFINITION

An **oracle** is the pronouncement of an officiant, offered at a shrine or in some other holy setting, as the divine answer to a believer's question. An oracle can also be the agency regarded as the source of that response.

One more point before we leave Greek religious observance: The region remained a cultural and religious center, and thus an influence on various ancient forms of worship, for some centuries after its annexation by Rome.

Ancient Mayan Worship

Renowned for their pyramidal structures, their arts, and their mathematical system, the Maya of ancient times operated under a complex theocracy that, like that of the Aztecs, emphasized calendar-making. Their descendants occupy roughly the same regions of what is now southern Mexico and Central America. Modest rural settlements have characterized the region for centuries.

Ancient Mayan Worship: The Cultural/Historical Setting

The zenith of the agriculturally centered Mayan civilization, one of the most important pre-Columbian peoples, occurred between 300 and 900 C.E. The reason for the gradual depopulation of their great cities between 900 and 1100 C.E. has been a subject of continuing debate.

SPIRITUAL SIGNPOST

Why did the Maya desert their cities? Was there an environmental collapse? An incursion from another tribe that forced the exodus, but did not subdue the people as a whole? Some other catastrophe? In recent years, some have argued that the available evidence indicates that large numbers of Maya commoners left population centers to avoid being selected as victims of human sacrifice rituals. It's an interesting notion; the debate continues.

At its height, the Mayan civilization appears to have operated not under a single ruler, but as a loosely organized gathering of semi-autonomous cities and villages. These units seem to have emphasized kinship and genealogy as important social and religious factors. Ties to the earth were always vitally important. Advances in agricultural techniques supported population growth in the ancient Mayan culture—and, by extension, the accompanying breakthroughs in mathematics, calendar-making, architecture, and the arts for which the old civilization is best known today.

The Ancient Mayan Creation Myth

In ancient times, before there were people, the gods Tepeu and Gucumatz reigned. If they thought something, it came into existence. When they thought about the earth, it was born. When they thought about trees, or mountains, or any other feature of the landscape, it came forth. The moment they thought about animals, the animals were there.

Tepeu and Gucumatz soon realized, though, that something important was missing. Nothing that they had created was capable of praising them. And so they decided to create people. The first people were made of clay—but the gods found that these dissolved when they got wet. The next people were fashioned from wood, but they were troublemakers, and so the gods sent a flood to rectify their mistake and start anew. Finally the gods appealed to the mountain lion, the coyote, the parrot, and the crow to help them find the right material from which to build superior beings. The animals found corn, and it was from corn that the gods created the Four Fathers from which all humanity traces its lineage.

Key Concepts from Ancient Mayan Observance

Among the most important points to remember about the ancient religious practices of the Maya are the following:

- The Maya placed a high degree of faith in the ability of the gods to control and order events and human undertakings within specific time periods.

- Nature, time, and agriculture were preoccupations of religious life—and, indeed, of life as a whole—in Mayan society.

- Like the religion of the Aztec peoples of central Mexico, Mayan religion incorporated elements of human sacrifice to appease key gods.

- Among the many other important deities were Kinich Ahau, the sun god; Chaac, the rain god; and the Maize god, strongly associated with the central obsession of the culture as a whole—ripened and healthy corn.

- Mayan mythology postulated four brother-gods who held up the sky. Each presided over a four-year span of time and represented one of the four directions. Colors associated with each of these deities were essential to Mayan religious and calendar-making practices.

- Current scholarship suggests that ancestor worship was an important part of life in ancient Mayan civilizations.

Descendants of the ancient Mayans are alive and well in the region. Roman Catholicism has been the dominant religion since the Spanish conquest of the 1500s; however, many original traditions (including native religious practices) have been intertwined with their European counterparts.

Ancient Druidic Worship

Druids were ancient priests who led nature-based religious ceremonies in Celtic Britain and other European regions. The Druids are known to have been active in the third century B.C.E. Archeological discoveries led to intense popular interest in Druidic practices during the eighteenth and nineteenth centuries.

> **BARRIER ALERT!**
>
> A common misconception associates the Druids with the creation of the huge primeval stone monuments of France and Britain. Although these mysterious edifices were once credited by scholars to the Druids and assumed to have been built as an expression of their religious practice, archaeologists have since concluded that the structures are actually older than even Celtic culture. The history and purpose of sites such as Stonehenge remain obscure. They may have been intended as observatories, or as centers of religious worship, or both.

The Druids: The Cultural/Historical Setting

What we know about the Druids' history arises primarily from what the Romans wrote about them. We learn from Julius Caesar that Druids in Gaul formed a federation that crossed over tribal boundaries, and it seems likely that a similar system operated in Britain. The Romans also noted that Druids met annually and exercised great influence over political and social matters.

In Gaul, Druids were fierce but ill-fated adversaries to Rome. Not even the Roman seizure of southern Britain in the first century C.E. and illegalization of native rituals, however, could completely eliminate Druidic practice, which moved to outlying areas and were branded as *pagan*, a term that endured for centuries.

Under attack from Rome, Druidic practice lost much of its political potency. It eventually yielded to the advance of Christianity in Britain circa 600 C.E., although suppressed rituals and oral teachings appear to have persisted in some quarters for many years after that. Modern practices based on Druidic concepts have become increasingly popular in recent years as contemporary seekers, eager to find or adapt alternative modes of religious expression, have become more familiar with the trials endured by early practitioners of Druidic rites.

It is important to bear in mind that the word "Druid" describes not a religion per se, but an elite class of revered and respected Celtic officiants gathered within a powerful network based on common practice and outlook. In their day, Druids appear to have performed the roles taken today by members of the clergy, scholars, judges, civic planners, teachers, and even entertainers. Druids also engaged in divination and nature-based worship rituals, leading to later (misleading) dismissals of their work as that of "soothsayers" or "wizards."

It is probably closer to the truth to think of the Druids as an ancient Celtic political and religious network that connected like-minded practitioners within a given region. They were far-sighted, experienced, and highly esteemed members of the community—the "movers and shakers" of their day.

SPIRITUAL SIGNPOST

The available evidence suggests the existence of female Druids, but the record is too sketchy for us to draw any meaningful conclusions about their role or social status within their communities.

(Conjecture on an) Ancient Druidic Creation Myth

Little is certain of how the Druids explained the origin of the universe, but some scholars have conjectured that the appearance of egglike objects and egg symbols in ancient Druid mysticism reflects a belief in a "hatching myth" involving an egg as the original source of all things. Such a myth would, of course, emphasize a powerful fertility symbol wholly appropriate within a creation account.

The egg's role in (hypothetical) Druidic creation stories remains a matter of debate, but it is certain that the Roman historian Pliny recorded having seen a "Druid's Egg," a diminutive relic purported to have been assembled from the dried expectoration of snakes. According to the Druid from Gaul described by Pliny, the egg was held to have restorative powers.

Key Concepts from Ancient Druidic Practice

Among the most important points to remember about the religious practices of the Druids are the following:

- The title "Druid" (which appears to mean "oak knowledge") was bestowed only on highly regarded members of the community—people who then served as religious officiants and performed a variety of other important social functions.

- Druidic practice seems to have focused on a vast array of nature gods (or, to use a modern term coined by Joseph Campbell, noted writer and lecturer in the field of mythology, "living presences"); sacrifice of animals and humans was part of religious practice.

- The Celts did have written language, but the Druids seem to have maintained an exclusively oral transmission of their rites. This may be a mark of the secrecy and exclusivity of their practice.

- Services took place near lakes and rivers and in tree groves. The oak and the mistletoe were regarded as holy plants.

- Suppression of the Druids led to the rise of the "bardic school," which kept Druidic practices alive by means of the relation of myths, quasi-historical heroic stories, and songs.

- Druidic practice today is associated strongly with Ireland because Roman authority did not extend as far as the Emerald Isle. Druidic practice thrived in Ireland until the people there were converted to Christianity and the old rites were put down.

Various Neo-Druid movements have gained popularity in the West in recent years.

Ancient Aztec Worship

The Aztec were the native people who had for centuries enjoyed primacy in central Mexico at the time the Spanish conquered the territory in the sixteenth century C.E. The Aztec priesthood and the religious practices it promulgated served as organizing elements of a centralized and highly developed civilization—one whose achievements in astronomy, engineering, and architecture astonished Europeans.

Aztec Worship: The Cultural/Historical Setting

The Aztecs were a small and struggling itinerant tribe when they wandered into the Valley of Mexico sometime in the twelfth century C.E. They founded their capital, Tenochtitlán, early in the fourteenth century C.E., and maintained a tenuous sovereignty by making tribute payments to nearby tribes.

Sometime in the fifteenth century C.E., a warrior culture began to flourish—reinforced, no doubt, by the creation myth that appears in the section that follows. Aztec leaders used a skillful combination of religious observance, diplomacy, careful social organization, flexibility in adapting the practices of other tribes, and expert warfare to raise their civilization to a position of supremacy in central Mexico.

Aztec religious tradition assumed a centrality that focused and galvanized the populace—and may well have led to the nation's undoing. When the Spaniard Hernán Cortés led his mission to Mexico in 1519, he and his men were seen by the Aztec ruling class not as European invaders, but as descendants of the ancient Toltec god Quetzalcoatl, long prophesied to return.

Playing upon this belief, Cortés was able to take hostage the emperor Montezuma II (himself regarded by the Aztec people as divine), thus paralyzing the Aztec social system for a time. Later, Cortés mobilized Indian groups that had been chafing under Aztec domination. So it was Cortés that put down the Aztec rebellion that eventually followed his kidnapping of the emperor. The Spanish soon overran Tenochtitlán, destroyed it, and assumed control of Mexico.

SPIRITUAL SIGNPOST

A social system comprised of a noble elite, a politically powerful priestly class, and a warrior/mercantile class led the Aztec people to extraordinary accomplishments in the arts, agriculture, mathematics, calendar-making, and many other areas.

The Ancient Aztec Creation Myth

The lord and lady of duality, Ometecuhlti and his wife, Omelcihuatl, brought into existence all things. The birth of Huitzilopochtli, the great god of the sun and of war, occurred in the following manner: Coatlicue, She Who Wears the Serpent Skirt, was mother of the moon goddess and her 400 brothers. Crisis and universal dissolution loomed, however, when she inadvertently became pregnant again after having tucked a blue feather in her serpent-skirt. The new birth was certain to infuriate her first brood of children, as a goddess was expected to give birth once and only once.

The new god within her, however, assured her that he would protect them both, and Coatlicue took a confident stance at the Serpent Mountain, Coatepec, as she awaited the onslaught of her own children. Huitzilopochtli came forth from her womb fully armed and slew his brothers and sister, scattering them across the face of the universe. His sister, the cold moon, he beheaded; his dead brothers are the shining stars.

Key Concepts from Ancient Aztec Observance

Among the most important points to remember about the religious practices of the Aztec people are the following:

- Ometecuhlti and his wife, Omelcihuatl, who brought about all creation, were regarded as having chosen the Aztec people above others for special favor.

- Aztec belief also held that friendly gods required constant appeasement; failure to keep benevolent gods happy would result in the destruction of the earth by malevolent deities.

- To keep the gods who protected them satisfied, the Aztec maintained a ritual of human sacrifice.

- Those sacrificed were generally prisoners of war. Occasionally, however, Aztec warriors would volunteer to be sacrificed.

- The Aztec people were closely focused on calendar-making; their intricate calendar combined a 365-day solar year with a 260-day holy period.

- Important Aztec deities included Tezcoptipcoca, the sun god, and Tlaloc, the rain god. There were many others.

One final observation on the Aztecs: The collapse of their theocracy in the face of Spanish forces was certainly hastened by their own suppression of neighboring peoples.

The Least You Need to Know

- Ancient Egypt boasted an almost incomprehensibly vast and diverse religious tradition, one highlight of which was the remarkably resilient cult of Isis and Osiris.
- Elements of ancient Greek mythology and religious practice have pervaded both ancient and modern life.
- The Maya of ancient times operated under a complex theocracy that emphasized calendar-making and ties to the earth.
- Druids were ancient priests who led nature-based religious ceremonies in Celtic Britain and other European regions.
- Aztec leaders used a skillful combination of religious observance, diplomacy, careful social organization, flexibility in adapting the practices of other tribes, and expert warfare to raise their civilization to a position of supremacy in central Mexico.

Nonscriptural Nature Religions

In This Chapter

- Common obstacles awaiting outsiders seeking to understand traditional faiths
- Some common elements of traditional Pacific Island, African, and Native American ritual and observance
- Huna Kupua, an indigenous Hawaiian worship tradition of great antiquity
- Important ideas that guide traditional African and Native American religious practice

In this chapter, you learn about the distinctive features of some important non-scriptural, nature-oriented religious traditions, and you find out about some of the obstacles to understanding indigenous faiths.

Before you proceed any further, please understand: there are countless indigenous religious traditions that operate beyond the scope of the regions selected for this chapter. We have chosen to look at some Pacific Island, African, and Native American religious practices because these practices have been the subject of keen interest in the United States in recent years. We acknowledge, though, that many other traditional patterns of devotion are worthy of study in other parts of the world.

Indeed, there are more than 100 million practitioners of traditional religions worldwide. Remember, though, that even the use of the word "religion" must be considered carefully in any discussion of indigenous faiths, because many of these traditions do not draw clear distinctions between everyday life and formal religious practices. All life, in other words, is religious and the systems discussed (in broad terms) in this chapter usually accept that principle.

Inside, Outside

Most of the faiths described by the word "traditional" are experiential, rather than intellectual. This makes any formulation of "core principles" something of a challenge. All these patterns of worship demand respect and understanding from the outsiders who wish to learn more about them.

This is another way of saying that assessing an indigenous set of traditions is a tricky business. Such observations may result in belittling designations such as "savage" or "primitive," or a well-intentioned but equally condescending tendency to romanticize "simpler" pre-technological societies.

Unique local traditions usually emphasize familiar cosmologies and the divinity of observable natural processes. Initially, they may not be set in opposition to any other system. It is a common mistake to define traditional religions outside of European or Asian experience by emphasizing the ways in which they differ from that experience. A similar problem arises in the description of traditional faiths by means of what they are not or do not possess.

As colonial expansion unfolded over the past 500 years, outsiders took on the task of creating labels for religions that remained free from colonial influence, or that somehow managed to survive in spite of that influence. Such labels are for the convenience of the outsiders themselves, and contribute little value to those inside the religions. Traditional religions exist on their own terms. They typically meet the needs of a body of believers who view themselves, not as a tribe or group separate from "dominant" (i.e., external) historical patterns, but simply as "the people."

Outsiders (such as the authors of this book) must always be careful in describing or assessing faiths that present racial, social, or cultural uniqueness. Such outsiders should be aware that in applying labels to these practices, they might be describing only their own preconceptions, not the most important facets of a differing tradition.

Ideas That Stay

Some traditional religious practices have been carefully preserved by native groups; there are also thousands of active contemporary tribal communities whose members subscribe to traditional religions. Most, but not all, of the practices in these groups are strongly associated with village or tribal settings.

Although it is dangerous to make too many generalizations about these groups and their belief systems, some commonalities are definitely worth exploring. The following three elements are familiar:

- The *shaman*
- The totem
- The fetish

> **DEFINITION**
>
> A **shaman** is a religious celebrant who is considered to possess more than human powers, including the ability to understand and treat diseases. Shamans may also, in some cases, bring about illness, a consideration that frequently leaves them both feared and respected in the community. Their powers derive from their interaction with, and influence over, certain spirits. Other English terms for the shaman include "medicine man" and "witch doctor."

The Shaman

There are many types of shamanistic practice, but a single idea guides those who operate as shamans within tribal societies: the world humans see is occupied by forces that cannot be perceived with the naked eye—forces that may exert positive or negative influence on human affairs. Unlike priests, for whom religious ritual and observance is a permanent vocation, shamans enter into temporary trances to perform their work as circumstances arise.

Shamans must acquire particular skills. They may inherit their titles from their forebears or be summoned to their calling through dreams, visions, or even possession. They are generally paid for their efforts. They may be either men or women, although male shamans are most common.

> **SPIRITUAL SIGNPOST**
>
> Traditions and rituals act as a binding force in indigenous African religious practice, just as they do elsewhere in the world. Tribal groups place special emphasis on community ties and values. Village elders and respected spiritual authorities are charged with the important task of handing down expressions of faith and rituals that will encourage harmonious social practices … and sustain and reinforce the group during times of trial.

The Totem

A totem is a particular object (generally a plant or animal) held in reverence and regarded as an ancestor or sibling by members of a group. Totemism is prevalent in both North America and Africa. Totems carry important social, ritualistic, and mystical associations, and are today strongly associated with indigenous peoples of the Pacific Northwest in North America. The word "totem" comes from the peoples of that region.

The spirit made manifest by the totem may serve as a powerful unifying element among members of a tribe, familial grouping, or other nonblood related grouping. Given its role as a protector and/or family member, a sacred animal or variety of plant may be declared off-limits by members of the totemic group in its "ordinary" use. (In other words, you can't eat them.) Symbolism associated with a totem may serve as an identifying mark for the group in question. In a number of societies, marriage among members of the same totemic group is prohibited.

SPIRITUAL SIGNPOST

For Native Americans, one of the more bitter legacies of the "settlement" of North America by European immigrants and their descendants is the mistreatment of natural forms. The tragedy of modern "development," from the Native American perspective, should be understood not merely as the desecration of particular sacred sites, but as a wide-ranging disrespect for the earth.

The Fetish

No, we're not talking about psychoanalysis. Before the term "fetish" was appropriated by Western clinicians to describe an erotic fixation, it was used by anthropologists to describe inanimate objects held by believers to hold magical powers or even an independent will. The term is employed here in a nonjudgmental way, and not as an indictment of "irrationality" or "superstition" among traditional believers.

Such reverence for and awe of natural or man-made objects is a distinctive feature of many traditional religions, many of which are considered potentially dangerous if mishandled, and so are subjected to rigorous controls. Although fetishism in traditional practice expresses itself in distinctive and recognizable ways, traditional religions are certainly not the only systems that promote or reinforce the reverence of objects. An argument can be made that some form of fetishism underlies virtually all religious worship and observance.

Huna Kupua

One particularly long-running example of nature worship can be found in the fiftieth state. The system of esoteric wisdom known as *Huna* Kupua found in the Hawaiian Islands is thought to have existed in Polynesia for many thousands of years. It celebrates nature and emphasizes ideas of deep self-perception and an ongoing interrelationship with all existence. Its worship practices were handed down across countless generations as part of an oral tradition. There is one basic commandment within Huna Kupua: "Harm no one and nothing with hate."

DEFINITION

Huna means "secret." It also reflects a deeper traditional concept that has been defined as follows: "The science of the control of universal life energies through the control of the mind and breath."

Here are some of the core ideas of the Huna tradition:

- The **Seven Principles** describe the initial assumptions of the Huna philosophy. They serve as a structural guide to the faith by offering insights on human perception of reality. (The first of the Seven Principles is "The World Is What You Think It Is.")

- The concept of the **Three Selves** (or the **Four Selves**) explores the Huna view of the self as existing in multiple levels. From the Huna viewpoint, each quality of "selfness" resides within a distinct realm of perception and contributes a unique aspect of personal experience. The development and interaction of the various qualities at each level is believed to have a direct relation upon one's connection to and integration with the Higher Self.

- The Huna understanding of the **Four Levels of Reality** holds all things to be simultaneously objective (reflecting scientific reality), subjective (reflecting psychic reality), symbolic (reflecting shamanic reality), and holistic (reflecting mystical reality). The Kupua (that is, healer or shaman) is able to exist in and move through these various realities to effect whatever changes are deemed necessary.

The practice of what is now known as Huna Kupua only narrowly survived contact with Western missionaries in the nineteenth and twentieth centuries. Most of what is now known about this religious practice arose from research begun in 1920, and was carried out over the next five decades by a remarkable gentleman named Max Freedom Long.

Long devoted his life to searching out and interviewing people with firsthand experience of the practice. His invaluable research led to a series of books on the subject. Max Freedom Long, quoted on www.huna.org: "We must be ready with understanding to love (through Aloha-Lani) and to welcome with open arms the drawing near of the Mate, our Beloved. We must have learned to give everything, holding back nothing of ourselves. We must be eager to learn and to serve and to love."

ON THE PATH

"In its simplest form, a Huna prayer works this way: the conscious mind, by conscious breathing and by conscious effort of will, calls mentally for a surcharge of energy to be created and brought up to its level. By continuous breathing and a further effort of the will the energy is stepped up even higher. Then with proper visualizations and words this high energy is sent down to the subconscious and … to the High Self. When all this is done correctly, miracles happen."

—Dr. Jonathan Parker, Ph.D., "Ancient Huna Secrets" (article available at www. quantumquests.com)

As the twentieth century wound down, more and more Americans and Europeans were, like Long, captivated by the beauty, subtlety, and profundity of this ancient body of belief and practice.

African Traditions

Traditional African believers pursue many paths and assign many names to the Supreme Being.

The Names of God

Some of these names emphasize the deity's creative capacity; others call attention to God's role as a great parent or ancestor, either male or female. Some African peoples revere the pervasive universal force as "the Source of All Being," "the One Who Is Ever Present," "the Great Providence Who Determines Destinies," or "the One Who Is Never Fully Known." A supreme God who acts as a universal sustainer is a common feature of African traditional observance.

Spirits, Good and Bad

Most groups also acknowledge the influence of spirits and ancestral entities who operate beneath the level of the high God. Practitioners rely on the most benevolent of these to overcome the influence of the wicked forces with which humans must always contend.

As a practical matter, traditional African spiritual groups accept the influences of these spirits as more immediate factors in everyday life than direct contact with the Supreme Being. In other words, immediate encounters with the Divine often prove as elusive for an African traditional believer as for her American Catholic counterpart, who might, for instance, appeal to St. Anthony for help in locating a lost article.

SPIRITUAL SIGNPOST

Developed by the Yoruba peoples of Western Africa many thousands of years ago, the tradition known as Ifa emphasizes internal tranquility and personal autonomy. Its practice was transmitted to the Americas by enslaved African tribespeople; today, it is the subject of renewed interest in America and continued practice in Africa.

Ifa practitioners hold that all things in the universe were created by the ever-constant and unchanging Supreme Head who retains the fullness of all things, known as Olodumare. They also regard Olodumare as the "source being" who imparts rationality, or essential being, to humanity. They believe that Olodumare determines and controls human destiny, and that all of existence operates within the control of Olodumare.

Ifa regards with reverence numerous orisa, or potent messenger spirits, whose energy and support humans may cultivate. For a discussion of a "new religion" that incorporates elements of traditional African and Roman Catholic practice, and that, like Ifa, venerates orisa, see the section on Santeria in Chapter 31.

The Ifa faith emphasizes piety, humility, concern for others, personal strength, tolerance, and a strict moral code that countenances no swindling or double-dealing. It is a joyous, practical system of belief that sets great store by social propriety and moral righteousness.

Native American Traditions

For all their tribal and historical differences (and these are not insignificant!), all Native American peoples share a profound and deeply spiritual reverence for the natural world and their land.

Within Native American spirituality, natural forms and processes are seen as containing fundamental creative powers; all processes, human and nonhuman, are seen as inextricably linked. Native American religion does not draw clear lines between natural and supernatural events. It's no wonder that societies that are out of balance with nature are regarded as spiritually deficient by many believers within these traditions.

The twentieth century's systematic desecration and abuse of systems formerly regarded as being in divine balance is seen as having left lasting wounds to the earth and to Native American spiritual practices.

BARRIER ALERT!

The many forms of Native American spirituality are often seen by believers as systems of belief and practice affecting all aspects of life, and not as formal or external matters of devotion that are somehow unrelated to other parts of life. Thus, attempts to separate "environmental issues" or "mythological accounts" from "religious matters" may be seen as insensitive and/or ill-informed.

All Together Now

Monotheism in the familiar sense of the word is not a primary feature of Native American religions. Instead, there is an understanding of physical and emotional interconnectedness among all beings. (Many of these groups, for instance, have preserved traditions that carry both spiritual and medical significance.)

All the same, a number of modern Native American groups have developed terminology that employs a single word or phrase for the collection of spiritual forces to be found in the six directions: North, South, East, West, Sky, and Earth.

SPIRITUAL SIGNPOST

The Vision Quest, common in many Native American systems, is a period during which a boy celebrates the onset of puberty by means of solitary meditation, fasting, and tests of physical endurance. (Girls are not generally permitted to engage in the ritual.) The participant's aim: to bring about a vision that will guide him in later life, and to earn the support and protection of a guardian spirit.

Integrity

Although there are many variations and cultural influences within Native American religious practice, an emphasis on balance, completion, and integrity is pervasive. Rituals within the various traditions are meant to promote an appreciation for the cycles of life and death and for harmonious community action.

Contact!

Many forms of observance involve purification rites, coming-of-age rituals (such as the Vision Quest), and mystical ceremonies meant to enable a fuller understanding of human life and the natural world. These rites frequently incorporate some form of direct contact with important spirits, contact that is seen as beneficial not only for the individual but for the community as a whole.

In other words, individuals may bring their own lives—and the day-to-day activities of their social groups—into greater coherence through personal contact and ongoing relationships with particular spiritual forces.

> **SPIRITUAL SIGNPOST**
>
> *Wakan Tanka* is a Lakota term describing the sum total of all spiritual entities. A parallel Ojibwa phrase is *K'che Manitou*. Such expressions do not reflect a personified single God, but rather the aggregate of various embodied spiritual forces.

The Least You Need to Know

- Traditional beliefs are often misunderstood by those who want to connect them to familiar outsider practices.
- Most of the faiths described by the word "traditional" are experiential, rather than intellectual.
- The shaman, the totem, and the fetish are important components of traditional religious systems.
- Huna Kupua is a particularly long-lived example of a nonscriptural nature religion.

- Many African religious systems acknowledge a supreme God (who goes by various names) and an array of lower spirits.
- Many Native American traditions emphasize personal wholeness within sacred natural processes.

Mystic Voices

In This Chapter

- What is mysticism?
- The Kabbalah
- Sufism and Rumi
- The Christian mystic tradition and Thomas à Kempis

Each of the world's major religious traditions carries, within it, one or more mystical movements. Mysticism is the desire for some kind of personal union with the Divine.

That's the simplest description we can offer; a longer one would have to consider a good many philosophical movements based on mysticism. These philosophical schools can be quite complex, but they all boil down to an interest in the specifics of a personal union with the Divine—and the means by which such a union is achieved.

Mystical movements, in other words, are all about direct contact. They are, frequently, less concerned with the social or practical questions a religion or social system must confront, and more concerned with encountering the Divine Reality straight on. Mystical movements have frequently suffered persecution and oppression from the religious authorities of the tradition they represent, yet they are remarkably persistent. They also have a way of "cross-pollinating" each other—that is, influencing complementary mystical movements that arise in very different faith systems.

This chapter introduces you to three of the most interesting and influential mystical traditions: the Kabbalah, Sufism, and the Christian mystic tradition reflected in the writings of Thomas à Kempis. Each is distinctive, and each stands alone. Yet each supports the desire for a complete and deeply personal union, within its own faith system, between God and the believer.

Let the Mystics Do the Talking

By definition, mystical religious movements are, well, hard to define. They frequently attempt to penetrate to the heart of their respective scriptures rather than simply engaging in weighty theological debates.

Because the focus of most mystical religious movements is usually on transcending dogma and intellectual analysis, this chapter will offer a brief historical summary of each of the three movements, and then let the texts and traditions of the movement in question do most of the talking.

The Kabbalah

The Kabbalah is a system of thought within Judaism that interprets the Hebrew scriptures in the light of a tradition believed to extend all the way back to the patriarch Abraham. Even though its adherents piously believe this lineage to be true, modern scholars are more skeptical and track the Kabbalah—at least in its present formulation—to eleventh-century France. Adherents of the system insist that there are important precedents to this eleventh-century Kabbalah, precedents that emphasize ways of deriving special spiritual insights from the texts and date from much earlier times.

The Kabbalistic interpretation of the Hebrew scriptures insists that there is spiritual value to be derived from the close study of their every syllable, and that the names of God possess special power. Understanding these mysteries, according to custom, is a goal requiring instruction from those well versed in the tradition.

Kabbalistic thought has been closely linked with both mystic experience and the historical development of the Hasidic Jews. Its main texts are the *Torah*, the *Zohar*, a commentary on the Torah, and the *Sefer Yezirah*, or Book of Creation.

Modern interpretation of the Kabbalistic tradition has taken many forms.

Following are some examples of the "voices" of the Kabbalah:

> *A person's highest spiritual potential is to reach the level of maaseh merkavah ("the act of rule"). He is able to correct himself to such an extent that Divine Providence over the world can be executed through that person.* (Talmud, Suka)

> *It is forbidden to study the Kabbalah for any purpose other than spiritual elevation.* (Talmud, Sanhedrin)

The Torah is concealed. It is only revealed to those who have reached the level of the righteous. (Talmud, Hagiga)

The Torah is the Light of the Creator, and only a person who receives this light is considered as learning Torah (rather than just acquiring mere wisdom). (Zohar, Metzorah)

The most important aspect of the process of self-improvement is the cultivation of one's sense of humility before the Creator. This, however, should not be an artificial undertaking, but a goal of one's efforts. If, as a result of working on the self, an individual gradually starts to develop this quality, then it means that he is proceeding in the right direction. (Talmud, Avodah Zarah)

A human being is born as an absolute egoist, and this quality is so visceral that it can convince him that he has already become righteous and has rid himself of all egoism. (Talmud, Hagiga)

The lower a person feels, the closer he comes to his true state and to the Creator. (Talmud, Sota)

When a person, by means of his studies, reaches the level at which he wants nothing but spiritual elevation and at which he accepts only the bare necessities of life to sustain his physical existence, not for pleasure's sake, this is the first step of his ascent to the spiritual world. (Talmud, Psachim)

Who can imagine a world that is not filled by the Creator? (Talmud, Shabbat)

SPIRITUAL SIGNPOST

To learn more about the Kabbalah, check out the article *Judaism 101: Kabbalah and Jewish Mysticism* by Dr. James Kiefer. It's available at www.jewfaq.org/kabbalah.htm.

Sufism

The Sufis were and are the sustainers of the great mystical tradition within Islam. The term refers to a variety of ascetic movements that have spun through Islam. As a point of history, some of the followers of these movements were persecuted for their beliefs, but the Sufi emphasis on direct contact with Allah remains strong to this day.

Sufism influenced, and was influenced by, some early Christian traditions.

The best-known Sufi figure is probably Rumi, the great Persian writer of the thirteenth century. A few of his extraordinary observations follow:

> *Quit thy wealth, even if it be the realm of Saba; Thou wilt find many realms not of this earth. What thou callest a throne is only a prison; Thou thinkest thyself enthroned, but art outside the door. Thou hast no sovereignty over thine own passions, How canst thou turn away good and evil? Thy hair turns white without thy concurrence, Take shame for thy evil passions. Whoso bows his head to the King of Kings Will receive a hundred kingdoms not of this world; But the delight of bowing down before God Will seem sweeter to thee than countless glories.* (Masnavi, Book 4, Story 2)

> *Would he had been less full of borrowed knowledge! Then he would have accepted inspired knowledge from his father. When, with inspiration at hand, you seek booklearning, Your heart, as if inspired, loads you with reproach. Traditional knowledge, when inspiration is available, Is like making ablutions in sand when water is near. Make yourself ignorant, be submissive, and then You will obtain release from your ignorance.* (Masnavi, Book 4, Story 2)

> *Sell your cleverness and buy bewilderment; Cleverness is mere opinion, bewilderment intuition.* (Masnavi, Book 4, Story 2)

> *Reason is like an officer when the king appears; The officer then loses his power and hides himself. Reason is God's shadow; God is the sun. What power has the shadow before the sun?* (Masnavi, Book 4, Story 4)

> *How long wilt thou dwell on words and superficialities? A burning heart is what I want; consort with burning! Kindle in thy heart the flame of love, And burn up utterly thoughts and fine expressions. O Moses! the lovers of fair rites are one class, They whose hearts and souls burn with love are another.* (Masnavi, Book 2, Story 7)

> *Why hast thou said "I have sinned so much, And God of His mercy has not punished my sins?" Thou sayest the very reverse of the truth, O fool! Wandering from the way and lost in the desert! How many times do I smite thee, and thou knowest not? Thou art bound in my chains from head to foot. On thy heart is rust on rust collected, So thou art blind to divine mysteries.* (Masnavi, Book 2, Story 15)

> *I regard not the outside and the words, I regard the inside and the state of the heart. I look at the heart if it be humble, Though the words may be the reverse of humble. Because the heart is substance and the words accidents.* (Masnavi, Book 2, Story 7)

Would you become a pilgrim on the road of love? The first condition is that you make yourself humble as dust and ashes. (Ansari of Heart)

O Thou that changest earth into gold, And out of other earth madest the father of mankind, Thy business is changing things and bestowing favours, My business is mistakes and forgetfulness and error. Change my mistakes and forgetfulness to knowledge; I am altogether vile, make me temperate and meek. (Masnavi Book 5, Story 3)

Fools laud and magnify the mosque, While they strive to oppress holy men of heart. But the former is mere form, the latter spirit and truth. The only true mosque is that in the heart of saints. The mosque that is built in the hearts of the saints Is the place of worship for all, for God dwells there. (Masnavi, Book 2, Story 13)

I pray God the Omnipotent to place us in the ranks of His chosen, among the number of those He directs to the path of safety; in whom He inspires fervour lest they forget Him; whom He cleanses from all defilement, that nothing remain in them except Himself; yea, of those whom He indwells completely, that they may adore none beside Him. (Al Ghazzali)

SPIRITUAL SIGNPOST

To learn more about Sufism, check out the article "Sufism's Many Paths," by Dr. Alan Godlas. It's available at www.uga.edu/islam/Sufism.html.

The Christian Mystic Tradition: Thomas à Kempis

There are many expressions of mysticism within Christianity. (The life and writings of the great Trappist monk Thomas Merton, for instance, is a recent example of celebrated Christian mysticism.) But the most influential piece of Christian writing remains *The Imitation of Christ*, attributed to the German Augustinian priest and monk Thomas à Kempis.

The book was written in the fifteenth century; for half a millennium it has stood as a preeminent faith-based document of commitment to pursuing the personal example of Jesus Christ.

ON THE PATH

Beware lest any man spoil you through philosophy and vain deceit, after the tradition of men, after the rudiments of the world, and not after Christ.

—Paul's Letter to the Colossians 2:8

Following are some examples of the "voices" of Christian mysticism (all from *The Imitation of Christ*):

First keep the peace within yourself, then you can also bring peace to others.

Some have (God) in their mouths, but little in their hearts. There are others who, being enlightened in their understanding and purified in their affection, always breathe after things eternal, are unwilling to hear of earthly things, and grieve to be subject to the necessities of nature; and such as these perceive what the Spirit of Truth speaketh in them. For it teacheth them to despise the things of the earth and to love heavenly things; to disregard the world, and all the day and night to aspire after heaven.

Love flies, runs, and rejoices; it is free and nothing can hold it back.

Never be entirely idle; but either be reading, or writing, or praying or meditating or endeavoring something for the public good.

Of two evils we must always choose the least.

Remember that lost time does not return.

The good devout man first makes inner preparation for the actions he has later to perform. His outward actions do not draw him into lust and vice; rather it is he who bends them into the shape of reason and right judgment. Who has a stiffer battle to fight than the man who is striving to conquer himself?

Who has a harder fight than he who is striving to overcome himself?

SPIRITUAL SIGNPOST

To learn more about Thomas à Kempis, check out the article *Thomas à Kempis, Priest, Monk, and Writer* by Dr. James Kiefer. It's available at satucket.com/lectionary/Thomas_a_Kempis.htm.

Be not angry that you cannot make others as you wish them to be, since you cannot make yourself as you wish to be.

If thou reliest more upon thine own reason or industry than upon the virtue that subjects to Jesus Christ, thou wilt seldom and hardly become an enlightened man; for God wishes us to be perfectly subject to Himself, and to transcend all reason by inflamed love.

The Least You Need to Know

- All major religious traditions include mystical traditions.
- Mysticism means acting on the longing for some kind of personal union with the Divine.
- Kabbalistic worship emphasizes traditional, and esoteric, close study of the words of the Hebrew scriptures, and holds that the names of God carry special power.
- Sufism is the great mystical tradition within Islam; its most celebrated figure is probably the Persian author Rumi.
- Thomas à Kempis is credited with authorship of a highly influential piece of Christian mystic writing, *The Imitation of Christ*.

New Religious Movements

In This Chapter

- Defining the term "new religion"
- Seven important new faiths you should know about
- The assortment of spiritual movements known as "New Age"
- New traditions and movements

Every religion was once a new religion to someone. In this chapter, you find out about some of the most important new religious movements to surface in the United States during the last hundred years.

What Is a "New Religion"?

The formal academic definition of a "new religion" is still a matter of scholarly debate, some of it pretty dry. For the (pragmatic!) purposes of this chapter, our working definition of the phrase "new religion" will be accessible, straightforward, and, so far as we can make it, consistent.

All of the new religions discussed within this chapter meet the following criteria:

- The movement represents a distinct set of spiritual traditions not widely practiced in the United States before 1900. (Such traditions sometimes, but not always, arise out of variations on or combinations of previously existing faiths.)

- The movement clearly emphasizes voluntary membership among newcomers to the system, in practice as well as in theory.

- Whether or not the movement features a formal hierarchy or set of doctrines, it has developed a basic structural viability. It is able to provide a continuing focus on fulfilling the spiritual needs of an identifiable body of practitioners, following the passage from the scene of its most important early figure(s).

- Even though it may embrace certain points of doctrine from an earlier tradition, the movement offers new and alternative patterns of authority, organization, or practice.

Note: This chapter does not focus on faith systems that could, in their present stage of development, still be described as "emerging" traditions.

Using these principles as a yardstick, this chapter focuses on the following new religions:

- The Nation of Islam

- The International Society for Krishna Consciousness (the ISKCON, or Hare Krishna movement)

- Transcendental Meditation

- Neo-Paganism

- The Baha'i Faith

- Santeria

- Rastafarianism

- The New Age Movement

The seven faiths examined in depth here are not the only spiritual movements that could be discussed, and no doubt some practitioners will argue that their tradition has been unfairly overlooked. In part to address this problem, we have also included very short summaries of some other recent traditions and movements at the end of this chapter.

Seven New Faiths—and a Movement

Covering every new religious movement in a book such as this is, however, an impossibility. Each group discussed in this chapter has been chosen simply to illustrate new points of view. Each reflects important trends that have emerged within the

American religious experience during the past century. By learning about these, you will be in a much better position to find out more about other traditions that you may encounter.

It's particularly important to bring a spirit of openness to your encounters with new systems of religious belief. After all, these believers are likely (by definition!) to offer perspectives that differ radically from your own experience of religious practice. Remember that fear and skepticism are not the best tools for encountering new systems.

BARRIER ALERT!

Throwing around terms such as "cult," "sect," or "charismatic group" will always close doors more quickly than open them. Avoid labels when you talk about the religious practices of others.

Many new and well-known religious groups have been passed over here because they appear to many observers to fail an important test: resisting the use of intimidation in recruiting and retaining members. We take the position that coercion is antithetical to spiritual seeking. However, it should be noted that traditions change, grow, and expand over time. (It's also worth noting that today's "major" religions were the persecuted "minor" faiths of centuries past.)

The Nation of Islam

The Nation of Islam (or Lost-Found Nation of Islam) was founded in Detroit in 1930 by Wallace Fard, a salesman whose early life remains something of a mystery. Fard claimed a prophetic vision from Allah directed specifically toward black Americans.

He taught that his version of Islam was the only valid faith for African Americans, and that blacks were the descendants of the race that had made human civilization possible. His followers considered him to be "Allah in person." In accepting such teachings, members of the Nation of Islam broke from established Islamic practice, which regards no human being as comparable to the Creator, and explicitly rejects racial discrimination of any kind.

When Fard vanished mysteriously from the scene in 1934, an associate named Elijah Poole, the son of former slaves, changed his name to Elijah Muhammad and assumed control of the church. Muhammad established himself as the "messenger of Allah" and began an economically focused separatist movement that promoted the social power of black communities and mandated rigorous obedience to his rules of cond some of which had been adapted from mainstream Islam.

A Separatist Practice

Despite its name, however, the movement was never a branch of mainstream Islamic worship. The Nation developed a distinctive obsession with race, one that rejected the American civil rights movement's campaign for integration among blacks and whites. The Nation of Islam promoted rigorous racial separatism—to the point of dismissing non-blacks as "white devils"—at the same time it preached a strict personal moral code. At one point, Elijah Muhammad called for the establishment of a separate black state.

SPIRITUAL SIGNPOST

Debates over racial separatism and doctrinal matters created a rift in the Nation in the late 1970s. One side of the rift, led by Wallace D. Muhammad, son of the group's late leader Elijah Muhammad, changed its name to the American Society of Muslims, renounced separatism, and adopted traditional Sunni Islamic practice. The other side, led by Minister Louis Farrakahn, has retained the name "Nation of Islam" and the separatist social vision enunciated by Elijah Muhammad.

The deep commitment of the faith's thousands of practitioners was reflected in their distinctive dress. In ever-larger numbers, converts in dark suits, white dress shirts, and bow ties began to proselytize in Elijah Muhammad's name. The Nation's most important convert to the faith was the outspoken and eloquent Malcolm X, a brilliant, vigorous, and effective agitator. Born Malcolm Little, the ex-convict-turned-minister followed established church practice and abandoned his "slave name" when he joined the church.

Malcolm X eventually broke with the group, embraced Sunni Islam, changed his name to Malik El-Shabazz, and established a separate organization. His assassination in 1965 was attributed to elements within the Nation of Islam; three members of the Nation were convicted of the killing, two of whom denied involvement. The planning behind the assault remains a subject of bitter dispute.

Pride and Action

Despite the criticism and controversy that has swirled around it since at least the late 1950s, the Nation of Islam remains an instrument of hope, pride, and self-determination for its practitioners. The impassioned, often-overheated rhetoric of Nation leaders has occasionally led to cycles of intense media scrutiny.

Even so, the Nation has unmistakably embraced hard work, piety, and accountability. Its practical emphasis on reclaiming drug-ridden urban areas deserves more attention than it has received. Media coverage of the group's role in the so-called Million Man March on Washington, D.C., in 1996 led to controversy about the (disputed) number of attendees and about Farrakhan's leadership role in the event. The stated aim of the march, to "convey to the world a vastly different picture of the Black male," was nevertheless fulfilled. Two years later, a Million Woman March drew similar nationwide attention.

The Nation of Islam has persistently run afoul of both established Muslim leadership (for its profound deviations from Islamic belief, practice, and theology) and the Jewish community (for its alleged anti-Semitism and its belligerent rhetoric concerning the State of Israel). At the same time, it has been among the most visible and dynamic new forms of religious expression on the American scene in the second half of the twentieth century, and one that has made a tangible difference in the lives of African Americans.

The International Society for Krishna Consciousness

Hare Krishna devotees, robed and chanting, have become a familiar sight around the world. Founded in 1966 in New York City by A.C. Bhaktivedanta Swami Prabhupada, ISKCON is a distinctive movement that explicitly rejects "the pantheism, polytheism, and caste consciousness that pervades modern Hinduism," according to the group's Internet site.

Outsiders often call the Hare Krishnas a "Hindu sect." Although ISKCON sees itself as continuing important traditions within the Hindu faith, the "sect" designation clearly makes insiders uncomfortable. The group sees itself as a platform for certain important and independent traditions, known as "divine culture."

BARRIER ALERT!

ISKCON devotees regard Krishna consciousness as transcending narrow sectarian forms. They reject the classification of their movement as representing Hinduism—or as being aligned with any other hierarchically organized religious structure.

"Krishna consciousness," the group's statement of purpose explains, "is in no way a faith or religion that seeks to defeat other faiths or religions. Rather, it is an essential cultural movement for the entire human society and does not consider any particular sectarian faith." Despite this cross-cultural emphasis, the group relies on the *Bhagavad Gita* as a central text.

ISKCON's Goals

The group has seven primary objectives:

- The propagation of spiritual knowledge ("to society at large") for the overall betterment of the human family.

- The encouragement and development of Krishna consciousness, as revealed in holy scriptures.

- The union of members of society with each other and "to Krishna, the prime entity, thus developing the idea within the members, and humanity at large, that each soul is part and parcel of the quality of Godhead (Krishna)."

- The promotion of the practice of chanting the names of the Deity.

- The establishment of places of "transcendental" religious worship and practice, sites devoted to Krishna.

- The support and promotion of a simpler way of life more in tune with the patterns of nature than that offered by contemporary society.

- The publication and circulation of written works that support the six preceding goals.

SPIRITUAL SIGNPOST

The Hare Krishna movement follows the teachings of the Vedas and the Vedic scriptures. It places a special emphasis on the Bhagavad Gita, and promotes Vaishnavism, a devotional school that inculcates "the essential and universal principle of all religion: loving devotional service to the one Supreme Personality of Godhead." ISKCON regards the chanting of the holy name of Krishna as a primary spiritual practice. It is a nonsectarian, nondenominational movement.

Core Practices and Beliefs

Beyond "chanting the name(s) of the Lord," members of ISKCON observe strict vegetarianism and accept the formal notion of the guru/disciple role as a component of individual spiritual development. In these respects, it shares points of contact with traditional Hinduism.

The group has sold more than 10 million copies of its vegetarian cookbooks. Its vegetarianism reflects deeply held spiritual principles. ISKCON maintains a vigorous environmental agenda that includes the development of new rural communities. Its members see eating meat as symptomatic of profound environmental, social, and spiritual imbalance. The group considers environmental activism for its own sake to be fundamentally shortsighted, and views the spiritual development of humanity as a whole as the only appropriate response to global social and environmental problems. In particular, any environmental campaign that does not acknowledge the sanctity of all life is seen as fatally flawed.

Although the focus within the ISKCON tradition is on veneration of the Lord Krishna through Hare Krishna mantra meditation, Prabhupada, its late founder, is regarded as the transmitter of truth within an established line of inspired teaching. "He is and will remain always the instructing spiritual master of all devotees in ISKCON," says a group statement.

Room for All

Dismissed by some observers as overemotional and lacking in theological depth, ISKCON actually represents a sophisticated, albeit direct, revision of familiar Hindu principles. Its unalterable egalitarian stance and its forthright rejection of sectarian conflicts have earned it a passionate following.

ISKCON'S preeminent goal, according to its members, is instructing people in the best and most immediate means of expressing love for God. The exuberance, openness, and complete dedication with which practitioners embrace that objective has become one of the tradition's most distinctive elements.

Transcendental Meditation

If ISKCON seeks to distance itself from the designation "Hindu sect," the Transcendental Meditation (TM) movement appears eager to reject the idea of formal religious observance altogether.

The group prefers to focus on the scientifically verifiable benefits of simple meditation techniques. Nevertheless, it has an identifiable group of practitioners and a discernible spiritual element based on Hindu Vedanta philosophy. It would also appear to have a metaphysical framework, given the group's emphasis on transcending physical boundaries through advanced meditation practice. Some meditators are held by practitioners to be capable of certain forms of levitation.

SPIRITUAL SIGNPOST

For many practitioners, TM's pragmatic, results-oriented practice is the perfect method for incorporating harmony and integrity into a modern world—a world that may, they argue, need those qualities far more than it needs another organized religious structure. That TM has thrived in its current form says much about the limited appeal of traditional religious practice for many today.

Remembered by many outsiders as the belief system that served as a spiritual way station for the Beatles, the Transcendental Meditation movement was introduced to Westerners by Maharishi Mahesh Yogi in 1959. It has attracted many practitioners over the years. It is not seen as exclusive. TM practitioners may use their meditation to supplement other faiths, or no faith at all.

Simple Meditation

One learns the TM method by means of (paid) introductory sessions with a certified instructor. The techniques are not at all complex, but formal instruction is a prerequisite to participation.

The meditation techniques are practiced twice a day for 15 to 20 minutes while sitting comfortably with closed eyes. Practitioners emphasize the effortlessness of the procedure, and many cite increases in overall health and well-being.

The organization, which promotes its activities via a network of Vedic Schools and affiliates, highlights an impressive number of studies linking Transcendental Meditation to increases in creativity, memory, happiness, energy, and overall stamina. Whether it is a scientifically validated method for personal growth and happiness, a nonscriptural devotional practice, a personal relaxation method, or some combination of all the above, TM has emerged as a popular and flexible discipline. It has attracted a number of passionate adherents who are uncomfortable with organized (and perhaps overly dogmatic) religious structures.

A Non-Faith "Faith"?

TM has evolved from an expression of the 1960s youth subculture to a kind of voluntary, open-ended vehicle for nondogmatic meditation principles—a vehicle with apparently benign capitalist overtones. Its insistence on fees for initial instruction has left some wondering at its motives, but the movement is not, to all appearances, an exploitative one.

Neo-Paganism

This "new" faith, which encompasses many groups, appeals to certain religious practices that are quite ancient in origin. In the distant past, tribal people all over the earth strove to understand the natural world and their place within it. They tended to hold all life in honor, revering the earth as the Mother from whom life springs. Some aspects of the European expression of these faiths have experienced a revival in recent years.

A perception of the giver of life responsible for forming and shaping both earth and heaven has been found in many cultures. Today, among many Neo-Pagans, this figure is called by some variation of the name "Goddess." Her role as all-pervasive Creator of life and of the universe is consistent with the cultural understanding of many indigenous peoples.

SPIRITUAL SIGNPOST

Ancient tribal peoples in pre-Christian Europe saw a profound order in the rhythms and cycles of the seasons, and they celebrated these guiding rhythms in their observances. Today, after centuries of suppression and neglect, many of these mysterious religions are being reanimated and adopted by contemporary followers. Most of these believers fall under the umbrella grouping "Neo-Pagan," and many of them elevate Goddess worship to high importance.

The Neo-Pagan groups in existence today emphasize personal responsibility and see divine force as residing in all things. Worshipping nature and the seasons, they associate particular physical locations with their sacred rites. Most members of these groups openly embrace the formerly derogatory label "pagan," embracing the original sense of its Latin root "country-dweller" while rejecting the negative associations that have accrued to this word over time.

Sun and Moon

The cycles of the sun and moon were among the powers early worshippers sought most fervently to understand. Some scholars suggest that the cycles of the moon were first noticed by women who connected them with another 30-day cycle, the menstrual cycle. It is likely that this initial "noticing" developed into ongoing understandings of important formal responsibilities and the relationship between the tribe, the earth, and the moon whose waxing and waning seemed so clearly to affect the human body.

In this way, many contemporary believers assume women came to perceive the moon itself as Goddess, directly and intimately related to the bringing forth of new life. Women of experience and wisdom eventually became priestesses within their tribes.

Persecution and Revival

The arrival of the invading Romans signaled the beginning of an assault on the cultures of many ancient tribes of Goddess worshippers. This assault continued throughout the Christian period, and was reinforced by the Muslim conquest in Europe and Asia Minor. Although suppressed (often violently), some of the old ways have, remarkably enough, managed to survive.

In recent years, many groups have revived or reconstructed ancient traditions centered on nature and Goddess worship. The belief systems of these gatherings have been eclectic and hard to define. All the same, it is true that the cycles of the year hold important religious meaning for Neo-Pagans.

The Dance of the Seasons

Seasonal and nature observances play a major role among members of Neo-Pagan groups. Accordingly, the following sections will make a modest attempt to look at major calendar observances of importance to these (frequently misunderstood) practitioners. It is important to recognize, though, that this summary is not an exhaustive list of all the holidays and observances of the Neo-Pagan movement. No such list exists! This is a many-layered movement, one that intuitively resists both dogma and centralized structures.

The Winter Solstice

The winter solstice marks the shortest day of the year in the Northern Hemisphere, the time when the least daylight is in evidence. After a spiraling-down of observable light to this single, shortest day, the year begins its ascent toward the summer solstice, the longest day of the year, six months later. The winter solstice is seen as a time to honor the darkness of night and the womb, and to celebrate emerging life. During this period, the Goddess is recognized as reborn, an infant.

The emphasis on renewal, on rebirth out of darkness, is thousands of years old, and predates the familiar observance of the Christian Nativity festival (Christmas) on December 25, very near to the winter solstice. The burning of candles and logs during the winter solstice is of similarly ancient origin.

Imbolc

This *cross-quarter holiday*, also known as Brigid, falls between the winter solstice and the spring equinox. It celebrates the increasing of the light and marks the progression from the newborn moon of winter to the infant moon of spring. This is a fire festival, a time of individual growth and healing, the period of inner power. During Imbolc, the Goddess is revered as a young virgin.

> **DEFINITION**
>
> **Cross-quarter holidays** occur at the points between the four natural solar "quarters" of the calendar (for instance, between fall equinox and the winter solstice). Neo-Pagan festivals marking these holidays incorporate fire as a central element.

The Spring Equinox

During the spring equinox, one of the two points in the year at which the daylight and the dark of night are in balance, practitioners honor and celebrate the awakening of plants and animals from the seeming death of winter. Signs of fertility (such as the hare and the egg, familiar symbols in the modern secular Easter) are important parts of this celebration. Signs of returning life are revered; the joyful promise of youth's renewal abounds.

Beltane

This cross-quarter holiday is after the spring equinox and before the summer solstice. It is a time of flowering for fertile Mother Earth.

During this holiday, young love and sexuality are celebrated with the ancient dance of the Maypole. The Goddess is honored as the maiden whose blood fertilizes the earth, and as the great mother. This is a time to honor personal sexuality and creativity as the source of life.

Celebrants leap across fires to release past injuries, and to warm and open the heart. During Beltane, the pleasure to be found in erotic pursuits is understood as innocent, and is expressed by means of rituals honoring the Goddess.

The Summer Solstice

This is the time of the longest day of the year in the Northern Hemisphere, and the most light. The Goddess is honored as being at the peak of her fertility, sexuality, and power. The summer solstice is regarded as a time of commitment to one's beloved, and also of the cultivation of healthy self-love.

The hope and promise of new life found in the winter solstice has been brought into existence through the ever-increasing light. Just at this moment of fertility and bounty, the journey back toward darkness begins with the waning half of the yearly cycle.

Lammas

Lammas is the cross-quarter holiday celebrated at the midpoint between summer and fall. The Goddess revered as the mother at the last cross-quarter holiday is now seen as the matron.

Slowly the days grow shorter and heat intensifies. That which has been planted is ripening but not yet harvested. The Grain Goddesses are celebrated as the bringers of the source of life; this is a time when practitioners honor Mother Earth in her ripeness. It is also a time for focusing on those things one hopes for in the coming harvest of one's own daily efforts.

The Fall Equinox

This is the second calendar-point of balance between light and dark. The harvest is seen as complete, and the earth no longer bears fruit. The Goddess is considered as passing into menopause. The fall equinox is a time to give thanks for the rich harvest that will see believers through the coming time of darkness.

Samhain

This cross-quarter festival celebrates the halfway point between the fall equinox and the winter solstice. It is regarded as the most powerful night of the year, a time when that which separates believers from other worldly forces may be transcended.

The Goddess, last revered as a matron, is now regarded as the crone, the old woman preparing for death. At this time of the year, the old falls to decay, making room, in the fullness of time, for the wonder of rebirth.

At this time, old habits and patterns are ritually burned, and the spirits of those who have passed are considered to be close at hand. Prayers for departed loved ones are offered during this festival.

Samhain (or Hallowmas) marks the Neo-Pagan New Year; it is seen as representing the beginning of the new.

The Baha'i Faith

Baha'i arose in nineteenth-century Persia (the country today known as Iran). Its central figure was a disciple of the man known as the Bab—the founder of a messianic sect of Shiite Islam known as Babism. This disciple, born Mizra Husayn Ali Nuri, was the son of a well-to-do government minister.

In 1852, after the death of the Bab, Nuri was in prison for his religious beliefs, when (according to Baha'i belief) he received a vision confirming his role as the one "whom God shall make manifest"—the Messiah-like figure foreseen by the Bab. During the following 40 years, he composed a body of scriptures that form the heart of what is now the Baha'i Faith. He became known as Baha'u'llah. He spent most of his adult life either imprisoned or under watch, and died in 1892.

The guiding ideas behind Baha'u'llah's writings are egalitarian, practical, and progressive. In keeping with the central principles of the Baha'i Faith, practitioners of this fast-growing tradition regard all previous religions as unified, and accept that God has been revealed to humanity through the influence of various manifestations at various points in history.

Unity

Although its followers were persecuted, the Baha'i tradition survived the death of Baha'u'llah without encountering major internal rifts. Under the leadership of Abdu'l Baha and Shoghi Effendi, the two men who, successively, headed the movement after 1892, the religion has grown and prospered around the world, most notably in Africa and North America. It now boasts approximately 6 million believers in 205 countries.

Equality and Harmony

The Baha'i Faith scriptures embrace the fundamental equality of men and women. Among other principles endorsed in the writings of Baha'u'llah are these:

- Humanity as a single race

- International government and a single language

- The necessity of the elimination of prejudice

- The importance of universal education

- The negative effects of economic inequality

- The necessity of avoiding forbidden activities (such as killing, theft, lying, sexual misbehavior, gambling, abusing drugs and alcohol, and engaging in malicious gossip)

Rapid Growth

Despite (carefully observed) scriptural injunctions against proselytizing, the Baha'i Faith has become one of the world's fastest-growing independent religions. In the past century, it has mushroomed from an obscure faith based in the Middle East to a global movement that has attracted believers in virtually every recognized nation. Followers of the Baha'i Faith have been subjected to persecution in contemporary Iran.

This vigorous, inclusive, and diverse faith may well emerge as one of the most dynamic in the twenty-first century.

Santeria

Santeria, in contrast to the global reach of the Baha'i Faith, is a small and frequently misunderstood religion that combines ancient African and Catholic practice in a remarkable religious synthesis. Although it was almost completely unknown in the United States until very recently, it has been gathering force for more than three centuries.

Santeria, which incorporates elements of prayerful animal sacrifice, reached American shores in the wave of immigration that followed the Cuban revolution of 1959. Its American practice is most notable among Afro-Cubans, Puerto Ricans, and African Americans in sections of New York City, but it has extended elsewhere in the country as well. This (currently) small hybrid religion combines elements of tribal African observance and Roman Catholic terminology and history. Today, Santeria is the subject of increasing devotional and scholarly interest.

Orisha

Santeria is inspired by the presence of orisha (spirits) known by both African and Spanish names. The strong African elements of the faith can be traced to the slave trade that brought people of the Yoruba nation to lives of forced labor in Cuba for three and a half centuries.

A New Form

The "conversion" of these slaves to Roman Catholicism resulted not in the eradication of existing African rituals but in their perpetuation in a new and extraordinary form. Santeria combines both indigenous name and ritual with the personifications of acknowledged Roman Catholic saints, a combination that may have been intended to appease religious authorities at first but are now an integral feature of the faith.

Saint Francis of Assisi, for example, is associated in Santeria with the orisha known as Orula, who embodies the principle of wisdom, the number sixteen, the colors green and yellow, and a particular distinctive dance involving the orisha known as Oshun, who in turn is associated with La Caridad del Cobre, the patron saint of Cuba.

Rastafarianism

The Rastafari movement honors Africa as the birthplace of humankind and issues an unmistakable call for autonomy and self-sufficiency among blacks. This distinctive religious practice was formulated by the descendants of slaves in the slums of Jamaica during the twentieth century.

The origin of Rastafarianism, which is as much a cultural movement as a religion, can be found in the teaching of the Jamaican-born advocate of black nationalism Marcus Garvey, famous for his "Back to Africa" movement. In the 1930s, Garvey's distinctive message of black unity and pride in African heritage found a new expression in Jamaica. News that Haile Salassie had been crowned emperor of Ethiopia was acclaimed not merely as a political development, but as confirmation of a prophecy that a black messiah had been crowned. Many Jamaicans honored Salassie as a living God for the black race. (Salassie's previous name was Ras Tafari, and it is from him that they chose the name of their movement.) Salassie, who died in 1975, was not a Rastafarian.

SPIRITUAL SIGNPOST

The founding ideals of the Rastafari faith are Freedom of Spirit, Freedom from Slavery, and Freedom of Africa. Devout Rastafarians emphasize austerity, purity, and a personal commitment to black solidarity.

Rastafarians are perhaps best known for their joyful reggae music and for their use of marijuana in meditation and for health purposes. They believe that the use of this herb is sanctioned by various references in the Bible. It is probably worth noting here that a particularly powerful strain of marijuana, also known as "ganja," grows wild in Jamaica.

True Rastas eat only food that has never been touched by chemical additives, is not canned, and is as nearly raw as possible. They use no condiments or preservatives. They drink only herbal drinks, believing that liquor, milk, and coffee are unnatural. They are vegetarians who emphasize the importance of living a peaceful life in study of holy scripture.

As a sign of their beliefs they let their hair grow into dreadlocks, which they see as the image of the lion of Judah. The colors used to represent Rastafarianism are red, gold (or yellow), and green, all adapted from the Garvey movement and associated with new concepts unique to Rasta practice.

Six out of ten Jamaicans are believed to be Rastafarians or allies of the movement. There are said to be hundreds of thousands of practitioners worldwide.

The New Age Movement

Also worthy of note, but too broadly scaled to fit within the grouping of traditions just named, is the assortment of spiritual and social movements known collectively as "New Age." This is a broadly inclusive, decentralized grouping of faith systems drawing on many existing traditions (not all of them harmonious with one another), and emphasizing personal choice and the full development of human potential.

To learn more about the many facets of the remarkably diverse New Age movement, which incorporates both ancient and modern influences, visit www.dmoz.org// Society/Religion_and_Spirituality/New_Age//.

SPIRITUAL SIGNPOST

Many other new religions exist; the ones discussed in detail in this chapter are representative traditions.

Some of the most interesting new spiritual movements are interfaith initiatives that do not possess the structures of formal religious communities. The Prayer Chain, for instance, is an online interfaith prayer effort proposing specific prayers in a variety of traditions. The website can be found at www.prayerchain. org.

The Least You Need to Know

- Every religion was once a new religion to someone.
- In recent years, the Nation of Islam, the Hare Krishna movement, Transcendental Meditation, Neo-Paganism, the Baha'i Faith, Santeria, and Rastafarianism emerged as important new spiritual traditions.
- The New Age movement also presents a diverse grouping of religious practices, with both modern and ancient influences.
- Many other new religions exist; the ones discussed in detail in this chapter are representative traditions.

A Matter of Life and Death

9

At the end of the day, religion offers us ultimate answers to ultimate questions. What happens when we die? What is right? What is wrong? What does God demand of us? And how should we respond when religion itself motivates people to do unspeakable things? In this part of the book, we explore both the questions and some of their possible answers.

The Afterlife

In This Chapter

- Misconceptions about life and death in religious traditions
- The dangers of generalizing
- Distinctive views on the afterlife
- The virtuous life as its own reward

In this chapter, you learn what five of the world's great faith systems have to say about the afterlife. Although many religious traditions, old and new, have clear—and often fascinating—teachings on these matters, the most influential teachings derive from five faiths. To address the positions most likely to be relevant to the largest number of people reading this book, this chapter focuses on the decisions and teachings of Judaism, Christianity, Islam, Hinduism, and Buddhism. Our hope is that, in helping you learn about the teachings of these religions about the hereafter, we will encourage you not only to seek out more specifics about their doctrines, but also to learn about the positions of other faith systems.

Judaism and the Afterlife

It is one of the peculiarities of human religious history that Judaism is, as a practical matter, so little concerned with questions of the hereafter. This fact is frequently overlooked.

These days, skeptical academics, intellectuals, agnostics, and atheists are fond of claiming that "all" human religious systems are basically elaborate intellectual justifications meant to secure social standing for some elite class of people: clerics, members of religious orders, scholars, or other groups supposedly eager to exploit humanity's inevitable fear of death. For instance, George Orwell, the brilliant political satirist and atheist, in his novel *Animal Farm*, lampooned the notion of "Sugarcandy Mountain," a simple-minded fable of eternal joy in a far-off place, used by shrewd agitators to secure earthly advantages.

Among the (many) facts that these blanket criticisms and misrepresentations of humanity's varied faith systems usually ignore, however, is the inconvenient truth that contemporary Judaism simply does not fit the pattern.

The Torah sets out 613 commandments. Some sense of the sacredness of human life within the Jewish faith tradition may be gained by considering that 609 of those commandments may be broken if doing so will save a human life. (The exceptions are the prohibitions against idolatry, murder, incest, and adultery.)

BARRIER ALERT!

Among the prominent contemporary intellectuals claiming that religious systems are essentially hierarchical exercises meant to subjugate followers is Desmond Morris, author of the 1970s bestseller *The Naked Ape*.

What Jewish People Believe

Practitioners of Judaism do not so much "dismiss" ideas of death, heaven, and hell as they choose to look beyond them and focus instead on the value of human life, which is regarded as sacred.

Judaism simply teaches that …

- The human soul is immortal

- The nature of that immortality is beyond the conception of mankind

- Drawing conclusions about the specific nature of our relationship with God after our death is not particularly useful or helpful from a theological point of view

This comparatively simple (and unemotional) approach to the subject has emerged over time, and it has helped to set Judaism apart from the other major monotheistic faiths.

As a matter of history, there have been various schools of thought within Judaism that emphasized detailed doctrines about punishment and reward relating to an afterlife. These, however, have not endured, and they are not a part of contemporary Jewish religious and ethical teaching. The prevailing view today is that emphasizing the literal specifics of the afterlife is essentially a distraction from the more pressing business of living the kind of life on Earth of which God approves.

Even the ancient Jewish teachings concerning what happens to the human soul after death tended to express themselves through the idea of the soul's remorse or joy, rather than a specific physical place where torments are administered to the damned or rewards bestowed upon the elect. The closest one comes to an enduring notion of heaven or hell in traditional Judaism—and it's not very close—is the idea of *Sheol.*

The great Jewish philosopher Maimonedes wrote passionately of what he considered to be the literal facts of the afterlife when he was a young man of twenty. In his later years, he held that the notion of divine rewards and punishments for human deeds was misguided, and argued that the reward of living a righteous life was righteousness itself.

> **DEFINITION**
>
> In early Jewish thought, **Sheol** was a shadowy realm where all people—virtuous and otherwise—were sent after completing life on Earth. Many people believe Sheol to have been simply a poetic metaphor for the notion of death. It does not carry anything like the theological importance of Heaven or Hell within Christianity and Islam.

A Stark Contrast

Although Islam and Christianity strongly emphasize eternal punishment for unrepentant sinners, eternal reward for those who win God's favor, and a Day of Judgment that will be faced by all humanity, Judaism has no such emphasis. Its approach to the question of what happens to the human soul after death is, in essence, to refer such matters to God alone, and to emphasize the importance, during earthly life, of emulating God's mercy, justice, and tolerance. The concise Jewish answer to the question, in other words, is simply to treat the question itself as an opportunity to re-emphasize the importance of winning God's favor. One does that through such activities as promoting learning, engaging in religious worship, and performing good deeds without expectation of reward.

An ancient Jewish rabbi once said: "We are required (by God) to feed the Gentiles who are poor, as well as the Jews we may encounter who are in need." This brief saying, focusing as it does on the practical requirements of righteous living, may well be Judaism's best answer to humanity's restless questioning concerning the specifics of the afterlife. It is an answer of interest to Jews, and to all people of goodwill.

> **ON THE PATH**
>
> "Jewish law requires that a tombstone be prepared, so that the deceased will not be forgotten and the grave will not be desecrated. It is customary in some communities to keep the tombstone veiled, or to delay in putting it up, until the end of the 12-month mourning period. The idea underlying this custom is that the dead will not be forgotten when he is being mourned every day. In communities where this custom is observed, there is generally a formal unveiling ceremony when the tombstone is revealed."—From "Life, Death, and Mourning," article posted on the Judaism 101 website at www.mechon-mamre.org/jewfaq/death.htm

Christianity and the Afterlife

Christians examining the Bible for information and instruction on the afterlife have found both clear guidance and room for dramatically differing interpretations. Let's take a look at some of the similarities and divergences of Christian belief in this area.

The Day of Judgment

The New Testament promises a Day of Judgment—a reckoning of all humanity following the Second Coming of Jesus, an event promised in the Book of Revelation.

The Day of Judgment, and the judgment of the living and the dead, is a clear and central component of virtually all Christian belief. Even so, different Christian groups over the centuries have developed distinctive, and varying, answers to questions about the afterlife.

Such questions include …

- Where are human beings sent after they die?
- What will win success in the afterlife?

- What is Heaven like? What is Hell like?

- What will happen to Christians who are still alive at the time of the Second Coming?

Let's look at each of these questions in turn; after that, we'll take a look at what some prominent Christians have to say about the afterlife.

Where Do People Go When They Die?

Reward in the afterlife for those who accept the divine mercy of redemption through Jesus Christ—and punishment in the afterlife for those who have turned away from God—are central themes of Christianity. Heaven can also be seen, not simply as a reward, but also as the culmination of a life lived in faith, hope, and charity.

Christian theology holds that Heaven awaits "the elect"—those who have earned salvation. This group is defined in various ways by various groups, but the formulation "those who die in God's grace and friendship," which is used in the Catechism of the Roman Catholic Church, would probably win agreement from a cross-section of Christians.

Most Christians understand admission to heaven to be life's supreme reward resulting in a state of supreme, incomprehensible happiness and union with God. Virtually all Christians see acceptance of Jesus Christ as Savior as a prerequisite to entry to Heaven.

The existence of a very different fate, Hell, is also a central component of Christian religious understanding. Residents of Hell—described by Pope John Paul II as "those who freely and definitively separate themselves from God"—endure horrific punishments.

Heaven, Hell, and the Gospels

The Christian belief in the existence of Heaven as a reward for the righteous, and Hell as a place of punishment for the unrepentant, is rooted not in the abstract theological principles of scholars, but in the words of Jesus Christ as reported in the Gospels.

Of Heaven, we read in the Bible that Jesus says:

> *Do not store up for yourselves treasures on earth, where moth and rust destroy, and where thieves break in and steal. But store up for yourselves treasures in heaven, where moth and rust do not destroy, and where thieves do not break in and steal.* (Matthew 6:19–20)

And of Hell, we read that he says:

> *And fear not them which kill the body, but are not able to kill the soul: but rather fear him which is able to destroy both soul and body in hell.* (Matthew 10:28)

It Depends on the Denomination ...

Beyond universally accepted Christian notions concerning Heaven and Hell, however, there are many questions about the afterlife whose Christian answer depends upon one's denomination and outlook on one's faith.

For instance: Is Heaven a physical place? Fundamentalist Christians are inclined to say "Yes." Many other Christians think of this destination as a locus of one's relationship with God.

How much time will elapse between the Second Coming and the final judgment of humanity? Different theologians and members of the clergy have different answers.

Is there any process that eventually yields the purified souls of imperfect human beings to God in Heaven? Again, opinions vary.

ON THE PATH

"[Heaven] is neither an abstraction nor a physical place in the clouds, but a living, personal relationship with [God]."—Pope John Paul II

The truth is that there is no single Christian answer to any of these questions. There is, rather, a wealth of answers and a series of ongoing discussions, some of them centuries old.

Perhaps the most interesting ongoing Christian discussion about the afterlife has to do with the question of Purgatory.

Purgatory

Catholic belief explicitly embraces the idea of Purgatory, a place of cleansing and purification. In the Catholic view, people who repented sinful activity, but have not yet been completely purified, are sent to Purgatory to be purged so that they may eventually enter Heaven.

As the Catechism of the Roman Catholic Church puts it:

> All who die in God's grace and friendship, but still imperfectly purified, are indeed assured of their eternal salvation; but after death they undergo purification, so as to achieve the holiness necessary to enter the joy of heaven. The Church gives the name Purgatory to this final purification of the elect, which is entirely different from the punishment of the damned. The Church formulated her doctrine of faith on Purgatory especially at the Councils of Florence and Trent. The tradition of the Church, by reference to certain texts of Scripture, speaks of a cleansing fire: As for certain lesser faults, we must believe that, before the Final Judgment, there is a purifying fire. He who is truth (Jesus Christ) says that whoever utters blasphemy against the Holy Spirit will be pardoned neither in this age nor in the age to come. From this sentence we understand that certain offenses can be forgiven in this age, but certain others in the age to come.

It is worth emphasizing here that Catholics believe that everyone who is sent to Purgatory is destined for Heaven. So it is not, strictly speaking, a place of punishment. Catholics believe that prayers for the souls of the dead, and indulgences, can shorten a person's stay in Purgatory.

ON THE PATH

"An *indulgence* is a remission before God of the temporal punishment due to sins whose guilt has already been forgiven, which the faithful Christian who is duly disposed gains under certain prescribed conditions through the action of the Church which, as the minister of redemption, dispenses and applies with authority the treasury of the satisfactions of Christ and the saints."

—Pope Paul VI

Most Protestant denominations do not accept the doctrine of Purgatory, and all of them reject the authority of the Catholic Church to grant indulgences. In fact, disagreement on these questions about the afterlife reflects a fundamental difference in outlook between these two branches of Christianity. Disagreements about indulgences were, of course, a motivating force behind the Protestant Reformation.

Strictly speaking, Orthodox Christians do not embrace the doctrine of Purgatory as outlined by the Roman Catholic Church. They do, however, offer prayers to God beseeching Him to show mercy and kindness to the dead. The Orthodox Church's doctrine of theosis, under which a person may experience greater and greater degrees of union with God—even after death—offers an interesting parallel with Catholic beliefs in Purgatory.

ON THE PATH

In 1507, Martin Luther wrote …

"Every truly repentant Christian has a right to full remission of penalty and guilt, even without letters of pardon. Every true Christian, whether living or dead, has part in all the blessings of Christ and the Church; and this is granted him by God, even without letters of pardon."

Then and now, Luther's words serve as a reminder that questions concerning the afterlife are addressed in very different ways by Catholics and Protestants.

What Will Win Success in the Afterlife?

Traditional Christian theology holds that, of those who lived after Jesus' time, only those who accept Jesus Christ as the Son of God and their personal savior will win entrance to Heaven. There have been a number of interesting discussions, however, regarding what, precisely, this means. The Roman Catholic Church's catechism, for instance, reads:

> *All are obliged to belong to the Catholic Church, in some way, in order to be saved.*

The words "in some way" are significant. Using this formulation, the possibility exists that Christ's mercy might be extended in the afterlife to a person not formally a member of the Catholic Church—in other words to people who have what is known as a "mysterious relationship" with the church. This is an example of the general movement away from pronouncements that all those who do not embrace a particular sect of Christianity are doomed to Hell. (Such pronouncements were particularly common in the period immediately following the Protestant Reformation.)

In the teachings of the Second Vatican Council, Catholics are reminded that the gift of salvation can be received in a way known only to God. Similar contemporary positions are put forth by the teachings of many other Christian denominations.

ON THE PATH

"Those who, through no fault of their own, do not know the Gospel of Christ or his Church, but who nevertheless seek God with a sincere heart, and, moved by grace, try in their actions to do his will as they know it through the dictates of their conscience—those too may achieve eternal salvation."—Lumen Gentium 16; *Dogmatic Constitution on the Church,* from the Roman Catholic Church's Second Vatican Council

What Is Heaven Like? What Is Hell Like?

The Bible describes Heaven as an eternal, joyful connection with God. It is strongly associated with light; it is sometimes referred to as a divine house:

> *For we know that if our earthly house of this tabernacle were dissolved, we have a building of God, a house not made with hands, eternal in the heavens.* (I Corinthians)

Christians believe that this mystery of blessed communion with God and all who are in Christ is beyond all understanding and description. Scripture speaks of it by means of a number of compelling images: life, light, peace, wedding feast, wine of the kingdom, the Father's house, the heavenly Jerusalem, paradise. In the final analysis, this communion is beyond analysis:

> *No eye has seen, nor ear heard, nor the heart of man conceived, what God has prepared for those who love him.* (I Corinthians 2:9)

By contrast, the Bible describes Hell as dark, flaming, and sulphurous. The Devil and his angels (also known as demons) watch over the condemned souls who reside there. Hell is notable for the suffering of its residents. Jesus tells us that there will be weeping and gnashing of teeth there. According to the New Testament, the residents of Hell suffer eternal torment.

> *It is better for you to enter the kingdom of God with one eye, rather than having two eyes, to be cast into hell fire—where the worm does not die, and the fire is not quenched.* (Mark 9:47–48)

What Will Happen on the Second Coming?

Many Protestant groups emphasize the concept of the Rapture, a theological doctrine traceable only as far back as the seventeenth century that is nonetheless quite important in many contemporary American Protestant circles.

The key Bible text with regard to the Rapture is 1 Thessalonians 4:16–17, which reads …

> *For the Lord himself will descend from heaven with a cry of command, with the archangel's call, and with the sound of the trumpet of God. And the dead in Christ will rise first; then we who are alive, who are left, shall be caught up together with them in the clouds to meet the Lord in the air; and so we shall always be with the Lord.*

This idea that living Christian believers will follow the dead believers to "meet the Lord in the air" at the time of the archangel's call is today known as the Rapture. (It has been called by a variety of other names throughout the history of Christianity.)

In recent years, the Rapture has been the subject of much discussion among Christians. There is much disagreement, though, about what will occur before the Rapture takes place.

There are three ways of looking at the Rapture:

- Premillennialist
- Amillennialist
- Postmillennialist

Some Protestants identify themselves as *premillennialists,* meaning that they believe that the Second Coming will occur before the thousand-year period of Christ's reign on Earth predicted in the twentieth chapter of the Book of Revelation—a prediction they take literally and see as not yet having taken place. Other Christian groups, categorized as *amillennialists,* view this prediction symbolically, and consider it to coincide with the present time; still others, the *postmillennialists,* see the Second Coming and the Rapture as occurring after a long period of Christianization corresponding to the period prophesied in the Book of Revelation. Postmillennialists, as with amillennialists, tend to view the "thousand years" as symbolic or figurative.

Historically, Catholics—along with many other Christian groups, including the leaders of the Protestant Reformation—have discouraged a literal reading of the "thousand years" prediction in Revelation, and have de-emphasized the importance of the Rapture as a motivation for spiritual preparation among believers. These more traditional groups point to the words of the Apostle Peter:

> *But do not ignore this one fact, beloved, that with the Lord one day is as a thousand years, and a thousand years as one day. The Lord is not slow about his promise as some count slowness, but is forbearing toward you, not wishing that any should perish, but that all should reach repentance …. Since all these things are thus to be dissolved, what sort of persons ought you to be in lives of holiness and godliness, waiting for and hastening the coming of the day of God, because of which the heavens will be kindled and dissolved, and the elements will melt with fire! But according to his promise we wait for new heavens and a new earth in which righteousness dwells. Therefore, beloved, since you wait for these, be zealous to be found by him without spot or blemish, and at peace. (2 Peter 3:8–14)*

Christians can hardly be said to speak with one voice on the subject of the Rapture. Nevertheless, discussion of the Rapture, preparation for the Rapture, and evaluation of contemporary events in the light of their relevance to the Rapture remain prominent features of religious life for today's premillennialist Protestants, who tend to embrace fundamentalism (that is, literal interpretation of Bible texts) and an evangelical viewpoint.

In recent years, many Christians have been captivated by novels whose storylines have revolved around the Rapture and the end of the world.

The Eternal Reward

The ministry of Jesus Christ was one that focused relentlessly on the notion of reward in the Kingdom of Heaven. Here are some thoughts on the attainment of this reward from some prominent Christians:

> *For a small reward, a man will hurry away on a long journey; while for eternal life, many will hardly take a single step.*—Thomas à Kempis (1380–1471)

> *Heaven is God's habitation, and when Christ came on earth He taught us to pray: "Our Father, which art in heaven." This habitation is spoken of as "the city of eternal life." Think of a city without a cemetery—they have no dying there. If there could be such a city as that found on this earth what a rush there would be to it! How men would try to reach that city!*—Dwight L. Moody

Heaven is not here, it's There. If we were given all we wanted here, our hearts would settle for this world rather than the next. God is forever luring us up and away from this one, wooing us to Himself and His still invisible Kingdom, where we will certainly find what we so keenly long for.—Elisabeth Elliot

We say, "I suppose I shall understand these things some day." You can understand them now: it is not study that does it, but obedience. The tiniest fragment of obedience, and heaven opens up and the profoundest truths of God are yours straight away. God will never reveal more truth about Himself till you obey what you know already. Beware of being wise and prudent.—Oswald Chambers

For the Christian, heaven is where Jesus is. We do not need to speculate on what heaven will be like. It is enough to know that we will be forever with Him. When we love anyone with our whole hearts, life begins when we are with that person; it is only in their company that we are really and truly alive. It is so with Christ. In this world our contact with Him is shadowy, for we can only see through a glass darkly. It is spasmodic, for we are poor creatures and cannot live always on the heights. But the best definition of it is to say that heaven is that state where we will always be with Jesus, and where nothing will separate us from Him any more.—William Barclay

Islam and the Afterlife

The Qur'an, the holy book of Islam, focuses relentlessly and with great eloquence on the importance of preparing for the life to come.

It also emphasizes the temporary nature of life on Earth, which is regarded as a test for the inevitable Day of Judgment, when human beings will receive just reward for their actions on Earth.

These two topics combine and overlap throughout the text of the Qur'an. Among the hundreds of Qur'anic passages addressing these twin ideas, is the following:

There are some people who say, Our Lord! give us (rewards) in the world (we see now); and they shall have no resting place. And there are some among them who say: Our Lord! grant us good in this world and good in the hereafter, and save us from the chastisement of the fire. They shall have (their) portion of what they have earned, and Allah is swift in reckoning. (The Qur'an 2:200–202)

The Trial

To a devout Muslim, all events in this life are seen as a trial from Allah for the life to come, and all circumstances in human experience, however they may appear to us now, are in fact preparations for our eventual encounter with the Divine. To a devout Muslim, this life is a test; and it is only a test.

This view of life—as a test—is certainly prominent in other faiths, but it is fair to say that the message is repeated with greater frequency in the Qur'an than in any of the world's other great religious texts. It is elaborated in dozens of ways, many with fascinating implications on the timeless question, "Why does God permit human beings to suffer?"

Here's just one example:

> We will most certainly try you with fear and hunger and loss of property and (loss of) lives and (loss of) crops; and give good news to the patient, who, when a misfortune befalls them, say: Surely we are Allah's and to Him we shall surely return. Those are they on whom are blessings and mercy from their Lord, and those are the followers of the right course. (The Qur'an 2:155–157)

Loss alone, however, is not the only test. Gain, too, is a test in Islam. Neither wealth nor poverty are seen as originating from anyone other than Allah. If someone is rich, Muslims believe that person is rich because Allah wants to make evident whether he or she will (for example) show generosity and mercy toward others, and help support the spread of Allah's religion on Earth.

If, on the other hand, someone is poor, Muslims believe that person is poor because Allah wants to test whether he or she will (for example) remain steadfast in the face of trial, show a good example to others, and avoid the sins of hopelessness and dishonesty.

In the Islamic faith, failing either the "wealth test" or the "poverty test"—or any of countless other tests—carries consequences in the life to come. Human beings have only this short span of life to prove (not just talk about) their devotion to the Creator.

The Reckoning

Within the Islamic faith system, there is no reincarnation and no Son of God. One's reckoning is with Allah alone, and it is for the choices and actions undertaken in a single human life.

According to the Islamic faith, each human being must accept direct personal accountability to Allah for his or her life. Failing in any human endeavor, Muslims believe, is nothing when compared with the tragedy of failing to please Allah and attain entrance to Paradise. There is no second chance to rectify such an error, according to Islam, nor is there any forgiveness of sins based on the blood-sacrifice of animals, or of any other entity.

SPIRITUAL SIGNPOST

The name of Allah is whispered both to the newborn Muslim baby and to the dying Muslim. It is, in the Islamic tradition, the first word one hears upon entering the world, and the last word one hears before leaving it.

On the Day of Judgment, Muslims believe, Allah will raise all of humanity to life and see to it that each individual is given an accurate accounting of deeds performed (or ignored) during life on Earth. That accounting will demonstrate clearly, for any who doubted the reality of the Judgment, what was actually important in human life.

Those who believed in Allah, who knew that the day of resurrection would come, and who did good deeds—such as showing generosity, praying, seeking forgiveness for sins, and fearing Allah—will be rewarded with entry to Paradise and unimaginable bliss. In describing Paradise, the Qur'an uses supremely evocative language to summon up images of rest, celebration, and joy. Its actual experience, Muslims believe, is beyond human comprehension or verbal summary.

Those who spent their lives blindly ignoring the communications of Allah—by denying His reality, imagining themselves to be the authors of whatever good fortune they encountered, piling sin upon sin without seeking forgiveness, or ignoring the suffering of others—will be cast into Hell. There they will suffer torments beyond description. The language of the Qur'an in describing the torments of Hell is among the most terrifying ever committed to paper.

A Reminder to Humanity

Christian theology, with which many people in Europe and the Americas are already familiar, sees death as the wages of sin—and sees Adam and Eve's disobedience to God as the Original Sin. The Islamic view, however, is rather different.

To the Muslim, death is a reality, not because of the misbehavior of the first human beings, but because Allah has determined that all human beings are to be tested by life and brought back to their Creator through death. In the Islamic view, Allah has determined that all of humanity is to experience death, and after undergoing the test of earthly life, to return to Him for judgment:

> *Blessed is He in Whose hand is the kingdom, and He has power over all things, Who created death and life that He may try you—which of you is best in deeds; and He is the Mighty, the Forgiving.* (The Qur'an 67:1–2)

(Interestingly, the story of Adam and his wife does appear in the Qur'an; in it, Eve is not assigned blame for the couple's disobedience, and Allah eventually forgives the pair for disobeying Him.)

SPIRITUAL SIGNPOST

There is no doctrine of Original Sin in Islam, as there is in Christianity. The Qur'an does not hold that human beings are inherently evil. Yet the Qur'an does maintain that human beings are inherently forgetful about matters of ultimate concern—notably the inevitable Day of Judgment—and it repeatedly describes itself as a "reminder" to humanity as a whole about the true definition of success: entry to Paradise in the afterlife.

Actual success, in the Islamic view, does not lie in the accumulation of material goods (because these all belong to the Creator anyway) or in the gratification of our physical desires (because these are potential distractions from the eventual reckoning) or even in seemingly virtuous actions such as bringing children into the world (because even the satisfaction of being a good parent can bring pride and cause one to lose sight of one's final destination).

Actual success, for a Muslim, lies in turning away from anything that causes one to lose sight of the will of Allah. Success means turning away from the temptations of the *dunya* and from any self-centered approach that causes one to focus on the creation in preference to the Creator.

DEFINITION

Dunya is an Arabic word meaning "lower world." It refers to the visible physical world, and all its attractions. Becoming distracted by it is, according to Islam, a grave error.

Destinations

Muslims believe that people who have earned the favor of the Lord will enter Paradise, and that those who have not will enter Hell:

> *There is no doubt that evil doers who are engulfed in sins are the companions of hell fire wherein they will live forever. As for the righteously striving believers, they will be among the people of Paradise wherein they will live forever.* (The Qur'an 2:81–82)

This passage from the Qur'an informs believers that all those who are "engulfed in sins" will be consigned to Hell forever. At the other end of the continuum are those immediately transported over Hell directly to Paradise, the "righteously striving" believers.

Not all human beings will fall into these two groups, however. Some people will be delivered to Hell for a period of (agonizing) purification; others, with better records in their books, will be transported to a place called the Heights until they are ready to enter Paradise.

ON THE PATH

There are very convincing reasons to believe in life after death.

Firstly, all the prophets of God have called their people to believe in it.

Secondly, whenever a human society is built on the basis of this belief, it has been the most ideal and peaceful society, free of social and moral evils.

Thirdly, history bears witness that whenever this belief is rejected collectively by a group of people in spite of the repeated warning of the prophet, the group as a whole has been punished by God even in this world.

Fourthly, moral, aesthetic, and rational faculties of man endorse the possibility of life after death.

Fifthly, God's attributes of Justice and Mercy have no meaning if there is no life after death.

—From "Life After Death," an article circulated by the World Assembly of Muslim Youth; Riyadh, Saudi Arabia

Non-Muslims and the Afterlife

Several passages in the Qur'an suggest that devout Christians and Jews can attain Paradise. Appeal to these verses is controversial, however, because many Muslims believe the verses in question have been superseded by verses revealed later by Allah to the Prophet Muhammad.

Islam on Death and Dying

Muslims believe that all human beings, without exception, will return to their Creator to face a reckoning:

> *In the end to Us shall you be brought back.* (The Qur'an 29:57)

This group will include (in a group of special honor) all the prophets of God, an assembly Muslims hold to include such figures as Abraham, Moses, John the Baptist, Jesus, and the Prophet Muhammad.

SPIRITUAL SIGNPOST

In the Islamic view, it is not any person who determines the ultimate fate of each human being, but Allah himself.

The Angel of Death

Muslims believe that a particular angel, whom tradition identifies as Izrael, has been given formal responsibility for separating the soul from the body at the time of death, and that other angels support him in this work:

> *The Angel of Death, put in charge of you, will (duly) take your souls: then shall you be brought back to your Lord.* (The Qur'an 32:11)

Interestingly, Muslims believe that the Prophet Muhammad was the only person in history who was consulted by the Angel of Death and asked whether he was prepared to conclude his life. All others were (and are), in the Islamic view, simply taken by Izrael and his subordinate angels at the appropriate time.

SPIRITUAL SIGNPOST

Muslim burial requirements include: the swift fulfillment of funeral rites; the custom of burying the deceased in a white seamless shroud; and ensuring that the dead person's face is toward Mecca.

Death Will Find You Out!

Islam emphasizes that humans must constantly be reminded that death is both unpredictable and inevitable. No protection can shield someone from it; when its time arrives, we must succumb to it:

> *Wherever you are, death will find you out, even if you are (hiding in) towers built up strong and high.* (The Qur'an 4:78)

Muslims believe that the removal of the soul from the body of the unbeliever at the time of death is an agonizing experience—regardless of whether or not it appears to be "peaceful" to outsiders here on Earth.

ON THE PATH

The Qur'an teaches that human beings who turn from Allah and abandon His commands will earn hell's punishment eternally. Atheists, we read, are among those who will earn membership in the group that earns eternal punishment:

Those who deny My existence and die with such attitude will be subject to the condemnation of God, the angels, and all people. They will live condemned forever, will have no relief from the torment, and no attention will be paid to them. (The Qur'an 2:161–162)

If you could see, when the angels take the souls of the unbelievers (at death), how they smite their faces and their backs, saying: taste the penalty of the blazing fire. Because of the deeds which your own hands sent forth: For God is never unjust to his servants. (The Qur'an 8:50–51)

A narration attributed to the Prophet Muhammad explains the process of death as experienced by the unbeliever:

> *If an unbelieving servant is more concerned with the worldly life than he is about the other life, tar-faced angels descend from the sky. These angels, who are carrying bad smelling fragrance, sit in near proximity to the dying unbeliever. Then the Angel of Death descends and places himself near the head of the unbeliever. The Angel of*

Death says: 'O bad soul! Come out to Allah's curse and anger.' … The soul disperses in the dying person's body. The Angel of Death grabs the soul like a sufud [a piece of metal stuck in wet wool]. The Angel of Death takes the soul without letting it stay in his hand for even an instant. Then the angels put a rough garment that smells bad on the deceased's soul. The soul comes out having a very foul smell.—Hadith attributed to the Prophet Muhammad

In another narration attributed to the Prophet Muhammad, we read of the very different experience of Muslims who die in Allah's good graces:

If the believing servant refrains from coveting material things in his temporal life and desires the hereafter, white-faced angels descend from the sky. Their faces shine as brightly as the sun. They carry with them funeral garb and hanut [fragrance] from Heaven. They sit in near proximity to the dying person. The Angel of Death (may Allah bless him) comes and sits near the dying person's head, saying: 'O good soul, come out to Allah's mercy and forgiveness.' … The soul comes out like a drop of water being poured out. Then the Angel takes the soul, without letting it stand in his hand, (and) releases it like a blink. The other angels take the soul and clothe it …. From that soul comes the best smell, one resembling the best musk on earth.—Hadith attributed to the Prophet Muhammad

Following the Example of the Prophet

In Islam, no believer's soul is expected to be perfect; the question is not whether one has succeeded in avoiding sin entirely, but whether one has repented and sought forgiveness for one's sins, as the Prophet himself did.

In the end, Muslims maintain, success or failure in the afterlife depends entirely upon one's willingness to cast one's entire faith and trust on Allah and his final prophet:

Therefore, believe in Allah and His Messenger, and in the Light which We have sent down. And Allah is All-Aware of what you do. (And remember) the Day when He will gather you on the Day of Gathering, that will be the Day of mutual loss and gain. And whosoever believes in Allah and performs righteous good deeds, He will remit from him his sins, and will admit him to Gardens under which rivers flow to dwell therein forever, that will be the great success. But those who disbelieved and denied Our Signs, they will be the dwellers of the Fire, to dwell therein forever. And worst indeed is that destination. No calamity befalls, but with the Leave of Allah, and whosoever believes in Allah, He guides his heart, and Allah is the All-Knower of everything. (The Qur'an 64:8–11)

Hinduism and the Afterlife

The Hindu doctrine of reincarnation puts this faith on a substantially different footing than Judaism, Christianity, and Islam in discussions of the afterlife, and deserves close study. Let's look more closely now at the specifics of this faith system's teaching about what happens after death.

Exiting the Body

Hindu scriptures tell us that at the time of death, the soul of the believer departs the body through a particular *chakra*, or spiritual channel in the body. Which chakra that is depends on the level of spiritual development appropriate to the person.

At the time of death, Hindus believe, one's destination depends on one's state of mind at the moment of passing, and the degree and nature of one's unresolved karma. Although there is no doctrine of hell in Hinduism, practitioners do believe that human beings who pass away full of rage, despair, or hopelessness are capable only of entering a spiritual realm populated by others with similar spiritual obstructions.

The Hindu practitioner who is aware that he or she is about to die and has ample time to prepare for the event is considered to have a significant advantage over those who die unexpectedly as a result of accidents or sudden catastrophic illness. For those with sufficient time to prepare, Hinduism promotes a vision of completing as many of one's earthly obligations as possible, and resolving all disputes, debts, and emotional entanglements before passing on to the next phase of existence. Ideally, the Hindu practitioner aims to avoid rebirth and attain permanent union with infinite intelligence.

In practice, Hindus believe this outcome is extremely difficult to attain, and the goal of freeing oneself from the cycle of birth and death is regarded as the appropriate object for highly advanced practitioners. It is important to note, however, that Hinduism does not rule out the possibility of rapid spiritual advancement and learning during the course of a single life, and that the motivation is high for attaining sufficient freedom from one's past karma is to be able to drop all attachments and resolve all outstanding problems.

Embracing the Death Experience

The Hindu conception of death is one in which a believer is both deeply grateful for the chance of having the ability to experience life in a given body, and hope for final union with the Ultimate after having discarded the current body. Many Hindu religious scriptures equate the process of death with that of falling asleep, and thus see the potential of advancing to a new stage in one's spiritual development as analogous to awakening. The final stage in spiritual development is seen as total and complete union with the universal creative force.

Unlike other religious systems, which have circled rather warily around the testimonies of those who have experienced "near-death experiences," modern Hinduism emphasizes these experiences, and sees in them evidence of a personal transformation at the time of death, and even an affirmation of the doctrine of karma. Hindus point to the fact that many people who experience these remarkable visions report not only common features—proceeding down a tunnel, encountering a beam of light, intense feelings of joy—but also a decision point at which one may decide to return to one's current body and resume life to work out current obligations and resolve problems with loved ones. The parallel with the principle of karma, under which no knot is left untied before union with God is possible, is indeed interesting.

Hindus believe that the time of death is not to be feared or denied, but rather welcomed as a new stage of personal growth. They refer to the process of death as *mahaprafthana.*

In the final analysis, Hinduism, as with other major faiths, believes that each individual is responsible for confronting his or her own mortality directly, and should not neglect doing so. It differs from many other faith systems, however, in that it takes as a given the doctrine that each individual human being has previously been born and previously died. Hinduism adds to this the belief that the principles of reincarnation and karma, and the inevitable approach of death, represent nothing more than the natural working-out of individual and group entanglements.

Each individual believer, Hindus maintain, will eventually come to a point of freedom from attachment and union with the creative force that will make it possible to break the cycle of birth and death. Hinduism teaches that the individual believer's experience of this transition, while it may be feared by some, is no more worthy of fear than the process of changing one's clothes.

DEFINITION

Mahaprafthana means "period of the great departure."

Death Rituals in Hinduism

Hindu death rituals are many and varied, and have been subject to a number of adaptations for employment outside of India. Ideally, the rites are pursued by family members, and priests may or may not take part in the rituals. Here as elsewhere, Hinduism displays a staggering diversity of modes of observance.

Hindus prefer to die at home, surrounded by members of the family. A dying person is reminded to repeat his or her mantra, and a source of light is placed near his or her head. At the time of death, a member of the person's family may chant his or her mantra softly into the ear of the person preparing to make the transition. After death, family members say formal goodbyes and sing near the body. There follows a number of mourning rituals. In some situations, cremation rites are appropriate; in others the body may be consigned to the waters of the Ganges. (For Hindus practicing outside India, cremation of the dead has been adopted in most situations.)

A series of memorial observances in the days immediately following the death are carried out; there is also a memorial observance at 31 days after the death, and at one year after. The Hindu funeral service can be carried out in a variety of ways, depending on the financial resources of the family and the prevailing customs of the group of believers.

Buddhism and the Afterlife

Buddhist approaches to questions about life after death can be complex, and they often defy easy summary. A full treatment of this multifaceted topic is beyond the scope of this book. What we can do, however, is examine some of the basic Buddhist concepts relating to the afterlife.

The Cycle of Life

Buddhism comes from Hinduism, and as a result retains, as a formal point of doctrine, its belief in a system of reincarnation. However, many contemporary Buddhists, notably those in the West, without explicitly rejecting the doctrine of reincarnation, choose not to emphasize it or make it a central component of their religious practice.

From a formal point of view, Buddhists believe that reincarnation is the proper answer to the question, "What happens to us after we die?" They believe that an individual spirit is reborn, undergoes a series of rebirths, and must continue that cycle until the ultimate, until reaching a position, until reaching a state of enlightenment.

Buddhists believe that the emotions and thoughts of a dying person have a great deal to do with his or her experiences after death. As a result, they emphasize a peaceful, tranquil transition, and suggest that a dying person be surrounded by family members, close friends, and others capable of promoting an atmosphere of support and spiritual assistance and spiritual guidance.

Karma and Death

Buddhist doctrine on the afterlife teaches that we will be made reborn into a human body, and that human beings may be reborn into groups other than human families. There are a number of realms to take into account, including that of the animals, that of the human beings, that of the "jealous gods," and the realm known as "the heavens." Many Buddhists believe, as a part of doctrine, the destination of one's soul after death is determined by the state of one's karma. A heedless life, lived to perpetuate desire, anger, and ignorance, is less likely to lead to a rebirth that moves one closer to enlightenment.

There is an old Buddhist story about a sage who was asked by a student whether the enlightened person was subject to the law of karma. He gave an incorrect answer— "No"—and was thus forced to be reincarnated as a fox for a number of lifetimes. As a fox, the story goes, he sought out the guidance of a prominent Zen teacher and asked how he could be released from his predicament. He asked the Zen teacher: "What is the correct answer to the question? Is the enlightened person subject to the laws of karma or is he not?" The Zen master decided to respond to the fox and help him attain rebirth in a different, human form. To help him escape the cycle of rebirth, he provided the answer to the question: "To the enlightened person, the law of karma simply becomes clear."

The fox instantly vanished.

SPIRITUAL SIGNPOST

It is worth noting here that the Buddhist conception of hell is transitory, one that encompasses a period of punishing and purification and eventually passes. (Nirvana, by contrast, is beyond conceptions of time, space, and duration.) To many Buddhists, of course, the very distinction between "heaven" and "hell" identifies a pair of opposites, and thus is an example of delusional human perception.

What's the Focus?

The other great religions have many sects, schools, and beliefs; Buddhism does as well. As a result, it is not accurate to suggest that all Buddhists hold the same beliefs on life, death, and reincarnation. Yet there are common threads.

Even questions of death, Buddhists are likely to suggest, revolve around managing one's attention and focus. Many Zen Buddhists, in particular, are more comfortable promoting the idea of focusing on what is in front of them than on explaining the intricacies of a system of reincarnation with which they are not presently concerned.

In the final analysis, the Buddhist approach to death is still about how an individual believer chooses to conduct his or her life in the now. In any given moment, the practitioner is obligated to identify what is good, what is righteous, and what is appropriate, and to turn away from desire, eliminate ignorance, and overcome anger.

If the believer can persistently pursue these seemingly simple activities—which in fact are the labor of a lifetime—then he or she is regarded as being in a good position, not only to save his or her own soul, but eventually to help bring about the redemption of all sentient beings. Attaining salvation, not simply for oneself, but for all of creation, is an important spiritual principle within Buddhism.

Perhaps the best-known Buddhist religious scripture dealing directly with the subject of death is the *Tibetan Book of the Dead*, which offers a kind of instruction manual for assisting the dying person in making a calm and successful passage.

ON THE PATH

"It is believed (in Tibet) that as soon as the death of the body has taken place, the personality goes into a state of trance for four days. During this time the person does not know they are dead. This period is called the First Bardo and during it Lamas (monks) saying special verses can reach the dead person.

"It is believed that towards the end of this time the dead person will see a brilliant light. If the radiance of the Clear Light does not terrify them, and they can welcome it, then the person will not be reborn. But most flee from the Light ….

"The person then becomes conscious that death has occurred. At this point the Second Bardo begins. The person sees all that they have ever done or thought passing in front of them …. Then comes the Third Bardo, which is the state of seeking another birth."

—From "The Light: Tibetan Views of Death," article on www.about.com

The Least You Need to Know

- Observant Jews tend to look past questions of punishment and reward in the afterlife, choosing instead to emphasize the sacredness of human life and the importance of living it virtuously.

- Some Christians (notably premillennialist Protestants) have emphasized the modern importance of the traditional Christian doctrine known as the Rapture.

- Islam focuses relentlessly on the importance of preparing for the afterlife by submitting to the will of Allah.

- Hinduism emphasizes the principle of reincarnation.

- Buddhism accepts the doctrine of reincarnation, which it shares with Hinduism. Some Buddhists choose to emphasize this doctrine; others don't.

Other Big Questions

In This Chapter

- War and peace
- Euthanasia
- Suicide
- Abortion

In the last chapter, you saw what some of the world's great faith systems had to say about the afterlife. In this chapter, you learn about specific teachings of the world's major faiths on the most momentous issues of daily life. These are the "Big Questions" that most of us will eventually address, directly or indirectly, during the course of our lives as citizens of the modern world.

Here, you get a sense of the divergences of approach—and the sometimes surprising areas of agreement—on questions of war and peace, euthanasia and suicide, and abortion.

War and Peace

It is common for media commentators and lay observers to suggest that one or another faith tradition features scriptures that aggressively endorse war as a concept, or actively promote hostilities that affect civilians. When applied to the world's major faith systems, these analyses are, frankly, off-base.

Take a moment now to consider the actual teachings of the world's great faith systems on the momentous issues of war and peace.

Judaism on War

The Hebrew scriptures give clear indications that God approves of war in certain circumstances, but they give equally clear indications that an earnest desire for peace is an essential component of Judaism.

The famous passage from the Book of Isaiah is one of the most memorable expressions of this desire for peace: "They shall beat their swords into ploughshares and their spears into pruning hooks: Nation shall not lift up sword against nation, neither shall they learn war anymore." (Isaiah 2:2–4)

For better or worse, many groups have emphasized the image of the God of the Hebrew scriptures as "warrior" and "defender" of the Jewish people. Although this image is certainly present in the Hebrew scriptures, there is a grave difficulty that goes along with focusing on it to the exclusion of the rest of Jewish practice.

For instance, emphasizing God's role in specific biblical conflicts may distract us from the ancient positions of scholarly Judaism regarding what is and is not morally permissible military action.

Judaism has long taught that the use of force is subject to certain important restrictions, most importantly the legitimate efforts of diplomats and other intermediaries to secure a viable peace. In other words, war undertaken for its own purposes, as a means of conquest or aggression against a neighboring state, with no attempt to come to terms with peace, is not permissible in Jewish thought.

The traditional Jewish interpretation of the Hebrew scriptures in the Talmud holds that the Jewish community may not engage in attacks on noncombatants, and must give civilians the opportunity to leave areas where military action is imminent. (The precise interpretation of these regulations in modern times, however, has been a subject of considerable debate.)

SPIRITUAL SIGNPOST

Interpretations of warfare in Jewish tradition are many and varied. One point on which all responsible commentators agree, however, is that both Jews and non-Jews are permitted to fight in self-defense, and that the intentional slaughter of civilians by military forces is morally indefensible.

Christianity and War

The early Christians were pacifists, and Jesus himself appears, from the Gospel indications at our disposal, to have pursued a pacifist lifestyle.

The question of how this strategy of pacifism equates to effective statecraft is a difficult one. The best understanding of Jesus' advice on, for instance, "turning the other cheek," may be that Christ, as with the Buddha, urged believers to take into account the important fact that hatred can never be overcome by hatred. Responding to hate with more hate, Christianity teaches, perpetuates the cycle of violence and aggression, and distances us from God.

The question is: How can this theological principle affect fundamental questions of war and peace?

DEFINITION

The Christian doctrine of the just war holds that military action is not wrong in and of itself, but may be right or wrong, depending on the purpose for which it is used.

When the Roman emperor Constantine mandated official acceptance of Christianity throughout his empire in the fourth century C.E., he helped to bring about a new set of ideas that replaced the traditional Christian notion of pacifism. This was the principle of the *Just War*, a product of Christian thinkers during this period that was to be elaborated on in the centuries that followed.

The line of reasoning defending the Christian conception of the Just War is, broadly speaking, as follows:

1. Human life is sacred, and taking it is morally wrong.

2. This means human life should be defended from attack.

3. To sustain and defend its citizens, the state has a right and a duty to maintain a military class.

4. The use of this military class in acts of war may sometimes be necessary—if the violence defends both innocent human beings and the survival of the basic moral precepts of Christianity.

The idea of the Just War has carried into modern Christian thinking, and has today, as it has always had, a strong group of Christians who argue that the use of war must always be seen as a necessary evil, and not as a morally praiseworthy choice.

SPIRITUAL SIGNPOST

Today, in the early years of the twenty-first century, there has been much discussion of a supposed "Culture War" between Islam and Christianity, and much criticism of the so-called doctrine of "Holy War" in Islam. It is important to understand, though, that, as a matter of history, Christianity's reliance on Holy War is just as pronounced as that of Islam.

Islam and War

The modern image of Islam in the West among non-Muslims has been one whose chief features are extremism, violence, and aggression. Serious students of the religion—both Muslim and non-Muslim—are likely to conclude that this image is not borne out in the scriptures and the teachings of the faith itself.

A word of caution. No faith—not Islam, not Christianity, not Judaism, not Hinduism, not Buddhism—can claim to have developed a system that makes it impossible for believers to violate key principles of the religion's scriptures as they relate to war and peace.

Having granted that, we suggest it is worth understanding what is actually taught (and, no doubt, sometimes misrepresented) within Islam.

As discussed in Chapter 15, the common conception that Islam promotes the slaughter of unbelievers is manifestly false. To the contrary, Islam promotes a clear code of ethics on the battlefield, a code that requires that prisoners of war be dealt with humanely and that civilians be spared. This fact is not well known among Islam's critics in the media—or, if it is known, it is routinely ignored.

There is a famous story of a wartime companion of the Prophet Muhammad. The companion was out on horseback when he came upon an undefended enemy; he raised his sword to kill him. The enemy blurted out the words "La Illaha Illah La!"—the Muslim profession of faith that translates as "There is no God, but God!" By doing this, the helpless enemy looked to escape death, but the Muslim warrior let his sword fall and killed the man.

Later, when the Prophet Muhammad heard what had happened, he condemned his warrior's action, and informed him that he had committed a grave sin by murdering a man who not only sought to submit as a prisoner of war, but who also was, at the moment the sacred words left his lips, a fellow Muslim.

The warrior protested: "But the man only said that in order to escape death!"

The Prophet said sternly: "And so you cut open his heart so that you could see whether or not he was telling the truth?"

Wanton, unrestrained violence in the name of victory is strictly forbidden in Islam. The first Caliph, or successor to the Prophet Mohammed, was a man named Abu Bakr. He was the Prophet's father-in-law, and was one of the earliest converts to Islam. Abu Bakr gave the following guidelines on conduct in battle:

> *Do not commit treachery or veer from the right path. Never mutilate a dead body. Never kill a child, or a woman, or an elderly person. Do not harm trees, or burn them, especially trees that bear fruit. Never kill the enemy's livestock, except if he disowns it. It is likely that you will encounter people whose lives have been given over to monastic devotion. Leave these people alone.*

It's hard to escape the conclusion that the modern non-Muslim understanding of Islamic teachings on the subject of warfare is woefully incomplete. Those interested in a fuller understanding of the history of this faith, however, should consider the example of the great Muslim warrior Saladin, who recaptured Jerusalem from the Christians in 1187 during the Crusades.

Saladin followed the example of the Prophet Muhammad, who, you will recall, took Mecca without reprisals against his many enemies there. After the city of Jerusalem yielded to Saladin, no killings or acts of revenge took place. (This is especially remarkable considering the carnage that had been inflicted on Muslims when the city was taken by Christian armies.) Christian residents in Jerusalem were seized as prisoners of war, but were granted an easy ransom and were soon set free.

Buddhism on War

The faith of Buddhism is, first and foremost, a religion of peace, and it must be said that it has, among the major faiths, probably the best record of living up to that creed.

There is no justification in any Buddhist scripture for the use of violence in human affairs. The scriptures advise believers to focus on their own mortality, encourage thoughts of compassion and love, help those in need, and turn away from retaliation or revenge. A famous story from the Buddha himself advises believers, "even if you should find yourself being carved up by thieves wielding a two-handed saw, you will not be a follower of mine if you hold hostility in your mind." (Kamcupamasutta, Majjhima-Nikkaya I, 28–29)

The Buddhist doctrine of pacifism is remarkably well established and has endured in more or less the same form from the Buddha's time to this period. Even so, it is important to understand that sound doctrines in any religion, including Buddhism, are no guarantee that those doctrines will always be observed by its followers.

It is understandable, then, that while Buddhism has a remarkable record in terms of promoting pacifism and nonviolence through the centuries, that record is not (as many of its practitioners mistakenly believe) perfect.

Fourteenth-century Buddhists, for instance, engineered an uprising that eventually drove Mongol warriors from China, and some twentieth-century Zen masters in Japan frankly supported nationalistic Japanese militaristic movements.

Having made this observation, however, it is important to understand that among the world's major faith systems, Buddhism has certainly done a remarkable job of enacting its peaceful teachings in a complicated and violent world. The agnostic Bertrand Russell, no great supporter of religious values, was once pressed to identify a single religion of which he approved. He cited Buddhism, because of its generally consistent record of avoiding being used as a justification for military conquests.

Hinduism and War

A word of warning is in order here. It is dangerous to make generalizations about Hinduism's attitude toward armed conflict, because it is dangerous to make generalizations about almost anything in regard to Hinduism. The faith simply covers too much ground and encompasses too many different religious groups. However, some fundamental beliefs are generally accepted by Hindus of various inclinations, including a belief in the legitimacy of self-defense; following certain humane procedures during times of war (for instance, not attacking children, women, the elderly, or the infirm); and not turning away from a clear religious duty to fight.

Hindu teachings about death in wartime are profoundly affected by the doctrine of karma. Hindus believe, with Buddhists, that what appear to human beings to be "life" and "death" are in fact part of a delusion, and that spiritual progress is the only true reality. Unlike Buddhism, Hinduism presents this way of thinking of human experience as (occasional) justification for armed conflict.

As a general rule, of course, Hinduism emphasizes nonviolence and forbids the doing of harm, and theological justifications for those wars. Among those modern Hindus who took exception to traditional Hindu teachings on war and peace was Mahatma Ghandi. Ghandi interpreted the ideal of Ahimsa, that of avoiding harming any person or living thing, as mandating a position of nonviolence.

Once, when asked whether he was willing to die for his beliefs, Ghandi thought for a long moment, and then responded: "I think it is a bad question."

Judaism on Euthanasia and Suicide

Judaism forbids the unnecessary taking of human life, and precludes physicians from taking any action that would make death advance more quickly. At the same time, however, Judaism does not force doctors to take extraordinary measures to prolong human life. Judaism also forbids suicide, and prohibits those who would assist another person in taking his or her own life.

There is a story in the Talmud of a rabbi who was being executed by the Roman authorities in a particularly ghastly way: he was being burned alive. His students urged him to hasten the onset of death by breathing the fire into his lungs. The rabbi shook his head and told them: "It is preferable that the One who gave it should take it, rather than that I should injure myself." He was speaking, of course, about God—the one who had given him his soul in the first place.

As with all modern religions, there is ongoing debate among practitioners regarding the wisdom or authority of these teachings, especially as they relate to so-called "mercy killing." These teachings are, nevertheless, clearly established within the formal precepts of Judaism.

Christianity on Euthanasia and Suicide

The vast majority of Christians oppose euthanasia under the justification that life is a gift from God, and that human beings are bound to respect God's decisions on when souls enter and leave the world. The same general approach applies to questions concerning suicide. The Roman Catholic Church, in particular, has been a vocal opponent of "mercy killing," seeing it as a sin that ignores the inherent validity and dignity of human life.

Pope John Paul II has been a vocal opponent of what he has identified as a "culture of death" in contemporary society. He has continued to emphasize traditional Catholic teachings on suicide and euthanasia.

Of so-called "mercy killing," the pope wrote: "True compassion leads to sharing another's pain; it does not kill the person whose suffering we cannot bear." (*Evangelium Vitae*, 1995)

ON THE PATH

"Euthanasia is a grave violation of the law of god, since it is the deliberate and morally unacceptable killing of a human person."

—Pope John Paul II, *Evangelium Vitae*, 1995

Although there are certainly differences of opinion and emphasis, it is fair to say that the majority of Protestant and Orthodox religious leaders agree in whole or in part with the pope's position. This is not to say that there have not been Christians of faith who have disagreed with the standard teachings on this matter. As yet, though, there is no sign of acceptance of suicide or euthanasia becoming a central component of Christian belief.

Islam on Euthanasia and Suicide

The Islamic faith does not accept immoral justification for "mercy killing" or for suicide. Both are rather briskly dismissed in the teachings of Islam. Suicide is specifically forbidden in any and all circumstances by the Qur'an.

A famous saying of the Prophet Mohammed clearly prohibits euthanasia: "Amongst the nations before you there was a man who had a wound, and who had no patience with it, and who took a knife and gave himself a wound on the hand, thus bleeding until he died. Allah said, 'My slave hastened to bring death to himself, and so I have forbidden paradise to him.'"

Buddhism on Euthanasia and Suicide

There is no clear teaching in Buddhism dealing with euthanasia. Many Buddhists are extremely skeptical of it, however, believing that anyone who attempts it is very likely to slip into a cynical or depressed state of mind.

Buddhists who encounter serious physical illness often decide to embark on sustained periods of meditation. As a guiding principle, Buddhists reject doing harm to others or taking human life. They also believe that consciously ending a human life is very likely to lead to difficulties with one's karma.

With regard to suicide, the situation is a little clearer, but not much. There appears to have been at least two cases where the Buddha sanctioned cases of monks killing themselves as a means of spiritual progression. There is no evidence that he approved of the practice for lay Buddhists.

Here, as elsewhere, Buddhism emphasizes the maintenance of a correct state of mind. It teaches that maintaining a peaceful and serene outlook on life is all the more important as the time of death approaches. Notions of anger, fear, or rage, Buddhists believe, must be overcome during this life.

Hinduism on Euthanasia and Suicide

There are a number of different viewpoints on euthanasia in the Hindu tradition. The majority view is that a doctor must not cooperate with the request to end a patient's life early. Giving into this request, most Hindus believe, is likely to lead to karmic difficulties for both doctor and patient. By the same token, however, there is a school of Hindu thought that holds that a doctor who helps to end a life that has become unbearably painful is giving aid to another person, and thus improving the karma of both doctor and patient.

The question is not definitively resolved, but majority interpretation appears to hold against the practice of euthanasia.

As to suicide, there is, within Hinduism, a suicide tradition known as *prayopavesa*. This is regarded as morally acceptable in certain circumstances, most involving the passing of aged practitioners whose health is failing. Hinduism teaches that prayopavesa must be undertaken in a spirit of serenity and wholeness, not out of cynicism, despair, or rage. It is the final gesture of someone who has attained a certain level of spiritual advancement. It may not be performed by someone who still has outstanding responsibilities to another human being.

DEFINITION

Prayopavesa, in Hinduism, is the practice of consciously refusing food until one dies.

Thoughts on Abortion

The world's major faith systems have remarkably similar positions on the question of abortion. All oppose, and view as deeply sinful, its casual use.

Hinduism describes the practice of abortion as "garha-batta" ("womb killing").

Many early Islamic scholars viewed abortion before the 120th day of the pregnancy as permissible in the presence of a compelling reason to end the pregnancy, such as a threat to the life of the mother. Other scholars, notably those of the Maliki school of jurisprudence, forbade the practice after the fortieth day, and strongly discouraged it before that point.

The Buddha not only forbade abortion, but forbade his monks from recommending it.

The prevailing view in Judaism is that a woman may not do harm to her own body, but may undergo surgical procedures, including abortion, in her own defense.

There is an array of positions in Christianity, with Catholics and Orthodox Christian leaders condemning the practice completely, and most other denominations tending to approve it only as a last resort when the life of the mother is endangered.

The Least You Need to Know

- The world's great faiths take distinctive approaches to the momentous issue of war and peace.
- No major faith system endorses war as a central doctrine, or sanctions the killing of innocent civilians.
- By the same token, no faith system is capable of developing a system of beliefs relating to war and peace that cannot be abused by its followers.
- The world's major faiths take differing approaches to questions of euthanasia and suicide. They condemn the casual use of abortion.

Religious Extremism in the Twenty-First Century

In This Chapter

- September 11th and its aftermath
- Reactions to religious extremism
- What religious extremists have in common
- The best response

The terrorist attacks upon the United States of September 11, 2001, highlighted, in an impossible-to-ignore way, the issue of violence committed in the name of religion. Although the scale of those attacks was unprecedented in the United States, it is important for Americans to remember that religiously motivated violence took place in their country before September 11 (for instance, when religious extremist Eric Robert Rudolph bombed the 1996 Olympic Games in Atlanta)—and after September 11 (for instance, when the anti-abortionist Scott Roeder murdered Wichita doctor George Tiller on May 31, 2009).

The question then becomes: What makes a follower of a particular religious system decide to turn to violence in the name of God? The answer is complex. When we look at these incidents closely, we see a common thread: abandonment of core principles of the religion supposedly followed by the perpetrators.

The Hand of Blind Rage

Following the shameful attacks on the United States in 2001, a wave of anti-Muslim violence and discrimination swept the nation. Some of the violence was even directed toward people who had no connection whatsoever to the faith claimed by the hijackers who turned passenger airplanes into deadly weapons.

In New York City, Sikhs wearing turbans were mistaken for Muslims and singled out for abuse. The long list of law-abiding citizens abused and assaulted in late 2001 deserves more than simple condemnation. Like the terrorist attacks themselves, the wave of anger and retaliation that followed deserves to be examined closely.

As many Americans realized in those dark days following the horrific events in New York, Pennsylvania, and Washington, D.C., the choice to retaliate by singling out a specific religious group for retaliation served only to mirror the misguided tactics of the people who had committed the crimes in the first place.

Blind rage has a way of begetting blind rage. It is not the foundation of any religious faith worthy of the name, or indeed of any functioning society. Recognizing this, people of goodwill began to disengage from the emotion of the situation, and began asking a number of difficult questions following the September 11 attacks. Among those questions was: What do religious extremists who resort to violence have in common?

A Global Phenomenon

The attacks by al Qaeda in 2001 were not the only such assaults on innocent persons in recent years. To the contrary, the September 11 attacks seemed to have a great deal in common with religiously themed violence that has spread across most major faith systems. There is religiously motivated violence by both Jewish and Muslim groups in the Middle East, and there are, as we have seen, religious groups that advocate violence in the name of Christianity in the United States, many around the issue of abortion.

These groups, despite their evident religious differences, are often startlingly similar to one another when it comes to motivation and worldview.

A Totalist Outlook

One common motivator of religious violence is what sociologists and political scientists call a *totalist* outlook on life. This is basically the belief that one's own cause is entirely good, and the cause of one's opponents entirely bad. Totalism has also been described as the belief that a single narrow set of ideas can and should permeate all of society, eradicating all ideas that oppose it.

> **DEFINITION**
>
> **Totalism** is the practice of seeing the world in black and white, and of actively rejecting all competing social and belief systems. It is a mark of political and religious extremism. Responsible religious leaders in Christianity, Judaism, Hinduism, Islam, and Buddhism have rejected totalist movements.

It's important to understand that totalist movements don't spring from within religious traditions spontaneously. They have social causes, among which are oppression, deprivation, psychological trauma, and prolonged periods of social instability.

Charismatic Figures, Feelings of Victimization

Those who coordinate religiously motivated attacks and campaigns of violence often recruit younger members who have psychological problems, unstable family backgrounds, or are simply immature.

People who carry out violent actions in the name of their religious faith may be encouraged through a relatively centralized organizational structure, such as the militia groups of the Middle East, or through a more open-ended organizational approach sustained by shadowy groups with no known specific location, such as al-Qaeda or the so-called *Christian Identity* groups of the United States.

> **DEFINITION**
>
> The so-called **Christian Identity** movement is a loosely knit coalition of nominal Christian splinter groups in the United States that advocate, but claim not to coordinate, domestic campaigns of violence against such targets as blacks, homosexuals, and Jews. The Internet is a primary recruiting and training ground for the "lone wolves" who adopt the principles espoused by prominent Christian Identity figures. The accused Olympic bomber Eric Robert Rudolph is believed to have been part of the movement.

Whether the religion being appealed to is Christianity, Islam, Hinduism, or any other faith, the pattern of a younger male with a traumatic family history and/or a deep-seated sense of having suffered injustice appears again and again in terrorist actions and campaigns. The task of recruiting, raising funds, and developing plans of religiously justified violence may or may not be coordinated by a single older figure who serves as a mentor to this younger male.

When there is such an older male mentor, he tends to present certain recognizable characteristics: he is likely to be a highly charismatic father figure; he may speak provocatively about the enemies of his cause, but is likeliest to do so by means of vague generalities (at least in public); and he may be, in personal demeanor, an apparently sober and thoughtful person, even withdrawn and passive. (Those who have met Osama bin Laden have claimed that his personality appears to reflect a calm, even retiring nature.)

Increasing Chaos and Injustice

Groups that act along religious lines to achieve political goals *without* recourse to violence are, of course, common around the world. These groups usually seek to resolve identifiable social problems. Groups that act along religious lines to achieve political goals *through violent means*, however, often aim to worsen the varied social and political problems they claim to oppose.

If there is violence on the ground, they want to accelerate it. If there is discrimination and racial strife, they want to increase it. Indeed, most members of these groups have concluded that the perpetuation of chaos and injustice is the likeliest, and perhaps the only, way to defeat their opponents. (Similar strategies were employed by the Nazis and Soviet Communists in the first half of the twentieth century; although these two groups were secular, rather than religious, in nature, the means selected to achieve their goals were essentially the same.)

It is frequently suggested that the best response to various global international terrorist groups is to undertake aggressive conventional military campaigns to "root them out." This approach, however, runs the risk of playing directly into the hands of the terrorists. Their objective is to accelerate whatever social chaos or dislocation they may find in their region or movement, because the greater the chaos, the more likely there are to be aggrieved young men or women to recruit to their cause. War inevitably brings suffering, disorder, and rage for these terrorist leaders to exploit.

The act of launching a military campaign against a terrorist organization has been compared, with some justice, to the act of shooting a swarm of mosquitoes with a machine gun.

Selective Interpretation

Religious extremists distort, quote out of context, and otherwise manipulate their own religious scriptures. The Christian Identity groups in the United States, for instance, conveniently overlook New Testament teachings concerning peace, reconciliation, and brotherhood, and choose instead to emphasize their own twisted interpretations of the apocalyptic visions of the Book of Revelation and the law of the Old Testament. The same phenomenon plays out in radical Jewish and Muslim groups around the world.

No major contemporary religious tradition on Earth—and certainly none of the major faiths we examined in depth in this book—promotes as an article of faith the killing of innocent people. By the same token, however, no major religious system is arranged in such a way as to make it impossible to misinterpret or manipulate its teachings in a destructive way.

Some deeply misguided believers, unfortunately, do fall prey to the promptings of charismatic figures who use selective interpretation of religious texts to justify such actions as launching suicide attacks upon skyscrapers, machine-gunning civilians, or bombing abortion clinics. Such cynical dealing can only be described as a fatal human disconnection with any divine message.

So What Is the Answer?

There is no easy response to the challenge of religious extremism and politically motivated religious violence in the twenty-first century.

The first and most important thing to do, however, is to understand that holding any single faith responsible for all deeds carried out in its name will only hasten and accelerate a cycle of mutual intolerance and increase the likelihood of new totalist factions. A Christian is not, by definition, a terrorist because some misguided person bombs an abortion clinic.

If we focus on the actions of an extremist group affiliated with any given faith, and repeatedly emphasize what we believe to be that faith's "terrorist" tendencies, we increase the likelihood that rank-and-file members of our faith will come to view all those who believe differently as extremists. *This is in fact the aim of many terrorists:* to accelerate the polarization of religious life and make it more difficult for people in different faiths to appreciate each other's humanity. This, in other words, is the triumph of totalism, and the failure of religion.

It is a common rhetorical trick of religious extremists to ask others to believe that any deed carried out by a believer within a given tradition is sanctioned by that believer's faith system. In other words, if a Muslim blows up the First National Bank, then (the argument goes) the tenets of Islam must somehow support the principle of detonating bank buildings. This is, of course, absurd. The acts of hatred, division, and violence that extremists undertake are their own responsibility, not those of the responsible teachers within their own faith.

ON THE PATH

"We may not always agree with every one of our neighbors. That's life. And it's part of living in such a diverse and dense city. But we also recognize that part of being a New Yorker is living with your neighbors in mutual respect and tolerance. It was exactly that spirit of openness and acceptance that was attacked on 9/11, 2001. On that day, 3,000 people were killed because some murderous fanatics didn't want us to enjoy the freedoms to profess our own faiths, to speak our own minds, to follow our own dreams, and to live our own lives. Of all our precious freedoms, the most important may be the freedom to worship as we wish …. Let us not forget that Muslims were among those murdered on 9/11, and that our Muslim neighbors grieved with us as New Yorkers and as Americans. We would betray our values and play into our enemies' hands if we were to treat Muslims differently than anyone else. On September 11, 2001, thousands of first responders heroically rushed to the scene and saved tens of thousands of lives. More than 400 of those first responders did not make it out alive. In rushing into those burning buildings, not one of them asked, 'What God do you pray to? What beliefs do you hold?' The attack was an act of war, and our first responders defended not only our city, but our country and our constitution …. (We should) repudiate the false and repugnant idea that the attacks of 9/11 were in any way consistent with Islam."

—New York Mayor Michael Bloomberg, August 3, 2010

In encouraging the process that allows members of a given faith to view all members of another faith as the "Other"—as members of a group that is essentially objectified and utterly different than our own—religious extremists from a variety of faiths hope to usher in the long period of conflict and suffering that they believe will make the realization of their own agendas possible.

The best response to this dark campaign is simply to learn the specifics about the teachings of other faiths, and to understand them as they are, and not as they are presented by others to be.

The Least You Need to Know

- Violent religious extremist groups have certain common elements.
- Religious extremists frequently rely on young men who have psychological problems or who perceive that they are victims of discrimination or injustice.
- No contemporary major religious faith advocates the murder of innocent civilians.
- The best response is probably to learn as much as you can about all faiths.

All Down in Black and White

In This Chapter

- How you can use scriptures from other traditions to build bridges
- The limitations of language (even holy language)
- What the world's great religions have to say in response to some of the most important human questions
- How even life's great challenges can be seen as "part of the plan"

In this part of the book, you discover important points of contact between familiar religious traditions—ideas that will allow you to find common ground with virtually anyone, of virtually any background, when it's time to address life's Big Questions.

Scripture as a Meeting Place

Although some religious systems (such as the Native American and African faiths discussed earlier) manage just fine without them, scriptures are important for most believers. Spiritual writings offer answers to important questions, identify fundamental points of observance and ritual, and lend a sense of permanence and continuity to a faith's essential teachings, whether those teachings are presented as ancient wisdom, timely contemporary instruction, or something in between.

Most important, perhaps, holy scriptures serve as a meeting point, a common resource and shared spiritual heritage that allows believers within a particular tradition to identify, support, and commune with each other. When we encounter someone who treats a sacred text with something akin to the respect that we do, we can begin to build a bridge with that person, even if he or she doesn't personally share our faith system. On the other hand, when someone offers neither curiosity nor respect, but instead attacks our scriptures, we may find dialogue is often difficult or impossible.

BARRIER ALERT!

Even "innocent" criticisms or "objective" analyses of another person's scriptural heritage can feel like direct attacks. Focusing on the "rightness" or "wrongness" of particular points of doctrine, or questioning the "logic" underlying someone else's religious scriptures, can undermine the most promising exchange.

Early in this book, you saw how the scriptures of the world's great religious traditions addressed questions of knowledge and experience of the Divine from very similar vantage points. This chapter aims to offer similar insights on some classic practical questions of everyday spirituality. It is meant to deepen understanding and to help you initiate dialogue, not impassioned debates, with people whose religious practices differ from your own.

Words and metaphors have their limits, and some religious traditions actively encourage the transcendence of written forms. In such traditions, religious observance is incomplete if it focuses too closely on texts. A famous Zen Buddhist story tells of an aging master who reverently passed along to the disciple who was to succeed him a carefully assembled book of their school's most essential teachings. The younger man immediately threw the texts into the fire. In the lineage he was to continue, this was a valid expression of the spiritual heritage.

A Sense of Purpose

Human beings, the core texts of the world's religions agree, are meant to be happy and to experience fulfillment through the cultivation of love that mirrors perfect divine love.

Most scriptures recognize that the quest for happiness and harmonious interaction among individuals and groups is not without its challenges and obstacles. It involves some kind of spiritual journey, whose completion is an experience of transcendence, homecoming, and contentment beyond the limits of human emotion and ordinary understanding. The fulfillment of this journey is also regarded as concluding all pain, trial, tragedy, distraction, worry, and confusion.

What Are We Doing Here?

Buddhism: Whatever grounds there be for good works undertaken with a view to [auspicious] rebirth, all of them are not worth one-sixteenth part of that goodwill which is the heart's release; goodwill alone, which is the heart's release, shines and burns and flashes forth in surpassing them. (Ittiuttaka 19)

Judaism: The Holy Spirit rests only on the one who has a joyous heart. (Jerusalem Talmud, Sukkat 5.1)

Islam: The greatest bliss is the good pleasure of God; that is the supreme felicity. (The Qur'an 9.72)

> **ON THE PATH**
>
> A sacred text within the Sikh faith celebrates human purpose as a communion of one's true self with God: "Completely fulfilled is myself, as the Master has granted a vision of the Supreme Being .... With Him seated on the throne of eternal justice, ended is all wailing and crying." (Adi Granth, Majh, M.5)

Christianity: Why take ye thought for raiment? Consider the lilies of the field, how they grow; they toil not, neither do they spin; and yet I say unto you, that even Solomon in all his glory was not arrayed like one of these. Wherefore if God so clothe the grass of the field, which today is, and tomorrow is cast into the oven, shall he not much more clothe you, o ye of little faith? Therefore take no thought, saying, what shall we eat? Or, what shall we drink? Or, wherewithal shall we be clothed? ... for your heavenly father knoweth that ye have need of all these things. But seek ye first the kingdom of God, and his righteousness, and all these things shall be added unto you. (Matthew 6:28–33)

Hinduism: Giving up all Dharmas (righteous and unrighteous action), come unto me alone for refuge. I shall free thee from all sins. Grieve not. (*Bhagavad Gita* 18.66)

The Importance of Personal Resolve

In pursuing a spiritual path, the religions of the world place a special emphasis on vigilance and wakefulness, reminding believers that even momentary inattention or disconnection from righteous action and observance can have disastrous consequences.

How Do We Stay on the Path?

Confucianism: Flood-like chi [primal energy] … is, in the highest degree, vast and unyielding. Nourish it with integrity and place no obstacle in its path, and it will fill the space between heaven and earth … It is born of accumulated rightness and cannot be appropriated by anyone through a sporadic show of rightness. (Mencius II.A.2)

Christianity: The day of the Lord so cometh as a thief in the night … But ye, brethren, are not in darkness, that that day should overtake you as a thief. Ye are all the children of the light, and the children of the day. We are not of the night, nor of darkness. Therefore let us not sleep, as do others; but let us watch and be sober. (1 Thessalonians 5:2–6)

Hinduism: Those journeying to heaven do not look back. (Satapatha Brahmana 9.2.3.27)

Islam: Surely there are Signs for those of understanding, those who remember God while standing, sitting, and lying down … (The Qur'an 3:190–191)

Jainism: One should not be swept away by the eddies of a mercurial mind. (The Acarangasutra)

Buddhism: Let me respectfully remind you, life and death are of supreme importance. Time passes swiftly and opportunity is lost. Each of us must strive to wake up, wake up. Take heed. Do not squander your lives. (Traditional reminder issued orally during Zen practice at the conclusion of the day.)

DEFINITION

Jainism is an ancient Indian religion that promotes a comprehensive code of nonviolence toward all living things and a commitment to nonviolence not merely in action, but in one's thoughts as well. Jainism emphasizes constant self-analysis and self-improvement as a means of ending the cycle of rebirth and attaining spiritual liberation. The religion dates to the prehistoric period; today, it claims over 4 million followers in India.

Loving Others as Ourselves

Is there a single idea that can guide all human behavior and bring it into line with divine purpose? For many the answer is yes. Nearly every religion, regardless of its age or range of geographical influence, emphasizes the ethical principle known to

Westerners as the Golden Rule. The world's religions formulate this principle in startlingly similar ways.

How Should We Act?

Judaism and Christianity: Thou shalt not avenge, nor bear any grudge against the children of thy people, but thou shalt love thy neighbor as thyself. I am the Lord. (Leviticus 19:18)

Christianity: Then one of them, which was a lawyer, asked him a question ... "Master, which is the great commandment of the law?"

Jesus said unto him, "Thou shalt love the Lord thy God with all thy heart, and with all thy soul, and with all thy mind. This is the first and great commandment, and the second is like unto it: Thou shalt love thy neighbor as thyself. On these two commandments hang all the law and the prophets." (Matthew 22:35–40)

Confucianism: Do not do to others what you do not want them to do to you. (*Analects* 15.23)

Hinduism: One should not behave toward others in a way which is disagreeable to oneself. (*Mahabharata*, Anusasana Parva 113.8)

Islam: We have created the human being to face a great deal of hardship. Does He think that no one will ever have control over him? (He boasts and shows off) saying, 'I have spent a great deal of money (for the cause of God).' Does he think that no one has seen him? Have We not given him two eyes, a tongue, and two lips? Have We not shown him the ways of good and evil? Yet, he has not entered into Aqaba. Would that you knew what Aqaba is! It is the setting free of a slave, or, in a day of famine, the feeding of an orphaned relative and downtrodden destitute person, (so that he would be of) the believers who cooperate with others in patience (steadfastness) and kindness. These are the people of the right hand. As for those who disbelieve in Our revelations, they are the people of the left who will be engulfed in the fire. (The Qur'an 90:4–20)

The Almighty as Protector and Sustainer

Even (perhaps especially!) when humans seem least to merit divine grace, it expresses itself. The world's great religious scriptures view divine power as a source of help, support, and unending compassion to the members of the human family. This sustenance is viewed as essential to the completion of life's journeys.

Who Is Watching Over Us?

Buddhism: I appear in the world like unto this great cloud, to pour enrichment on all parched living beings, to free them from their misery to attain the joy of peace, joy of the present world, and joy of Nirvana. (Lotus Sutra 5)

Islam: He is the only God. God is Absolute (sustaining all, without requiring sustenance); He neither begets nor was He begotten. There is no one equal to Him. (The Qur'an 112:1–4)

Judaism and Christianity: The Lord is my shepherd; I shall not want. He maketh me to lie down in green pastures; he leadeth me beside the still waters. He restoreth my soul; he leadeth me in the paths of righteousness for his name's sake. Yea, though I walk through the valley of the shadow of death, I will fear no evil: for thou art with me. Thy rod and thy staff, they comfort me. Thou preparest a table before me in the presence of mine enemies: thou anointest my head with oil; my cup runneth over. Surely goodness and mercy shall follow me all the days of my life: and I will dwell in the house of the Lord forever. (Psalm 23)

Taoism: Tao never acts, yet nothing is left undone. (Tao Te Ching 37)

Constant Praise to the Almighty

The faiths of the world agree that the Ultimate is to be openly praised and celebrated. Although praise takes countless forms, the earnestness of spirit and intent guiding this devotion is always recognizable. So, according to the scriptures, are the positive effects upon the individual believer of rendering praise.

Doctrinal and theological disputes aside, the idea of sustained, continual praise to that which is revered as eternal is one of the most exhilarating and dramatic elements unifying human religious practice.

A holy text of Zoroastrianism summarizes the purifying effect of praising God as follows: "The deeds which I shall do and those which I have done ere now, and the things which are precious to the eye, through Good Mind, the light of the sun, the sparkling dawn of the days, all this is for your praise, O Wise Lord, as righteousness!" (Avesta, Yasna 50.10)

How Do Human Voices Glorify the Divine Presence?

The Hare Krishna Movement: Hare Krishna, Hare Krishna, Krishna Krishna, Hare Hare; Hare Rama, Hare Rama, Rama Rama, Hare Hare.

Islam: He is the Living One; there is no God but He: call upon Him, giving Him sincere devotion. Praise be to God, Lord of the Worlds. (The Qur'an 40.65)

Hinduism and Buddhism: Gate, gate, paragate, parasamgate, bodhi svaha. (Gone, gone, gone beyond, gone beyond—hail the goer!)

Judaism/Christianity: Praise ye the Lord! Praise God in his sanctuary! Praise him in the firmament of his power! Praise him for his mighty acts! Praise him according to his excellent greatness!

Praise him with the sound of the trumpet! Praise him with the psaltery and harp! Praise him with the timbrel and dance! Praise him with stringed instruments and organs! Praise him upon the loud cymbals! Praise him upon the high-sounding cymbals! Let everything that hath breath praise the Lord! Praise ye the Lord! (Psalm 150)

Striving Toward the Infinite

All major religious scriptures emphasize the importance of a continual effort to align ourselves with an infinite, sustaining force.

What Guides Our Relationship with God?

Islam: O man! Surely you must strive (to attain) to your Lord, a hard striving until you meet Him. (The Qur'an 84:6)

Buddhism: Neither abstinence from fish and flesh, nor going naked, nor shaving the head, nor wearing matted hair, nor dressing in a rough garment, nor covering oneself with dirt, nor sacrificing to Agni, will cleanse a man who is not free from delusions. (The Buddha, *The Sermon at Benares*)

Christianity: What woman having ten silver coins, if she loses one of them, does not light a lamp, and search carefully until she finds it? When she has found it, she calls together her friends and neighbors, saying, 'Rejoice with me, for I have found the coin that I had lost.' (Luke 15:8–9)

The Divine Plan

As you may have gathered in Chapter 33, there is no use pretending that the scriptures of the world's religions are in agreement on the answers to fundamental human questions concerning death. They aren't.

As this book nears its end, we appeal not to competing excerpts from ancient religious scriptures, but to a very recent observation from one of today's most influential spiritual writers. The author is the Buddhist monk Thich Nhat Hanh. Although his views do not possess scriptural authority in any tradition, they seem to us to be profound. Perhaps you will agree. Here, then, is one response to what may be the ultimate human question: Why do we suffer and die?

Why Do We Suffer and Die?

When we have a compost bin filled with organic material (that) is decomposing and smelly, we know that we can transform the waste into beautiful flowers. At first, we may see the compost and the flowers as opposite, but when we look deeply, we see that the flowers already exist in the compost, and the compost already exists in the flowers. It only takes a couple of weeks for a flower to decompose. When a good organic gardener looks into her compost, she can see that, and she does not feel sad or disgusted. Instead she values the rotting material and does not discriminate against it. It takes only a few months for the compost to give birth to flowers. (Thich Nhat Hanh, "Peace Is Every Step," *Parabola*, Winter, 1991)

Within the Christian tradition, there is scripture that closely parallels Thich Nhat Hanh's inspiring words. This saying of Jesus can be found in the Gospel of John.

"I tell you most solemnly, unless a wheat grain falls on the ground and dies, it remains only a single grain; but if it dies, it yields a rich harvest." (John 12:24–46)

As we conclude this book, we acknowledge the enduring power of the force that reconciles all endings and all beginnings, and we look forward to the bountiful harvest that is the birthright of all humankind.

The Least You Need to Know

- Scripture can be used to build bridges between people of different religious traditions.
- Words and metaphors have their limits, and some religious traditions actively encourage the transcendence of written forms.
- The world's great scriptural traditions offer complementary answers to important human questions about human purpose, individual resolve, basic ethical conduct, grace, spiritual effort, and the glorification of the divine force.
- Even death and suffering can be understood as elements of the divine plan.

Fellow Travelers

Some remarkable people have had thoughts on the sacred, on everyday life, and on the intersection of the two. Here are some of our favorite observations.

"Tell him your future plans."—Woody Allen, on "how to make God laugh."

"The Japanese, concentrating on the abdomen, rid their minds of useless luggage. The Sufi dervishes, using their feet, also rid their minds of useless luggage. The ridding of luggage is more important than the method. What is needed is a method that works, not a philosophy about method, which can be very confusing."—Sufi Ahmed Murad

"Call it Nature, Fate, Fortune; all these are names of the one and selfsame God."—Seneca

"All the different religions are only so many religious dialects."—G. C. Lichtenberg

"Religion is like the fashion: one man wears his doublet slashed, another laced, another plain, but every man has a doublet; so every man has a religion. We differ about the trimmings."—John Selden

"My reason tells me that God exists, but it also tells me that I can never know what He is."—Voltaire

"I feel that there is a God, and I do not feel that there is none. For me that is enough."—Jean de la Bruyere

"Every man recognizes within himself a free and rational spirit, independent of his body. This spirit is what we call God."—Leo Tolstoy

"'There are quicksands all about you, sucking at your feet, trying to suck you down into fear and self-pity and despair. That's why you must walk so lightly …'

"'The Light,' came the hoarse whisper, 'the Clear Light. It's here, along with the pain, in spite of the pain.'

"'And where are you?'

"'Over there, in the corner. I can see myself there.'

"'Brighter,' came the barely audible whisper, 'brighter.' And a smile of happiness intense almost to the point of elation transfigured her face."

—Aldous Huxley, *Island*

"I think that the leaf of a tree, the meanest insect on which we trample, are in themselves arguments more conclusive than any which can be adduced that some vast intellect animates Infinity."—Percy Bysshe Shelley

"If you can serve a cup of tea right, you can do anything."—George Gurdjieff

"For the wonderful thing about saints is that they were human. They lost their tempers, got angry, scolded God, were egotistical or testy or impatient in their turns, made mistakes and regretted them. Still they went on doggedly blundering toward heaven."—Phyllis McGinley

"A woman once came to Mahatma Gandhi with her little boy. She asked, 'Mahatma-ji, tell my little boy to stop eating sugar.'

"'Come back in three days,' said Gandhi.

"In three days the woman and the little boy returned and Mahatma Gandhi said to the little boy, 'Stop eating sugar.'

"The woman asked, 'Why was it necessary for us to return after only three days for you to tell my little boy that?'

"The Mahatma replied: 'Three days ago I had not stopped eating sugar.'"

—Ram Dass, *Be Here Now*

"We trust, sir, that God will be on our side. It is more important to know that we are on God's side."—Abraham Lincoln

"All evil vanishes from life for him who keeps the sun in his heart."—Ramayana

"Some very humane, simple-minded old lady sees the play *King Lear* performed, and she is outraged that a poor old man should be so humiliated, made to suffer so. And in the eternal shade she meets Shakespeare, and she says to him, 'What a monstrous thing to make that poor man go through all that.' And Shakespeare says, 'Yes, I quite agree. It was very painful, and I could have arranged for him to take a sedative at the end of Act I, but then, ma'am, there would have been no play.'"—Malcolm Muggeridge

"When I lay these questions before God I get no answer. But a rather special sort of 'No answer.' It is not the locked door. It is more like a silent, certainly not uncompassionate, gaze. As though He shook His head not in refusal but waiving the question. Like, 'Peace, child; you don't understand.'"—C. S. Lewis

"The essence of civilization consists not in the multiplication of wants but in their deliberate and voluntary renunciation."—Mahatma Gandhi

"I have loved to hear my Lord spoken of; and wherever I have seen the print of His shoe in the earth, there I have coveted to set my foot, too."—John Bunyan

"As soon as a man is fully disposed to be alone with God, he is alone with God no matter where he may be; in the country, the monastery, the woods, or the city. The lightning flashes from East to West, illuminating the whole horizon and striking where it pleases and at the same instant the infinite liberty of God flashes in the depths of that man's soul, and he is illumined. At that moment he sees that though he seems to be in the middle of his journey, he has already arrived at the end. For the life of Grace on earth is the beginning of the life of Glory. Although he is a traveler in time, he has opened his eyes for a moment in eternity."—Thomas Merton

"God will be present, whether asked or not."—Latin proverb

"Lord God of hosts, be with us yet,
Lest we forget, lest we forget."

"—Rudyard Kipling

"He who desires to see the living God face to face should not seek Him in the empty firmament of his mind, but in human love."—Fyodor Dostoevsky

"Here is God's purpose—for God, to me, it seems, is a verb, not a noun, proper or improper."—R. Buckminster Fuller

"The soul has the means. Thinking is the means. It is inanimate. When thinking has completed its task of release, it has done what it had to do, and ceases."—Vishnu Parana

"To get into the core of God at his greatest, one must first get into the core of himself at his least, for no one can know God who has not first known himself."—Meister Eckhard

"Well, God's a good man."—William Shakespeare

"Lord, who art always the same, give that I know myself, give that I know Thee."—St. Augustine

"Religion is a way of walking, not a way of talking."—Dean William R. Inge

"Religion is doing; a man does not merely think his religion or feel it, he 'lives' his religion as much as he is able, otherwise it is not religion but fantasy or philosophy."—George Gurdjieff

"We have committed the Golden Rule to memory; let us now commit it to life."
—Edwin Markham

"God is a busy worker, but He loves help."—Basque proverb

"Compulsion in religion is distinguished peculiarly from compulsion in every other thing. I may grow rich by an art I am compelled to follow; I may recover health by medicines I am compelled to take against my own judgment; but I cannot be saved by a worship I disbelieve and abhor."—Thomas Jefferson

"If you see a child making progress in Bible, but not in Talmud, do not push him by teaching him Talmud, and if he understands Talmud, do not push him by teaching him Bible. Train him in the things which he knows."—Anonymous author on Jewish school practices in Germany, circa 1200 C.E.

"If a pickpocket meets a holy man, he sees only his pockets."—Hari Dass Baba

"A wise architect observed that you could break the laws of architectural art provided you had mastered them first. That would apply to religion as well as to art. Ignorance of the past does not guarantee freedom from its imperfections."—Reinhold Niebuhr

"And even in his corrections, let him act with prudence, and not go too far, lest while he seeketh too eagerly to scrape off the rust, the vessel be broken."—Time-honored monastery instructions concerning the governance of monks, cited in *Be Here Now*, Ram Dass

"God is a being absolutely infinite; a substance consisting of infinite attributes, each of which expresses His eternal and infinite essence."—Baruch Spinoza

"Though the mills of God grind slowly, yet they grind exceeding small;

Though with patience he stands waiting, with exactness grinds he all."

—Friedrich von Lorgas

"But he learned more from the river than Vasudeva could teach him. He learned from it continually. Above all, he learned from it how to listen with a still heart, with a waiting, open soul, without passion, without desire, without judgment, without opinions."—Herman Hesse, *Siddartha*

"In the faces of men and women I see God and in my own face in the glass, I find letters from God dropt in the street, and every one is signed by God's name, and I leave them where they are, for I know that wheresoever I go others will punctually come for ever and ever."

—Walt Whitman

"God is day and night, winter and summer, war and peace, surfeit and hunger."—Heraclitus

"Whatever you are, be a good one."—Abraham Lincoln

"Hath God obliged himself not to exceed the bounds of our knowledge?"—Montaigne

"God is subtle, but he is not malicious."—Albert Einstein

"God must not be thought of as a physical being, or as having any kind of body. He is pure mind. He moves and acts without needing any corporeal space, or size, or form, or color, or any other property of matter."—Origen (c. 254 C.E.)

"If you have love you will do all things well."—Thomas Merton

"Men of sense are really all of one religion. But men of sense never tell what it is." —Anthony A. Cooper, Earl of Shaftsbury

"Quit this world, quit the next world, quit quitting."—Sufi saying

"The Buddhist doctrine [is] that real riches consist not in the abundance of goods but in the paucity of wants."—Alfred Marshall

"You must also own religion in his rags, as well as when in his silver slippers; and stand by him, too, when bound in irons, as well as when he walketh the streets with applause."—John Bunyan

"Imagine the Sanskrit letters in these honey-filled foci of awareness, first as letters, then more subtly as sounds, then as most subtle feeling. Then leaving them aside, be free."—Paul Reps, on the use of a mantra

"God is a circle whose center is everywhere and circumference nowhere."—Voltaire

"Rain water falling upon the roof of a house flows down to the ground through spouts shaped grotesquely like a tiger's head. One gets the impression that the water comes from the tiger's mouth, but in reality it descends from the sky. In the same way the holy teachings of godly men seem to be uttered by those men themselves, while in reality they proceed from God."—Ramakrishna

"Fear God, yes, but don't be afraid of Him."—J. A. Spender

"Talk to me about the truth of religion and I'll listen gladly. Talk to me about the duty of religion and I'll listen submissively. But don't come talking to me about the consolations of religion, or I shall suspect that you don't understand."—C. S. Lewis

"… on Sunday go to church. Yes, I know all the excuses. I know that one can worship the Creator and dedicate oneself to good living in a grove of trees, or by a running brook, or in one's own house, just as well as in a church. But I also know that as a matter of cold fact the average man does not thus worship or dedicate himself." —Theodore Roosevelt

"It is time now for us to rise from sleep."—St. Benedict

"Human endeavor must always remain short of perfection; besides, no one will ever weed out the tendencies innate in his particular nature. The point is to change their force into life power."—Ouspensky

"Faith consists in believing when it is beyond the power of reason to believe. It is not enough that a thing be possible for it to be believed."—Voltaire

"The finding of God is the coming to oneself."—Meher Baba

"It takes place every day."—Albert Camus, on the Last Judgment

"We cannot too often think that there is a never-sleeping eye that reads the heart and registers our thoughts."—Francis Bacon

"To study Buddhism is to study ourselves. To study ourselves is to go beyond ourselves. To go beyond ourselves is to be enlightened by all things. To be enlightened by all things is to free our body and mind, and to free the bodies and minds of others. No trace of enlightenment remains, and this no-trace continues endlessly." —Zen Master Dogen

"We live to work out a drama which is God's drama, and therefore anything that happens to us is in some degree God's will. We are participating in the unfolding of God's will. Supposing it's true, for instance, at this moment—which I think it probably is—that what we call Western civilization is guttering out to collapse. If you take that in purely human historical terms this is an unmitigated catastrophe. You and I must beat our breast and say that we lived to see the end of everything, what we love is coming to an end. But the point is, that is a catastrophe only to the extent that you don't see it as part of the realization of God's purposes."—Malcolm Muggeridge

"God does not die on the day when we cease to believe in a personal deity, but we die on the day when our lives cease to be illuminated by the steady radiance, renewed daily, of a wonder, the source of which is beyond all reason."—Dag Hammarskjold

"Guru, God, and Self are one."—Ramana Maharishi

"The Buddha, the Godhead, resides quite as comfortably in the circuits of a digital computer or the gears of a cycle transmission as he does at the top of a mountain or the petals of a flower."—Robert M. Pirsig

"God is over all things; under all things; outside all; within but not enclosed; without but not excluded; above but not raised up; below but not depressed; wholly above, presiding; wholly beneath, embracing; wholly within, fulfilling."—Hildebert of Lavardin, Archbishop of Tours

"Time and space are not God, but creations of God; with God, as it is a universal Here, so is it an everlasting Now."—Thomas Carlyle

"I have ever been fed by his bounty, clothed by his mercy, comforted and healed when sick, succored when tempted, and everywhere upheld by his hand."—Jarena Lee, black nineteenth-century evangelist

"God shall be my hope, my stay, my guide, and lantern to my feet."—William Shakespeare

"God alone is Real."—Meher Baba

"God is best known in not knowing Him."—St. Augustine

"In the mid-1650s, the small Jewish community living in lower Manhattan petitioned Dutch governor Peter Stuyvesant for the right to build a synagogue, and they were turned down. In 1657, when Stuyvesant also prohibited Quakers from holding meetings, a group of non-Quakers in Queens signed the Flushing Remonstrance, a petition in defense of the right of Quakers and others to freely practice their religion. It was perhaps the first formal political petition for religious freedom in the American colonies, and the organizer was thrown in jail and then banished from New Amsterdam. In the 1700s, even as religious freedom took hold in America, Catholics in New York were effectively prohibited from practicing their religion, and priests could be arrested. Largely as a result, the first Catholic parish in New York City was not established until the 1780s, St. Peter's on Barclay Street ... which still stands just one block north of the World Trade Center site, and one block south of the proposed mosque and community center .... The simple fact is, this building is private property, and the owners have a right to use the building as a house of worship, and the government has no right whatsoever to deny that right. And if it were tried, the courts would almost certainly strike it down as a violation of the U.S. Constitution. Whatever you may think of the proposed mosque and community center, lost in the heat of the debate has been a basic question: should government attempt to deny private citizens the right to build a house of worship on private property based on their particular religion? That may happen in other countries, but we should never allow it to happen here. This nation was founded on the principle that the government must never choose between religions or favor one over another. The World Trade Center site will forever hold a special place in our city, in our hearts. But we would be untrue to the best part of ourselves and who we are as New Yorkers and Americans if we said no to a mosque in lower Manhattan."—New York City mayor Michael Bloomberg, August 2010

"I consider myself a Hindu, Christian, Moslem, Jew, Buddhist, and Confucian."
—Mahatma Gandhi

Scriptures to Keep You Company

B

The following books will offer you a deeper insight into the beliefs and histories of the world's religions.

The World's Faiths, Old and New

Champion, Selwyn Gurney, and Dorothy Short, ed. *Readings from World Religions.* London: Watts & Co., 1951.

International Religious Foundation. *World Scripture: A Comparative Anthology of Sacred Texts.* New York: Paragon House, 1991.

Judaism

Berg, Rav P.S., ed. *The Essential Zohar: Source of Kabbalistic Wisdom.* New York: Crown Publishing Group, 2002.

Birnbaum, Philip, ed. *Daily Prayer Book.* Rockaway Beach, New York: Hebrew Publishing Company, 1949.

Danby, Herbert, trans. *The Mishnah.* London: Oxford University Press, 1933.

Feinsilver, Alexander, trans. *The Talmud for Today.* New York: St. Martin's Press, 1980.

Montefiore, C.G., and H. Loewe, ed. *A Rabbinic Anthology.* New York: Schocken Books, 1974.

Christianity

The Apocrypha, Revised Standard Version. New York: National Council of the Churches of Christ in the USA, 1957.

The Holy Bible, Revised Standard Version. New York: National Council of the Churches of Christ in the USA, 1946, 1971.

Jones, Alexander, ed. *The Jerusalem Bible: Reader's Edition.* Garden City, New York: Doubleday and Company, 1968.

Miller, Robert J., ed. *The Complete Gospels: Annotated Scholars Version.* Sonoma, California: Polebridge Press, 1992.

Islam

Ahmad, Ghazi, trans. *Sayings of Muhammad.* Lahore, Pakistan: Sh. Muhammad Ashraf, 1968.

Ali, Maulana Muhammad, ed. *A Manual of Hadith.* London: Curzon Press, 1978.

Khan, Muhammad Muhsin, trans. *The Translations of the Meanings of Sahih Al-Bukhart.* Chicago: Kazi Publications, 1976–1979 (9 vol.).

Pickthall, Muhammad Marmaduke, trans. *The Meaning of the Glorious Qur'an.* Mecca and New York: World Muslim League, 1977.

Shrawardy, Abdullah, trans. *Sayings of Muhammad.* London: John Murray, 1941.

Wilcox, Lynn, ed. *Sayings of the Sufi Sages.* Washington, D.C.: M T O Shahmaghsoudi, 1997.

Hinduism

Bose, Abinash Chandra, ed. *Hymns from the Vedas.* Bombay: Asia Publishing House, 1966.

Hume, R.E., trans. *The Upanishads.* Petaluma, California: Nilgiri Press, 1985.

Prabhavananda, Swami, and Christopher Isherwood, trans. *The Song of God: Bhagavad-Gita.* Hollywood, California: Vedanta Press, 1944, 1972.

Thibault, George, trans. *Vedanta Sutra—The Vedanta Sutras of Badarayana*. New York: Dover Press, 1962.

Van Buitenen, J.A.B., trans. *The Mahabharata, volume 1, The Book of the Beginning*. Chicago: University of Chicago Press, 1973.

Buddhism

Babbitt, Irving, trans. *The Dhammapada*. New York: New Directions, 1965.

Batchelor, Stephen, trans. *A Guide to the Bodhisattva's Way of Life Shantideva*. Dharamsala, India: Library of Tibetan Works and Archives, 1979.

Blofield, John, trans. *The Zen Teachings of Huang Po*. New York: Grove Press, 1959.

Conze, Edward, ed. *Buddhist Texts Through the Ages*. New York: Philosophical Library, 1954.

———. *Buddhist Wisdom Books: Concerning the Diamond Sutra and the Heart Sutra*. London: Allen & Unwin, 1958.

———. *Perfection of Wisdom in Eight Thousand Lines and Its Verse Summary*. San Francisco: Four Seasons Foundation, 1983.

Evans-Wentz, W.Y., ed. *The Tibetan Book of the Dead: Or The After-Death Experiences on the Bardo Plane, According to Lama Kazi Dawa-Samdup's English Rendering*. London: Oxford University Press, 1960.

Confucianism

Lau, D.C., trans. *Mencius*. London: Penguin Books, 1979.

Legge, James, trans. *Book of Ritual (Li Chi): A Collection of Treatises on the Rules of Propriety of Ceremonial Usages*. Oxford: Clarendon Press, 1885.

———. *Book of Songs (Shih Ching)*. Oxford: Clarendon Press, 1895.

———. *Classic of Filial Piety (Hsiao Ching)*. Oxford: Clarendon Press, 1879.

———. *Doctrine of the Mean (Chung Yung)*. Oxford: Clarendon Press, 1893.

Waley, Arthur, trans. *The Analects of Confucius*. London: Allen & Unwin, 1938.

Waltham, Clae, trans. *Book of History (Shuh Ching): A Modernized Edition of the Translations of James Legge*. Chicago: Henry Regnery, 1971.

Wilhelm, Richard, and C.F. Baynes, trans. *The I Ching, or Book of Changes*. Princeton: Princeton University Press, 1977.

Taoism

Legge, James, trans. *The Texts of Taoism: The T'ai Sahng Tractate of Actions and Their Retributions*. Oxford: Clarendon Press, 1891.

Tzu, Lao. Victor Mair, trans. *Tao te Ching: The Classic Book of Integrity and the Way*. New York: Bantam Books, 1990.

Watson, Burton, ed. and trans. *The Complete Works of Chuang Tzu*. New York: Columbia University Press, 1968.

Shinto

Ashton, W.G., *Shinto: The Way of the Gods*. London: Longmans, Green & Co., 1905.

Havens, Norman, trans. *The World of Shinto*. Tokyo: Bukkyo Dendo Kyokai, 1985.

Philippi, Donald L., trans. *Kojiki*. Tokyo: University of Tokyo Press, 1959.

Sikhism

Trumpp, Ernest. *The Adi Granth: The Holy Scriptures of the Sikhs*. Gujarat, India: Abm Komers, 2004.

Native American Religions

Erdoes, Richard, and Alfonso Ortiz, ed. *American Indian Myths and Legends*. New York: Pantheon, 1984.

Traditional African Religions

Ikenga-Metuh, Emefie. *Comparative Studies of African Traditional Religions*. Onitsha, Nigeria: IMICO Publishers, 1987.

The Baha'i Faith

Baha'u'llah. *Kitab-i-Iqan: The Book of Certitude*. Wilmette, Illinois: National Spiritual Assembly of the Baha'is of the United States, 1931.

———. *Epistle to the Son of the Wolf*. Wilmette, Illinois: National Spiritual Assembly of the Baha'is of the United States, 1941.

———. *The Seven Valleys and the Four Valleys*. Wilmette, Illinois: National Spiritual Assembly of the Baha'is of the United States, 1945.

———. *The Hidden Words of Baha'u'lla*. Wilmette, Illinois: National Spiritual Assembly of the Baha'is of the United States, 1985.

Timelines of Major World Religions

Following are condensed timelines, drawn from a variety of sources, for five of the world's major religious traditions. Many of the dates are subject to disagreement among the best scholars; we have tried to present the most generally accepted chronologies.

Hinduism

Pre-2000 B.C.E.: Harrapa culture exists in Indus Valley.

Circa 2000 B.C.E.: Aryans migrate into region now known as India. Interplay of cultures and religious practices takes place.

Circa 1500 B.C.E.: Compilation and development of the Vedas is thought to have begun at around this time.

Circa 800 B.C.E.: Compilation and development of the Upanishads is thought to have begun at around this time.

Pre-sixth century B.C.E.: Development of Samkhya (classical school of thought and practice).

Circa sixth century B.C.E.: Development of Nyaya (classical school of thought and practice).

Circa sixth century B.C.E.: Development of Vaisheshika (classical school of thought and practice).

Circa second century B.C.E.: Development of Yoga (classical school of thought and practice).

Circa second century B.C.E.: Development of Purva Mimamsa (classical school of thought and practice).

Circa 200 B.C.E.–200 C.E.: *Bhagavad Gita* refined.

Circa first century C.E.: Development of Vedanta (classical school of thought and practice).

711: Muslim incursions into India.

1498: Portuguese incursions into India.

1750–1947: Period of British control over India.

1869: Mohandas Gandhi (later known as Mahatma Gandhi) is born.

1947: India wins independence.

Judaism

Circa 2085 B.C.E.: Accounts of Abraham's life reflective of events in this period. Hebrew peoples leave Mesopotamia for Canaan.

Eighteenth century–circa 1500 B.C.E.: A portion of the Hebrews who end up on the outer edge of Egypt are enslaved.

Circa thirteenth century B.C.E.: Moses leads the Hebrews out of Egypt. Scriptures relate a divine encounter and the transmission of the Ten Commandments during this period.

Circa 1000–circa 900 B.C.E.: Palestine conquered, Judea united; David reigns in Jerusalem. Solomon succeeds him. On Solomon's death, chaos and secession within David's kingdom turn Judah, to the south, into the only remaining tribe within the house of David.

Ninth–eighth centuries B.C.E.: Under the sway of the Assyrians, the northern kingdom (Israel) enters a period of decline and corruption. Prophets foresee doom. Assyrian kings eventually carve Israel into subjugated provinces, but leave Judah intact.

Sixth–fifth centuries B.C.E.: Jerusalem falls to Nebuchadnezzar; period of exile to Babylon is marked by retention of religious traditions, and terminates in a return to the holy city. Restoration of the Temple, originally constructed by Solomon, also occurs during this period.

Circa 440–430 B.C.E.: Formulation of legal code under Ezra. First public reading of the Torah.

Fourth–third centuries B.C.E.: Egypt emerges as the dominant force in Palestine and permits a significant measure of autonomy to the Hebrews.

Second century B.C.E.: Syrian power is ascendant in Palestine, resulting in the desecration of the Temple.

165 B.C.E.: The Maccabee family leads a revolt against the Syrians that culminates in the restoration of the Temple.

63 C.E.: Rome's period of tolerance of Judean social institutions comes to an end as Pompey subjugates Jerusalem.

66–70: Period of revolt culminates in the destruction of the Temple by the Romans.

Circa 90: Canon of Hebrew scriptures is completed.

Circa 200: Mishnah is completed.

Circa 400: Palestinian Talmud is completed.

Circa 600: Babylonian Talmud is completed.

Circa 1135–1204: Life of the scholar and philosopher Moses Maimonedes, probably the most gifted Jewish thinker of the Middle Ages.

1492: Jews are expelled from Spain; the event is representative of a long period of segregation, abuse, legal persecution, and expulsion of Jews in many European nations.

Eighteenth century: Founding of Hasidic movement in Poland.

1810: Beginning of the Reform movement in Germany.

Late nineteenth century: Huge numbers of Jews emigrate to the United States, fleeing persecution in Russia and Eastern Europe.

1896: Founding of Zionist movement.

1937–1945: Nazis systematically murder six million Jews during World War II.

1948: State of Israel is born.

Buddhism

Circa 560 B.C.E.: Birth of Gatauma Buddha. (Note: Buddha's birth is placed at various points in time by various sects. This is the most commonly accepted dating.)

483 B.C.E.: Council at Rajagrha.

Circa 440 B.C.E.: King Kolasoka's Council.

250 B.C.E.: Council of Asoka.

Circa 30 C.E.: Council at Sri Lanka.

Circa 100: Mahayana ("Greater Vehicle") Buddhism emerges, focusing on goals of compassion and service to others. The new school's approach contrasts with the previous emphasis on solitary practice, which comes to be known as Hinayana ("Lesser Vehicle") Buddhism.

Second century C.E.: Life and ministry of Nagarjuna.

Second–sixth centuries: Refinement of scriptures known as pitakas (baskets) after centuries of oral transmission.

470–534: Period attributed to the life and teachings of Bodhidharma.

Sixth century: In China, Mahayana practice combines with the teaching of Bodhidharma. The result is Ch'an, or sitting meditation practice.

817: Great Council (Tibet).

Twelfth century: Ch'an practice spreads to Japan, where it takes the name by which it is best known today, Zen.

1160: Council of Anarahapura, Ceylon.

1870: Council at Mandalay.

1893: First World Parliament of Religion takes place; based in the United States, it exposes many Westerners to Zen Buddhism for the first time.

1930: Founding of Japanese Soka Gakkai school.

1950: Council at Rangoon.

Christianity

Circa 30 C.E.: Ministry and crucifixion of Jesus of Nazareth.

Circa 33: The Apostle Peter (the first pope) leads the new church. Stephen, early deacon of the Christian Church, is stoned to death.

Circa 36–67: Saul of Tarsus suppresses Christians in Jerusalem; later, he experiences a powerful conversion, changes his name to Paul, and becomes apostle to the Gentiles, author of many epistles, and the foremost early Christian theologian. During this period, early Christians spread through Judea; time of oral transmission of Jesus' sayings and life story.

Circa 65–125: Period of composition of the four Gospels: Matthew, Mark, Luke, and John.

Circa 66–70: Period of the Roman-Jewish war; destruction of Herod's Temple.

125–300: Christians vigorously persecuted in Rome.

300–400: Formal Christian doctrine set forth; unorthodox practices branded heretical.

313: Constantine I and Licinius issue the Edict of Milan, making toleration of Christianity official Roman policy.

325: First Council of Nicaea. Attended by major bishops and papal legates, this Ecumenical Council addressed doctrinal and theological issues and standardized the observance of Easter. Other councils included those of Arles (314), Constantinople (381), Ephesus (431), and Chalcedon (451), and the Second Council of Nicaea (787), which addressed the vexing issue of the role of religious imagery.

800: Pope Leo III crowns Charlemagne emperor on Christmas Day in Rome. The event marks the inauguration of the political entity that would become the Holy Roman Empire, and helps to legitimize Charlemagne's position as ruler over Western European lands once controlled by the Roman Empire.

Eleventh and twelfth centuries: Rifts between secular and ecclesiastical authorities are common.

1054: Formal split between Eastern Orthodox and Roman Catholic churches; Eastern Orthodox authorities reject the jurisdiction of the pope, but accept the pronouncements of the first seven Ecumenical Councils.

1096–1291: The Crusades.

1233: Inquisition founded to counter heretical practices.

Fourteenth century: Excesses in Rome lead to calls for reform and the foundation of the Franciscan and Dominican orders.

1517: Martin Luther initiates the Protestant Reformations; John Calvin follows suit in later years.

1529: Henry VIII defies the Pope and declares himself head of the Church of England.

1545: Council of Trent. This, the nineteenth Ecumenical Council of the Roman Catholic Church, addressed issues raised by the Protestant Reformations and produced significant internal reforms. It took place between 1545–1547, 1551–1552, and 1562–1563.

Sixteenth and seventeenth centuries: Missionary activity in Asia; many Christian groups emigrate to North America.

Eighteenth century: Secular understanding of social groupings becomes more pronounced after European Age of Reason; powerful "revival" movements reinvigorate specific Christian practices in England and the United States. Missionary activity vigorous, particularly in Africa and Asia.

1869: First Vatican Council proclaims that the pope is infallible when he speaks *ex cathedra*, that is, when he, in the exercise of his office of his supreme apostolic authority, decides that a doctrine concerning faith or morals is to be held by the entire church.

1948: World Council of Churches founded to promote dialogue and cohesion among Protestant churches and to acknowledge areas of agreement between Protestant and Catholic practice.

1962–1965: Second Vatican Council incorporates observers from Protestant and Eastern Orthodox faiths; promotes diversity, liturgical reform, and involvement of lay people in Catholic worship.

Islam

571 C.E.: Birth of the Prophet Muhammad in Mecca. The city will be the destination of countless pilgrimages in the centuries to follow.

610: Muhammad receives his first revelation in the cave at Mt. Hira; this event regarded as holy initiation of the Qur'an.

622: Muhammad organizes a Hegira (exodus) of his followers at Mecca to go to Medina.

632: Death of Muhammad.

656–661: Caliphate of Ali. Bitter division over his legitimacy as leader of the faith causes a split resulting in two divisions of Islam, Shiite, and Sunni. Shiites regard Ali as the first Imam (leader).

661: Founding of the Umayyad dynasty under Muawiya.

750: Umayyad dynasty overthrown by Abbasid family, which is descended from the uncle of Muhammad. (Abbasid dynasty endures until 1258.)

780–1031: Period of the Western caliphate (based in Spain), founded by a surviving member of the Umayyad family.

909–1171: Period of the Fatimid caliphate (based in Africa).

1258: Baghdad falls to the Mongols; Abassids flee.

1517: Capture of Egypt by the Ottomans; Selim I is proclaimed caliph. A long period follows during which Ottoman sultans retain the title of caliph.

1924: Title of caliph abolished.

1968: Enlargement of Haram in Mecca is completed.

1979: A group of extremists led by Theological University of Medina students occupy the Haram in Mecca and hold out against military forces for two weeks before they are overcome by superior power. The holy mosque, revered by millions of Muslims, is recovered.

The Names of God

The following article from Wikipedia.org is reproduced with permission.

Jewish Names of God

The most important name of God in Judaism is the Tetragrammaton, the four-letter name of God. This name is first mentioned in the book of Genesis and is usually translated as "the Lord." Because Jews for quite a long period of time considered it sinful to pronounce, the correct pronunciation of this name was forgotten—the original Hebrew texts only included consonants. Modern scholars conjecture that it was pronounced "Yahweh." The Hebrew letters are named Yod-Heh-Vav-Heh. In English it is written as YHVH. Only its Hebrew expression is considered sacred.

In appearance, YHVH is the third person singular imperfect of the verb "to be," meaning, therefore, "God is," or "God will be," or, perhaps, "God lives," the root idea of the word being, probably, "to blow," "to breathe," and hence, "to live." With this explanation agrees the meaning of the name given in Exodus 3:14, where God is represented as speaking, and hence as using the first person—"I am." The meaning would therefore be "He who is self-existing, self-sufficient," or, more concretely, "He who lives," the abstract conception of pure existence being foreign to Hebrew thought.

The idea of life was intimately connected with the name YHVH from early times. God is presented as a living God, as contrasted with the lifeless gods of the heathen, and God is presented as the source and author of life (comp. 1 Kings 18; Isaiah 41:26–29, 44:6–20; Jeremiah 10:10, 14; Genesis 2:7; etc.).

Adonai

Jews also call God Adonai, or "my Lord." Because pronouncing YHVH is considered sinful, Jews would use Adonai instead in prayers. When the Masoretes added vowel pointings to the text of the Tanach in the first century C.E., they gave the word YHVH the vowels of Adonai, to remind the reader to say Adonai instead. Many Christian Bible translators misinterpreted this to mean that God's name was Jehovah, which is the result of combining Adonai's vowels with YHVH's consonants, written using Latin orthography in which "J" is pronounced as the English "Y." This name may be etymologically related to the Phoenician god Tammuz or Adonis.

Pronouncing the Tetragrammaton

All denominations of Judaism teach that the four-letter name of God, YHVH, is forbidden to be uttered except by the High Priest, in the Temple. Because the Temple in Jerusalem is no longer extant, this name is never pronounced in religious rituals by Jews. Orthodox Jews never pronounce it for any reason. Some non-Orthodox Jews are willing to pronounce it, but for educational purposes only, and never in casual conversation or in prayer. Instead of pronouncing YHVH during prayer, Jews say "Adonai."

Jewish law requires that "fences" be built around the basic laws, so that there is no chance that the main law will ever be broken. As such, it is common Jewish practice to restrict the use of the word "Adonai" to prayer only. In conversation many Jewish people will call God "HaShem," which is Hebrew for "the Name" (this was first used in Leviticus 24:11). Many Jews also write "G-d" instead of "God." Although this later substitution is by no means required by their religion (only the Hebrew name, not the English, is holy), they do it to remind themselves of the holiness attached to God's name.

English translations of the Bible generally render YHVH as "LORD" (in small capitals), and Adonai as "Lord" (in normal case).

Elohim

A common name of God in the Hebrew Bible is Elohim.

Despite the -im ending common to many plural nouns in Hebrew, the word Elohim, when referring to God, is grammatically singular, regularly taking singular predicate forms in the Hebrew Bible. The word Elohim likely had an origin in a plural grammatical form, because, when the Hebrew Bible uses elohim not in reference to God, it takes plural forms (e.g., Exodus 20:3).

Some scholars interpret the -im ending as an expression of majesty (pluralis majestatis) or excellence (pluralis excellentiae), expressing high dignity or greatness: compare with the similar use of plurals of ba'al (master) and adon (lord). (For these reasons, Christian theologians have generally pointed out that it is a fallacy to draw support for the Christian doctrine of the trinity from the apparently plural ending of the word Elohim.)

In Ethiopic, Amlak ("lords") is the common name for God. The singular, Eloah, is comparatively rare, occurring only in poetry and late prose (in Job, 41 times). The same divine name is found in Arabic (ilah) and in Aramaic (elah). The singular is used in six places for heathen deities (2 Chronicles 32:15; Daniel 11:37, 38; etc.); and the plural also, a few times, either for gods or images (Exodus 9:1, 12:12, 20:3; etc.) or for one god (Exodus 32:1; Genesis 31:30, 32; etc.). In the great majority of cases both are used as names of the one God of Israel.

The root-meaning of the word is unknown. One theory is that it may be connected with the old Arabic verb alih (to be perplexed, afraid; to seek refuge because of fear). Eloah, Elohim, would, therefore, be "He who is the object of fear or reverence," or "He with whom one who is afraid takes refuge."

El

The word El appears in Assyrian (ilu) and Phoenician, as well as in Hebrew, as an ordinary name of God. It is found also in the South-Arabian dialects, and in Aramaic, Arabic, and Ethiopic, and also in Hebrew, as an element in proper names.

It is used in both the singular and plural, both for other gods and for the God of Israel. As a name of God, however, it is used chiefly in poetry and prophetic discourse, rarely in prose, and then usually with some epithet attached, as "a jealous God." Other examples of its use with some attribute or epithet are: El 'Elyon ("most high God"), El Shaddai ("God Almighty"), El 'Olam ("everlasting God"), El Hai ("living God"), El Ro'i ("God of seeing"), El Elohe Israel ("God, the God of Israel"), El Gibbor ("Hero God").

Shaddai

The name Shaddai, which occurs along with El, is also used independently as a name of God, chiefly in the Book of Job. According to Exodus 6:2, 3, this is the name by which God was known to Abraham, Isaac, and Jacob.

Elyon

The name Elyon occurs with El, with YHVH, with Elohim, and also alone. It appears chiefly in poetic and later Biblical passages.

YHVH Tzevaot

The names Yhwh and Elohim frequently occur with the word tzevaot ("hosts"), as YHVH Elohe tzevaot ("YHVH God of Hosts") or "God of Hosts"; or, most frequently, "Yhwh of Hosts." To this last Adonai is often prefixed, making the title "Lord Yhwh of Hosts."

This compound divine name occurs chiefly in the prophetic literature and does not appear at all in the Pentateuch or in Joshua or Judges. The original meaning of tzevaot may be found in 1 Samuel 17:45, where it is interpreted as denoting "the God of the armies of Israel." The word, apart from this special use, always means armies or hosts of men, as, for example, in Exodus 6:26, 7:4, 12:41, while the singular is used to designate the heavenly host.

The Latin spelling Sebaoth led to identification by Romans with god Sabacius.

Ehyeh-Asher-Ehyeh

The name Ehyeh denotes God's potency in the immediate future, and is part of YHVH. The phrase "ehyeh-asher-ehyeh" (Exodus 3:14) is interpreted by some authorities as "I will be because I will be," using the second part as a gloss and referring to God's promise, "Certainly I will be [ehyeh] with thee" (Exodus 3:12). Other authorities claim that the whole phrase forms one name. The Targum Onkelos leaves the phrase untranslated and is so quoted in the Talmud (B. B. 73a). The "I AM THAT I AM" of the Authorized Version is based on this view.

Yah

The name Yah is composed of the first letters of YHVH. The Rastafarian Jah may derive from this.

Jewish Laws of Writing Divine Names

According to Jewish tradition, the sacredness of the divine names must be recognized by the professional scribe who writes the Scriptures, or the chapters for the tefillin and the mezuzah. Before transcribing any of the divine names he prepares mentally to sanctify them. After he begins a name he does not stop until it is finished, and he must not be interrupted while writing it, even to greet a king. If an error is made in writing it, it may not be erased, but a line must be drawn round it to show that it is canceled, and the whole page must be put in a genizah (a cemetery for worn-out Hebrew language books and papers on religious topics) and a new page begun.

The Tradition of Seven Divine Names

According to Jewish tradition, the number of divine names that require the scribe's special care is seven: El, Elohim, Adonai, Yhwh, Ehyeh-Asher-Ehyeh, Shaddai, and Tzevaot.

However, R. Jose considered tzevaot a common name (Soferim 4:1; Yer. R. H. 1:1; Ab. R. N. 34). R. Ishmael held that even Elohim is common (Sanh. 66a). All other names, such as Merciful, Gracious, and Faithful, merely represent attributes that are common also to human beings (Sheb. 35a).

The prohibition of blasphemy, for which capital punishment is prescribed, refers only to the Name proper, YHVH (Soferim iv., end; comp. Sanh. 66a).

In many of the passages in which "elohim" occurs in the Bible it refers to gentile deities, or in some instances to powerful men (comp. Genesis 3:5), to judges (Exodus 21:6), or to Israel (Psalms 81:9, 82:6). Adonai sometimes refers to a distinguished person.

Shalom

The Talmud says Shalom ("Peace"; Judges 6:23) is a name of God; consequently one is not permitted to greet another with the word "shalom" in unholy places (Talmud, Shabbat 10b). The name Shelomoh (from shalom) refers to the God of Peace, and the Rabbis assert that the Song of Solomon is a dramatization of the love of God: "Shalom" to His people Israel = "Shulamite."

Other Jewish names of God include ...

> Emet (Truth)
>
> Tzur Yisrael (The Rock of Israel)
>
> Elohei Avraham, Elohei Yitzchak ve Elohei Yaacov (God of Abraham, God of Isaac, God of Jacob)

Ehiyeh sh'Ehiyeh (I Am That I Am)

Avinu Malkeinu (Our Father, our King)

Ro'eh Yisrael (Shepherd of Israel)

Ha-Kadosh, Baruch Hu (The Holy One, Praised be He)

Melech ha-Melachim (The King of Kings)

Makom (literally, "the place"; meaning "The Omnipresent")

Magen Avraham (Shield of Abraham)

YHVH-Jireh: The Lord will provide (Genesis 22:13, 14).

YHVH-Rapha: The Lord that healeth (Exodus 15:26).

YHVH-Nissi: The Lord our Banner (Exodus 17:8–15).

YHVH-Shalom: The Lord our Peace (Judges 6:24).

YHVH-Ra-ah: The Lord my Shepherd (Psalms 23:1).

YHVH-Tsidkenu: The Lord our Righteousness (Jeremiah 23:6).

YHVH-Shammah: The Lord is present (Ezekiel 48:35).

Christian Names of God

Historically, Christianity has professed belief in one deity, three divine persons (the Trinity), that make up one deity or Godhead, known as "God."

Thus, most Christians are trinitarian monotheists, although there have been dissenters. Most of these unitarian groups believe or believed that only God the Father is a deity; Latter-Day Saints believe that the Father, the Son (Jesus Christ), and the Holy Spirit are three distinct deities.

For most Christians, however, the most important names of God are the names of the Trinity.

The following is from the Athanasian Creed (fourth century, c.e.):

"The Father Uncreated, the Son Uncreated, the Holy Spirit Uncreated"

For there is one person of the Father, another of the Son, and another of the Holy Spirit.

But the Godhead of the Father, of the Son, and of the Holy Spirit is all one, the glory equal, the majesty coeternal.

Such as the Father is, such is the Son, and such is the Holy Spirit.

The Father uncreated, the Son uncreated, and the Holy Spirit uncreated.

The Father incomprehensible, the Son incomprehensible, and the Holy Spirit incomprehensible.

The Father eternal, the Son eternal, and the Holy Spirit eternal.

And yet they are not three eternals but one eternal.

As also there are not three uncreated nor three incomprehensible, but one uncreated and one incomprehensible.

So likewise the Father is almighty, the Son almighty, and the Holy Spirit almighty.

And yet they are not three almighties, but one almighty.

So the Father is God, the Son is God, and the Holy Spirit is God;

And yet they are not three Gods, but one God.

So likewise the Father is Lord, the Son Lord, and the Holy Spirit Lord;

And yet they are not three Lords, but one Lord.

Islam and the 99 Names of Allah

The primary name for God in Islam is Allah, which means simply "the God."

Allah is regarded by Muslims as having 99 Names. They are …

Ar-Rahman: The Most Compassionate, Most Kind

Ar-Rahim: The Most Merciful

Al-Malik: The Master, the King, the Monarch

Al-Quddus: The Pure, the Holy One

As-Salaam: The Peace, the Tranquility

Al-Mu'min: The Faithful, the Trusted

Al-Muhaymin: The Protector, the Vigilant, the Controller

Al-'Aziz: The Almighty, the Powerful

Al-Jabbar: The Oppressor, the All Compelling

Al-Mutakabbir: The Haughty, the Majestic, the Lord

Al-Khaliq: The Creator, the Maker

Al-Baari': The Inventor

Al-Musawwir: The Fashioner, the Organiser, the Designer

Al-Ghaffar: The Forgiving, the Forgiver

Al-Qahhar: The Almighty, the Dominant

Al-Wahhab: The Donor, the Bestower

Ar-Razzaq: The Provider, the Sustainer

Al-Fattah: The Opener, the Revealer

Al-'Alim: The All Knowing, the Omniscient

Al-Qabid: The Contractor, the Restrainer, the Recipient

Al-Basit: The Expander, the Increaser

Al-Khafid: The Abaser, the Humbler

Ar-Rafi': The Raiser, the Exalter

Al-Mu'iz: The Honourer, the Exalter

Al-Muzil: The Abaser, the Subduer

As-Sami': The All Hearing, the All Knowing

Al-Basir: The All Seeing, the Insightful

Al-Hakam: The Arbitrator, the Judge

Al-'Adl: The Justice, the Equitable

Al-Latif: The Most Gentle, the Gracious, the One Who is Kind

Al-Khabir: The Aware, the Segacious

Al-Halim: The Gentle, the Most Patient, the Benevolent

Al-'Azim: The Great, the Mighty

Al-Ghafoor: The Forgiving, the Pardoner

Ash-Shakur: The Grateful, the Thankful

Al-'Aliy: The Most High, the Exalted

Al-Kabir: The Greatest, the Biggest

Al-Hafiz: The Guardian, the Preserver

Al-Muqit: The Maintainer, the Nourisher

Al-Hasib: The Noble, the Reckoner

Al-Jalil: The Majestic, the Honorable, the Exalted

Al-Karim: The Most Generous, the Bountiful

Ar-Raqib: The Guardian, the Watcher

Al-Mujib: The Answerer

Al-Wasi': The Enricher, the Omnipresent, the Knowledgeable

Al-Hakim: The Most Wise, the Judicious

Al-Wadud: The Affectionate, the Loving

Al-Majid: The Glorious, the Exalted

Al-Ba'ith: The Resurrector, the Raiser from Death

Ash-Shahid: The Witness

Al-Haqq: The Truth, the Just

Al-Wakil: The Guardian, the Trustee

Al-Qawee: The Powerful, the Almighty, the Strong

Al-Matin: The Strong, the Firm

Al-Walee: The Supporter, the Friend, the Defender

Al-Hamid: The Praiseworthy, the Commendable

Al-Muhsi: The Counter

Al-Mubdi': The Beginner, the Creator, the Originator

Al-Mu'eed: The Restorer, the Resurrector

Al-Muhyee: The Bestower, the Life Giver

Al-Mumeet: The Bringer of Death, the Death Giver

Al-Hayy: The Ever-Living

Al-Qayyum: The Self-Subsistent, the Eternal, the Self-Sustaining

Al-Wajid: The All Perceiving, the Bountiful, the Finder

Al-Wahid: The One, the Unique

Al-Majid: The Noble, the Illustrious

Al-Ahad: The Only, the Unique

As-Samad: The Perfect, the Eternal

Al-Qadir: The Able, the Capable, the Omnipotent

Al-Muqtadir: The Capable, the All Powerful

Al-Muqaddim: The Presenter, the Advancer, the Expediter

Al-Mu'akhkhir: The Fulfiller, the Deferrer

Al-'Awwal: The First

Al-'Akhir: The Last

Az-Zahir: The Apparent, the Exterior, the Manifest

Al-Batin: The Hidden, the Interior, the Veiled

Al-Waali: The Governor, the Ruler, the Master

Al-Muta'ali: The Exalted, the Most High, the One Above Reproach

Al-Barr: The Benefactor, the Beneficient, the Pious

At-Tawwab: The Acceptor of Repentance, the Forgiver, the Relenting

Al-Muntaqim: The Avenger

Al-'Afuww: The Forgiver, the Pardoner

Ar-Ra'uf: The Merciful, the Ever Indulgent

Al-Muqsit: The Just, the Equitable

Aj-Jami': The Collector, the Comprehensive, the Gatherer

Al-Ghanee: The Richest, the All Sufficing, the Self-Sufficient

Al-Mughnee: The Enricher, the Sufficer, the Bestower

Al-Maani': The Supporter

Ad-Daarr: The Distresser, the Afflictor, the Bringer of Adversity

An-Nafi': The Beneficial, the Benefactor

An-Nur: The Light

Al-Hadi: The Guide

Al-Badi': The Wonderful, the Maker, the Incomparable

Al-Baqi: The Enduring, the Everlasting, the Eternal

Al-Warith: The Inheritor, the Heir

Ar-Rashid: The Rightly Guided, the Conscious, the Guide

As-Sabur: The Most Patient, the Enduring

Malik Al-Mulk: The Ruler of The Kingdom, the King of The Universe

Zul-Jalali wal-Ikram: Lord of Majesty and Generosity

According to some Islamic traditions, the believer who memorizes and recites these names will achieve Paradise. Some Muslims speak of a hundredth name of God, one that only God knows.

Glossary

Adi Granth   Sacred text of the Sikhs.

Advent   Season of preparation for Christmas; begins on the Sunday nearest November 30, and lasts until Christmas itself. (Christianity)

agnostic   A person who believes that the existence of God, or a primal cause, can be neither proven nor disproven.

ahimsa   Hindu principle of reverence for life.

akikah   Birth or welcoming ceremony. (Islam)

Al-Isra Wal Miraj   Holiday marking Muhammad's divinely supported journey from Mecca to Jerusalem, where he is said to have ascended to meet with God. (Islam)

apostolic succession   Doctrine that, in transmitting authority to the apostles, Jesus initiated a chain of authority that has extended in an unbroken line to current Christian bishops. (Christianity)

arhat   In the Theravada Buddhist tradition, one who attains enlightenment through solitude and ascetic practices.

asceticism   A practice or set of practices such as fasting, going without sleep, and putting up with rough conditions, that disciplines the body and helps the practitioner concentrate on achieving spiritual perfection and union with God.

Ash Wednesday   The seventh Wednesday before Easter. The first day of Lent, marked by the imposition of ashes onto the foreheads of worshippers. (Christianity)

atheist   A person who believes that there is no such reality as God or a primal cause.

atman   In Hinduism, the essential, unending self or soul.

Bardo Thodol   Tibetan Buddhist text that sets out instructions for the dying and for their spiritual guides. Popularly known as *The Tibetan Book of the Dead*.

Bhagavad Gita   Epic poem relating the dialogue between the human Prince Arjuna and the beloved Lord Krishna, one of the most important Hindu deities. A hugely influential religious text. (Hinduism)

Bodhi Day   Day celebrating Gautama's decision to sit beneath the bodhi tree until he attained enlightenment. (Buddhism)

Bodhi tree   Sacred fig tree under which Gautama is believed to have received the supreme enlightenment that marked his emergence as the Buddha. (Buddhism)

bodhisattva   In the Mahayana school of Buddhism, one who deserves Nirvana but postpones entry to it until all sentient beings are rescued from rebirth and suffering.

Brahma   Personification of the Absolute, the creator of the world, which is perpetually destined to last for 2,160,000,000 years before it falls to ruin, at which time Brahma re-creates it. One of the three supreme gods in the Hindu triad. (See also: *Vishnu, Shiva.*)

Brahman   Ultimate Reality. (Hinduism)

Brahmin   Member of a priestly Indian social caste. (Hinduism)

Buddha   A fully enlightened being. Siddhartha Gautama became known as Buddha Tathagata ("he who has gone through completely"). Other names for this revered figure include Bhagavat (Lord) and, simply, the Buddha.

Buddha Day   Day on which the Buddha's birth is celebrated.

caliph   Title bestowed on the designated successor to Muhammad in leading the Islamic faith. (The office is now abolished.)

Chanukah   Festival of Lights celebrating the victory of the Maccabees over the Syrians in the second century B.C.E. (Judaism)

Christmas   The feast of the Nativity, celebrating the birth of Jesus. (Christianity)

chun-tzu   Noble individual. (Confucianism)

chung   "Faithfulness to oneself." (Confucianism)

Conservative Judaism   Branch of Judaism between Reform and Orthodox, willing to accommodate some contemporary social trends. (See also: *Reform Judaism, Orthodox Judaism, Reconstructionist School of Judaism.*)

covenant   Agreement; specifically, the agreement between God and the ancient Israelites, under which God promised protection in return for obedience and faithfulness. (Judaism, Christianity)

Decalogue The Ten Commandments that appear in the Hebrew Bible. (Judaism, Christianity)

dharma In Buddhism, sublime religious truth; also, any particular facet of experience or existence. In Hinduism, a religious obligation, social convention, or individual virtue.

dualism The attempt to explain phenomena by means of opposing poles: good and evil, black and white, old and new, "I" and "other," God and creation, and so on.

Duhsehra/Durga Puja Hindu holiday celebrating the triumph of good over evil.

Easter The central Christian festival, celebrating the resurrection of Jesus after his crucifixion and proclaiming the spiritual rebirth of believers through their union with the risen Christ.

ecumenism Gathering of initiatives promoting greater understanding and tolerance among the various branches of the Christian churches. (The words *ecumenical* and *ecumenicism* are also sometimes used to refer to the process of attaining greater cooperation and understanding among widely differing faiths.)

Eightfold Path The path that leads to the cessation of craving and attachment; marked by right understanding, right purpose, right speech, right conduct, right livelihood, right effort, right alertness, and right concentration. (Buddhism)

Epiphany Holiday commemorating the visit of the Wise Men to the newborn Jesus; Jesus' baptism; and Jesus' first miracle, the changing of water into wine; as recounted in the Gospels. (An epiphany may also be a manifestation of the Divine in one's own experience, through a vision, for example.)

The Five Classics The *Book of Changes (I Ching)*, the *Book of History (Shu Ching)*, the *Book of Poetry (Shih Ching)*, the *Book of Rites (Li Chi)*, and the *Spring and Autumn Annals (Ch'un Chi)*, which chronicle major historical events. (Confucianism)

Five Pillars Five obligations, outlined in the Qur'an, essential to the lives of Muslims. They include confession of one's faith in God and in his prophet Muhammad, ritual worship, almsgiving, fasting, and pilgrimage. (Islam)

The Four Books Confucian texts incorporating the works of Confucius and Mencius (372–289 B.C.E.) and the commentaries of their followers, considered the fundamental teachings of early Confucianism. They include the *Analects (Lun Yu)*, the *Great Learning (Ta Hsueh)*, the *Doctrine of the Mean (Chung Yung)*, and the *Book of Mencius (Meng-tzu)*. Together with the Five Classics, the Four Books make up the basic texts of Confucianism.

Four Noble Truths   The most important principles of the Buddhist faith; they hold that life is suffering, that suffering is caused by craving and attachment, that craving and attachment can be overcome, and that the means of overcoming craving and attachment is the Eightfold Path. (See also: *Eightfold Path*.)

Godhead   The essential being of God.

Good Friday   The Friday before Easter, when believers recall the death of Jesus on the cross. (Christianity)

guru   Personal spiritual guide, typically one who develops an important personal relationship with a disciple or practitioner. (Hinduism)

Hajj   A pilgrimage to the holy city of Mecca, required at least once in the lifetime of every Muslim who is of sound body, sane, and able to afford the journey. (Islam)

Hinayana   Another name for the Theravada school of Buddhism. (See also: *Theravada*.)

Id al-Fitr   A feast period that takes place at the end of Ramadan and lasts for three days. (Islam)

Jainism   Ancient religion of the Indian subcontinent emphasizing nonviolence personal progress toward spiritual liberation.

jananzah   Islamic funeral service.

jen   The compassion and humanity arising from genuine love. (Confucianism)

K'che Manitou   An Ojibwa (Native American) term describing the sum total of all spiritual entities; the aggregate of various embodied spiritual forces. (See also: *Wakan Tanka*.)

Kami   Japanese word for "spirit" or "one residing above." (Shinto)

Kami-dana   Shelf of the Spirits in the home of a Shinto believer; a miniature depiction of the holy central section of a shrine.

karma   Doctrine embodying an impartial principle of moral cause and effect, under which actions have unavoidable implications and even affect one's future incarnations. Only those who escape the cycle of birth and death may be said to go beyond the reach of karma. (Hinduism, Buddhism, and other faiths, in different forms)

koan   Zen Buddhist riddle that invites the responding student to overcome potential barriers to enlightenment.

Krishna   Popular Hindu deity; an incarnation of Vishnu. (Hinduism)

Krishna Janmashtami   Holiday celebrating the birthday of Krishna. (Hinduism)

Lailat ul-Qadr   The final 10 days of Ramadan, when Muslims celebrate Muhammad's first experience of divine revelation. (Islam)

Law   In the Jewish tradition, the written account of the revelation of God.

Lent   A season of repentance and fasting that serves as a spiritual preparation for the joy of the Easter festival. (Christianity)

Li   Correct ritualistic and etiquette-based behavior between individuals. (Confucianism)

liturgy   Public worship or ritual.

Mahayana   Younger of the two major schools of Buddhism; venerates the bodhisattva (see separate listing) and emphasizes the necessity of helping all living beings attain liberation. (See also: *Theravada*.)

mantra   Word or phrase repeated in meditation and religious ritual. (Hinduism, Buddhism, other systems)

Maulid al-Nabi   Holiday celebrating the birth of Muhammad. (Islam)

monotheism   Belief in a single personal God, usually a figure seen as unifying the entire universe.

mosque   Building used by Muslims for worship and prayer. (Islam)

Muslim   Literally, "one who submits." A follower of Islam.

mysticism   Pursuit of a direct, often ecstatic, inner experience of the Ultimate.

Nichiren Buddhism   Term describing a number of Japanese Buddhist schools.

nirvana   State of final liberation from the cycle of birth and death. (Hinduism, Buddhism)

Nirvana Day   Day on which the Buddha's passing is observed.

Nukhagni   Hindu cremation ritual.

Orthodox Eastern Church   The dominant form of Christian worship in Greece, a large region of Eastern Europe, and parts of the Middle East, within which individual national churches share liturgical traditions but operate independently of their counterparts. (Christianity)

Orthodox Judaism   Branch of Judaism notable for its emphasis on the supreme authority of the Torah, and for followers' scrupulous adherence to tradition. (See also: *Reform Judaism, Conservative Judaism, Reconstructionist School of Judaism*.)

Palm Sunday   The final Sunday of Lent and the last Sunday before Easter; the first day of Holy Week. (Christianity)

Passover   Major holiday honoring the delivery of the Jewish people from slavery in Egypt.

Pauline Epistles   Ancient letters, attributed to the Apostle Paul, offering guidance to particular congregations and to the Christian church as a whole. (Christianity)

Pentecost   Feast commemorating the gift to the disciples of the Holy Spirit following Jesus' resurrection and ascension. (Christianity)

Pesach   See *Passover*.

proselytize   To make an effort to convince another to convert, typically to another faith or sect.

Protestant   Umbrella term for a diverse set of Christian traditions that came into existence following the Protestant Reformations, and that deny the authority of the pope. (Christianity)

Protestant Reformations   Series of religious and political upheavals in sixteenth-century Europe, leading to the formation of Protestant denominations that rejected the authority of the pope. (Christianity)

puja   Ritualized worship of a particular deity or holy figure. (Hinduism)

Pure Land School   Buddhist movement emphasizing absolute reliance on the Buddha's grace and unwavering faith in the Buddha Amitabha (Amida), who is held to have vowed, in the second century B.C.E., to save all sentient beings.

Purim   A festival celebration commemorating the deliverance of Persian Jews from destruction. (Judaism)

Qibla wall   In a mosque, the wall that faces Mecca. (Islam)

Qur'an   Sacred text held by Muslims to consolidate and fulfill all past revelations from God; regarded by the faithful as the Word of God, whose instrument was the Prophet Muhammad. (Islam)

rabbi   A respected teacher and leader of worship, usually connected to a particular synagogue.

Rama   In the epic *Ramayana*, a deity whose story celebrates the commitments of family life and the virtue of right living; an incarnation of Vishnu. (Hinduism)

Rama Navami   Important holiday centered on the god Rama. (Hinduism)

Ramadan   The name of both a month of the year and a period of religious observance. During the holy festival, which occupies the entire month, adults embark on a rigidly observed period of abstinence, reflection, and purification. (Islam)

Reconstructionist School of Judaism   Movement holding that Judaism is a fundamentally social (rather than God-centered) religious civilization.

Reform Judaism   Wing of Judaism notable for its attempts to adapt the faith to the demands of the modern world, and for its liberal approach to matters of criticism and interpretation of the Law. (See also: *Orthodox Judaism, Conservative Judaism, Reconstructionist School of Judaism*.)

Rig Veda   Earliest and among the most revered of the holy scriptures of Hinduism.

Roman Catholic Church   Those Christians worldwide who identify themselves as being in communion with the bishop of Rome, the pope. (Christianity)

Rosh Hashanah   The Jewish New Year (observed in September/October).

samadhi   In Buddhism, a state of single-minded concentration; an important tool for pursuing a path of self-awakening. In Hinduism, the point at which an individual's consciousness merges with the Godhead.

samsara   The process of accumulated, karma-driven birth, in which the thoughts and deeds of past lives are addressed. (See also: *Karma*.) (Hinduism, other faiths)

sangha   A monastic community, much like a Western monastery. (Buddhism)

Second Vatican Council   Roman Catholic gathering convened in 1962 that eventually led to dramatic reforms in church practice. (Christianity)

Shabbat   Sabbath, day of rest. (Judaism)

shahada   Ritual marking a young Muslim's formal entry to the Islamic faith.

shaman   Religious celebrant who is considered to possess more than human powers, including the ability to understand and treat diseases—and sometimes bring them about. (Traditional religions)

Shavuot   Holiday celebrating the spring harvest season and God's gift of the Torah. (Judaism)

Shiite sect   Smaller of the two dominant sects of Islam; emphasizes the authoritative role of religious leaders and their teachings. (See also: *Sunni sect*.)

Sikhism   A monotheistic faith founded in the fifteenth century by Guru Nanak Dev Ji and successive Gurus.

Shiva   Deity symbolizing the various potent forms of the energy of the Ultimate; usually depicted with four arms and surrounded by fire. One of the three supreme gods in the Hindu triad. (See also: *Vishnu, Brahma*.) (Hinduism)

Shiva Ratri   All-night celebration of the Divine as manifested in the god Shiva. (Hinduism)

Sufism   A variety of movements within Islam that stress *mysticism* and *asceticism* (see separate entries).

Sunni sect   Larger of the two dominant sects of Islam, often according more authority to the sacred writings of Islam than to human religious authorities. (See also: *Shiite sect*.)

sunyata   (Sanskrit: "emptiness") Principle that all ultimate entities including the Buddha and the state of Nirvana are empty, that is, completely undivided from the rest of the Supreme Reality. (Buddhism)

Talmud   Extensive compilation of rabbinical discussions, commentaries, and clarifications; the Oral Law and its commentaries. (Judaism)

Tao   Literally "path" or "way." According to the scriptures of this faith, the "eternal Tao" cannot actually be named. However, it has been described as a sublime "Natural Order" marked by the effortless alternation of cycles (night and day, growth and decline). The Tao may best be described as "the way the universe works."

te   Controlling power, virtue, or magical energy; also, integrity or moral rectitude. (Taoism)

Theravada   Older of the two major schools of Buddhism; historically one that re-emphasizes the spiritual progress of the individual. (See also: *Mahayana*.)

Torah   The scroll containing the Five Books of Moses; also, in a broader sense, the accumulated sacred Jewish writings of the centuries.

tori   Gateway identifying the entrance to a Shinto shrine.

totem   Particular object (generally a plant or animal) held in reverence and regarded as an ancestor or sibling by members of a group. (Traditional religions)

Upanishads   (Sanskrit: "sitting near") Texts that mark the final phase of the sacred Vedas and contain direct accounts of advice from spiritually advanced mystics. (Hinduism)

Vajrayana   A Tibetan strand of Buddhist tradition emphasizing yogic discipline.

Veda   (Sanskrit: "knowledge") The great collection of early Hindu religious scriptures. The Vedas outline spiritual principles accepted by Hindus as fundamental to their religion.

Vedanta   Classical school of Indian philosophy that gave rise to disciplines emphasizing the transcendent messages of the *Upanishads*. (See also: *Upanishads*.) (Hinduism)

Vishnu   Deity who is seen as a force of transcendent love and whose many incarnations include Krishna and Rama. One of the three supreme gods in the Hindu triad. (See also: *Brahma, Shiva*.) (Hinduism)

vision quest   Period during which a boy celebrates the onset of puberty by means of solitary meditation, fasting, and tests of physical endurance. The participant seeks a vision that will guide him in later life, and the support and protection of a guardian spirit. (Native American systems)

wadu   Ritual washing before prayer. (Islam)

Wakan Tanka   A Lakota (Native American) term describing the sum total of all spiritual entities—the aggregate of various embodied spiritual forces. (See also: *K'che Manitou*.)

Waleemah   Wedding reception. (Islam)

Wu-wei   Taoist concept of an inaction that is really a kind of sublime efficiency.

yoga   Classical school of Indian philosophy meant to help instill personal, physical, and spiritual discipline. (Hinduism)

Yom Kippur   A Day of Atonement marked by fasting and prayer. (Judaism)

Yorozu-yomi   Doctrine of flexibility that allows Shinto to be adapted easily to the lives of many people.

Zen   Influential school of Buddhism originally known as "Chan." Bodhidharma is acknowledged as the founder of Zen.

Index

D

I

J

O

P

T

U

V

CHECK OUT THESE BEST-SELLERS

More than 450 titles available at booksellers and online retailers everywhere!

978-1-59257-115-4

978-1-59257-900-6

978-1-59257-855-9

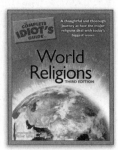

978-1-59257-222-9

978-1-59257-957-0

978-1-59257-785-9

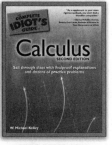

978-1-59257-471-1

978-1-59257-483-4

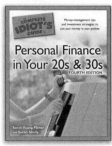

978-1-59257-883-2

978-1-59257-966-2

978-1-59257-908-2

978-1-59257-786-6

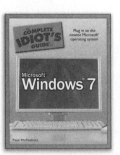

978-1-59257-954-9

978-1-59257-437-7

978-1-59257-888-7

idiotsguides.com